BEATS AT NAROPA

Beats

AT NAROPA

AN ANTHOLOGY

Edited by Anne Waldman
and Laura Wright

COFFEE HOUSE PRESS • MINNEAPOLIS • 2009

Coffee House Press books are available to the trade through our primary distributor, Consortium Book Sales & Distribution, www.cbsd.com. For personal orders, catalogs, or other information, write to info@coffeehousepress.org.

Coffee House Press is a nonprofit literary publishing house. Support from private foundations, corporate giving programs, government programs, and generous individuals helps make the publication of our books possible. We gratefully acknowledge their support in detail in the back of this book.

LIBRARY OF CONGRESS CATALOGING-IN-PUBLICATION DATA
Beats at Naropa / edited by Anne Waldman and Laura Wright.
p. cm.
Includes bibliographical references.
ISBN 978-1-56689-227-8 (alk. paper)
1. Beat generation.
2. Authors, American--20th century--Interviews.
3. Beat generation--Interviews.
I. Waldman, Anne, 1945-
II. Wright, Laura.
III. Naropa University.
IV. Title.
PS228.B6B4675 2009
810.9'0054—dc22
[B]
2009011462

ACKNOWLEDGMENTS
Thanks to Kathryn Beam (Special Collections, Hatcher Graduate Library, University of Michigan), Lisa Birman, Chris Fischbach, Tim Hawkins, Andy Hoffmann, Anselm Hollo, Ann Hunter, David Kessler (Bancroft Library, University of California, Berkeley), Allan Kornblum, Daron Mueller, Jenn Quinn, Randy Roark, Ed Bowes, and Ivan Suvanjieff.

Dedicated to all the students,
past, present, and still to come,
of the Jack Kerouac School of Disembodied Poetics.

"I learned . . . from thirty years of observing Allen [Ginsberg] to try to bring that spontaneity and creativity and pizzazz and élan into your activism, into the social concerns you have, to give them a patina of joy and happiness. Because we cannot be dour, stodgy, robotic claw-mouths out there chewing away on issues. We have to bring our vision of a new world, a better world, and our dancing shoes, into our social concerns."

—EDWARD SANDERS

from a panel on Poetic Activism, July 16, 1994

CONTENTS

11 **INTRODUCTION;** Anne Waldman

15 **THE FIRST READING OF THE ENVIRONMENTAL MOVEMENT: THE SIX GALLERY READING;** Michael McClure

19 **KEROUAC'S SOUND;** Clark Coolidge

23 SIDEBAR: **ALLEN GINSBERG ON WILLIAM BLAKE**

24 **BASIC DEFINITIONS;** Gary Snyder

39 **PULLING IT DOWN OR THE GOOD MANNERS OF VAMPIRES;** Amiri Baraka

45 **WOMEN AND THE BEATS;** Hettie Jones, Joanne Kyger, Janine Pommy Vega, Anne Waldman

60 SIDEBAR: **JOYCE JOHNSON**

62 **ALLEN GINSBERG'S LANGUAGE GAMES: A WITTGENSTEINIAN PERSPECTIVE;** Marjorie Perloff

70 **RECOLLECTIONS AND GOSSIP: FIRST MEETINGS WITH JACK KEROUAC;** David Amram, Gregory Corso, Allen Ginsberg, John Clellon Holmes, Edie Parker Kerouac,

80 SIDEBAR: **TED BERRIGAN**

81 **READING, WRITING, AND TEACHING KEROUAC IN 1982;** Ann Charters

94 **KEROUAC, CATHOLICISM, BUDDHISM;** Gregory Corso, Allen Ginsberg, John Clellon Holmes

100 SIDEBAR: **FERLINGHETTI ON COLLABORATION**

102 **COMMONPLACE DISCOVERIES: LEW WELCH;** Philip Whalen

113 **THE BEATS AND BEYOND;** Lorna Dee Cervantes

117 **BOB KAUFMAN: BEAT, SURREAL, BUDDHIST, AND BLACK;**
David Henderson

135 **AN INTERVIEW WITH EDWARD SANDERS;** Junior Burke

144 SIDEBAR: **ABBIE HOFFMAN, WARRIOR IN THE WORLD**

145 **YOU CAN'T WIN: AN INTERVIEW WITH WILLIAM
BURROUGHS;** John Oughton and Anne Waldman

164 SIDEBAR: **TENDREL;** Anne Waldman

166 **"FRIGHTENED CHRYSANTHEMUMS": POETS' COLLOQUIUM;**
William Burroughs, Rick Fields, Allen Ginsberg, W. S. Merwin,
Chögyam Trungpa, Rinpoche, Anne Waldman, Philip Whalen,
David Rome, Joshua Zim

195 **BY ANY MEANS NECESSARY;** Diane di Prima

209 **REMEMBER THE FUTURE: ARCHIVAL POETICS AND THE
WAR ON MEMORY;** Steven Taylor

216 SIDEBAR: **ALLEN GINSBERG ON WILLIAM BLAKE**

217 Notes

219 Biographies

INTRODUCTION

Anne Waldman

I T WAS 1974, THE SUMMER BEFORE THE LAST AMERICAN TROOPS LEFT VIETNAM. The country was weary of the war. Visible protest had gone on for years. Images of the bloody carnage were not being censored or screened as they had been during World War II and Korea, and as they are once again. There was palpable burnout, exhaustion, and nihilism operating on many levels. The promise of the sixties, which once seemed so close, appeared out of reach. Deaths from drug and alcohol excess were legion. People were looking for alternatives to political rhetoric and the horrors of the war. Many of us in the artistic and political counterculture had begun to feel that our confidence that our protests would result in a saner more holistic world had been naïve. We were still committed to activism, but instead of just protesting, we became more centered on creating discrete cultural alternatives to the status quo.

What else was going on in 1974? The House Judiciary Committee adopted three articles of impeachment charging President Richard Nixon with obstruction of justice, failure to uphold laws, and refusal to produce material subpoenaed by the congress. India successfully tested an atomic device, becoming the sixth country with nuclear power. The first class stamp went to ten cents. Mohammad Ali kayoed George Foreman in Kinshasa, Zaire. Duke Ellington died. Gary Snyder published *Turtle Island*, which won the Pulitzer Prize. And Patti Smith recorded her first punk single, "Hey Joe."

It was during that summer that Allen Ginsberg, Diane di Prima, and I were invited by Chögyam Trungpa, Rinpoche, a Tibetan Buddhist lama and meditation instructor, to attend a summer festival in Boulder, Colorado, organized by his students. Among us, we felt a commonality of spirit, a spirit that morphed into a chrysalis from which emerged the Jack Kerouac School of Disembodied Poetics. Since its inception, the program has been a stimulating site for alternative poetics, weaving together the various literary movements identified in Donald Allen's breakthrough anthology, *The New American*

Poetry, with the experimental pedagogies growing out of the particulars and practices of the Beats, Black Mountain School, the San Francisco Renaissance, and the New York School, in which I was engaged and considered a second generation and a half "member." (I had been an assistant director and by 1968 was director of the Poetry Project at St. Mark's Church In-the-Bowery, an earlier and ongoing site for poetic experiment and community which has always been a sort of older sibling to the poetry scene in Boulder.)

Student activists, bohemians, hippies, Zen, Tibetan, and Native American spiritual teachers, journalists, theater and dance folk, artists, and students representing every conceivable discipline have been drawn over the years to the nexus of energy surrounding the Naropa "experiment." The Beat ethos of candor and community provided the initial impetus for the founding of the Kerouac School, and has served as a continuing source of inspiration.

Buddhism has also played a key role in the lines and work of many of the writers represented here. Diane di Prima had been engaged with Buddhist teachings for a number of years, becoming an early student of Suzuki Roshi at the Zen Center in San Francisco. Gary Snyder received a scholarship from the first Zen Institute, which led to spending nearly fifteen years in Japan studying Japanese poetry and Zen Buddhism. He was joined in the early years by his wife (at that time) Joanne Kyger, herself a longtime Buddhist. Allen Ginsberg, an inveterate seeker, traveled to Japan and India with Gary Snyder, Peter Orlovsky, and Joanne Kyger. Jack Kerouac, for whom the poetics school was named, had written *Some of the Dharma*, and a *Life of the Buddha*. In 1973 Philip Whalen was ordained as a Buddhist monk and in 1991 was subsequently ordained as the abbot of the Hartford Street Zen Center in San Francisco.

And so it seemed a natural fit for the Jack Kerouac School of Disembodied Poetics to develop and evolve within the Naropa Institute (now Naropa University), as a dharma-based school, a promising haven or temporary autonomous zone for a new kind of "academy" that would welcome unorthodox poets and magpie scholars who had not had careers in the academic mainstream. The vision was to foster principles of non-competition, contemplative education, and to encourage investigation of consciousness, imagination, and the "wild mind." Gary Snyder defines "wild mind" as "elegantly self-disciplined, self-regulating." The practice of the "wild" also, as he says, encourages an "etiquette of freedom." It was apt that the "wild mind" of the Beats and the radical poetics of the New American Poetry landed in the high Rockies close to the Continental Divide. An important mythic geographical locus, Denver and environs loom large in the Beat mythology. It was the home of Neal Cassady, and a destination in *On the Road*.

Thus, five years after Jack Kerouac's death, Allen and I agreed (after some push on my part to consider The Gertrude Stein School as an alternative) to name our burgeoning school for him, because he had realized the First Noble Buddhist Truth, the truth of suffering. The term "Beat Generation" had sprung out of a conversation Kerouac had with John Clellon Holmes in 1948, as they were recalling the nature of generations, "recollecting the glamour" of the "Lost Generation," as Allen tells it and Kerouac said, "Ah, this is nothing but a beat generation." Allen also went on to describe the subtler definitions of the term, including beatitude, beatific, the hipster perspective of everything being exhausted, which had also Buddhist connotation, the framing of the historical period, and then the broader view of resonance and association of a range of people, including editors, filmmakers, musicians, and several generations of writers, activists, thinkers, and what we call at Naropa the "outrider" tradition.

Albeit most of the pieces in this anthology—unscripted talks, interviews, panels, colloquia, and documents from the principle writers associated with the Beat literary movement—were the most part selected from the Naropa Audio Archive. Some were transcribed and edited with the help of the authors, and in a few cases (such as Philip Whalen) by the editors of this anthology. There's an early colloquium that includes the Tibetan Buddhist founder, Chögyam Trungpa, Rinpoche, who enjoyed challenging Allen's politics. Also included are pieces about major Beat authors, such as Clark Coolidge's salient piece on Kerouac's "sound," Marjorie Perloff on Allen Ginsberg's "language games," David Henderson's historical perspective on Bob Kaufman, and Diane di Prima's memoir around the exigencies of small press publishing and community. Steven Taylor, a principle teacher at Naropa for many years and close friend to Allen Ginsberg as well as being his music collaborator, concludes the volume with a discussion of the implications and value of the Naropa Archive itself.

While many of the authors in this collection do not feel comfortable with the term "Beat," or feel their identity does not lie under a "Beat" rubric, they have nevertheless been historically linked (guilt by association?) through friendships and associations with Jack Kerouac, who named it and Allen Ginsberg who ran with it. It was Ginsberg who single-handedly created the Beat literary/cultural mythology and was invested in its perpetuation for a number of reasons, not the least being a grandiose need to foist an alternative poetics onto the larger "official verse culture" mainstream. There is an interesting disparity between the views of say, Michael McClure, who seems to embrace the term, and expands the notion to include even younger "out-riders," to Amiri Baraka (LeRoi Jones) scholars who name a "Beat period" for Baraka's oeuvre, to considerations of Bob Kaufman's "erasure" as a Beat. Diane di Prima disparages the term, rightly so, as reductive and one must put on the feminist lens here to expand the sense of her major role in trou-bling the waters through a uniquely original far-ranging body of work (as one must do with Joanne Kyger, another intensely independent writer). Yet Kyger and di Prima both have appeared in a number of anthologies under the Beat banner. Gary Snyder, on whom Jack Kerouac's character Japhy Ryder is based, is adamantly opposed to being so facilely labeled. It is unsub-tle, and I agree. He is a translator, scholar of Japanese and Chinese poetries and world ecologies, working far beyond any boundaries and cliches around the Beat trope. Ferlinghetti has often protested he is not a Beat!

As Hettie Jones once notoriously said: they couldn't be a "generation" because they could all fit in her living room.

So why the title *Beats at Naropa?* To some extent the term beat "covers the waterfront," as Ted Berrigan would say. Naropa's role in all this is complex, being for so many years a place where writers associated with the Beat Literary Generation were honored and often provided with a first teaching gig.

I believe the term applied here coalesces—maybe for just a brief moment—a kinship that was so important to Allen Ginsberg. It magnetizes a lot of inquiry that has gone on at Naropa, a place that also includes Language Poetry, the New York School, Black Mountain, and San Francisco Renaissance in its years-long pedagogy. May they all bloom! What, in fact, does *Beats at Naropa* really mean? I invite you to consider this provocative notion.

The founding of a school such as Naropa was an auspicious event, a "cultural intervention" of ongoing influence, and a resource for advancing poetic investigation. Such a creative environment, inflected by Buddhist principles, was able to meet a need in our culture and in the educational realm. Students have come from all over the world to study poetics at Naropa and then continue to be active as poets, writers, scholars, political and cultural activists, small press publishers, printers, and brilliant profes-sors. And the doings of the Kerouac School in particular have helped build an even stronger and robust literary community for several generations that branches out energetically throughout the world. This anthology represents some of the history, continuity, and conviction of our endeavor.

—Anne Waldman

THE FIRST READING OF THE ENVIRONMENTAL MOVEMENT: THE SIX GALLERY READING

Michael McClure

THE FIFTIES WERE NOT THE WAY SOME PEOPLE IMAGINE THEM TODAY, lovely, retro, sentimental, charming, that the young folks danced a certain way, and television was just coming in and it was black and white and sort of valentiney. The truth is the time was serious. It was the Cold War, the time of the House on Un-American Activities Committee, the time of Joe McCarthy, the time of the Korean War. It was the beginning of the U.S.'s new series of massacres of people around the world, particularly in Asian countries. Citizens were tremendously oppressed by their need for conformity after having been through the celebrated and homicidal WW II, and after having been ground up by the "educational machine" of the military-industrial propaganda system that was created by WWII. Americans believed that being absolutely miserable and loveless and owning a Buick with a torpedo hood ornament and a tract home and feeling heartless, unloved, and unlovable, was the way to go—as long as they had a deep freeze and the right kitchen appliances. They were told they desperately needed sirens to warn about the imminent Russian hydrogen bomb, in time to dive under the dining room table and put their head between their knees. It was an ugly and stressed time.

All the same there were small communities that were self-exiled so to speak; they comprised artists and dissenters who supported and stood up for one another, believed in one another, and were not living the conformity and political commandments or following the morés, but doing things their own way, living much like some people manage today, and as a matter of fact, with considerably more freedom. One enclave was the North Beach area in San Francisco—that's where artists went when we first arrived in San Francisco in the early fifties.

In San Francisco on October 7, 1955, I gave my first poetry reading. It was also Philip Whalen's first poetry reading and it was Gary Snyder's first reading. It was also Allen Ginsberg's first reading and he read "Howl." The other reader that night was Philip Lamantia, a young American surrealist poet who had been recognized by André Breton. He read poems by his friend John Hoffman who had died recently in Mexico. Our master of ceremonies was anarchist-philosopher and poet Kenneth Rexroth. The evening is sometimes called the first reading of the Beat Generation. But it wasn't the first poetry reading in San Francisco. It was in the air. I remember seeing readings in San Francisco months before ours. One had belly dancers and musicians playing bongo drums, and I thought dubiously, "Boy, that's pretty far out."

San Francisco was a home base for conscientious objectors and radical groups from all over, it was one of the remaining outposts for the Wobblies, and the city had its radical politics—ranging from Trotskyism to anarcho-pacifism to socialism. Our MC, Kenneth Rexroth, had introduced many artists to the ideas of those groups.

I was deeply concerned with the new American painting of Pollock and Kline, and I knew the young artists around the Six Gallery. I'd been in a play by Robert Duncan that was staged at the Six Gallery earlier, in 1955. The Six Gallery was an artists' gallery, the artists were the students of the most intense, most radical, most far-out stances, students from Clyfford Still and Mark Rothko. If you know the paintings by Jay DeFeo from having seen them in the Whitney Beat show, you'll have an idea of what the Six artists were like. One of the founders of the Six was poet Jack Spicer. The artist who ran the gallery, Wally Hedrick, asked me if I'd set up a poetry reading. I agreed but there was a lot going on in my life; my wife was pregnant at the time, and I was working. I could not get around to organizing the reading. It was on my mind when I ran into Allen Ginsberg in North Beach one day. Allen asked what I was up to, and I said that I was supposed to be organizing a poetry reading. He said he'd like to do it. And I turned it over to him. Allen and I had met earlier that year at a party for W. H. Auden, at the first poetry reading of the San Francisco Poetry Center. Ginsberg and I were the wallflowers at the academic event. Leaning against the wall, Allen told me about his visions of Blake, I told him about my dreams that I was William Blake, and we hit it off. Though his Blake was a long ways from mine. We were interested in knowing each other and we'd get together in Chinatown. A few times Allen read me letters from his pal Jack Kerouac; I didn't know exactly what to make of them, but I thought the stanzas contained in the letters from Mexico City Blues were beautiful. Allen also read me letters from William Burroughs. We had developed friends in common. We all went to Rexroth's apartment where Kenneth had a soirée once a week.

The reading at the Six Gallery was on a typical foggy October San Francisco evening, in the Marina District in a building that had once been an automobile repair garage, which had a small show up of sculptures by Fred Martin, which looked like, and I'm sure were, orange crates that had been swathed with gauze and then dipped in plaster of Paris, so they were hanging surrealist sculptures. About a hundred and fifty people came at the most, and we were surprised by that. I don't think anyone expected much attendance. What we found out quickly, on stage, is that we were speaking for the audience. We were saying what they would like to have us say, because they wanted to hear it out loud, it was time to hear it out loud. "Howl" was part of it, of course; I was reading nature poems about the murder of whales that was taking place in Iceland; Gary Snyder was reading powerful poems about nature and the environment; Philip Whalen was reading poems of unutterable Zen humor and beauty, and also about nature, and about trail hiking in the woods. It was almost startling to see people in the audience ranging from elderly women who were wearing fur coats and were college professors, to the young radical carpenters, to the bartender at your favorite bar in North Beach, The Place. But he was an anarchist student of Clyfford Still's anyway. Kerouac was there, in the audience, that night. And he started yelling, "go, go, go," while Allen was reading "Howl." People were sitting on the concrete floor, and they were leaned up against the walls, or standing. This was nothing too elegant. I'm always surprised nowadays when I see it written of as the "Gallery Six reading." Sort of Parisian sounding. I don't think anybody would have known what to make of that. It was the Six Gallery. The walls were one board thick and the floor was concrete.

The remarkable thing was that we were able to go out, lift the poetry off the page with our voices, and find ourselves speaking for people. As Rexroth said, San Francisco was for the artists like Barcelona was for the Spanish anarchists. It was a kind of a reservation, but there were reservations like Greenwich Village in New York too, and there were many others.

The poetry that we wrote began to become popular, some of it began to foster other poetry. The next thing you knew there was a group called The Beatles, before that they'd been named the Silver Beetles—b-e-e-t-l-e-s. They became the b-e-a-t-l-e-s and their lyrics became much more intelligent. They'd been listening to Allen's poetry, or Ed Sanders's poetry, or someone's poetry, and the lyrics became intelligent. Then their music fed back into what we were doing. At the same time, people were listening to black music, blues; there was an enormous influence coming in of black music. A lot of that charged rock 'n' roll, which for a time was not yet co-opted by cologne merchandising, tennis shoes, beer, and hi-fi equipment—music was a radical force. And there was an exchange between music and poetry. We hear some music groups continuing on, who are still speaking in an old, furious and imaginative way.

Jack Kerouac being in the audience heard all of the poems of nature, and soon after wrote *Dharma Bums,* and then *Big Sur.* I begin to see Allen's poetry, starting with "Howl," as a kind of nature poetry. So it seemed like we were the first reading of the environmental movement. Why not call it that? And the reading aloud has continued, not because any of us have anything against the page, but because it's entirely different to hear it out aloud, and it's an entirely different thing to hear it with music. It's shaped, it's become part of the culture. Some young person comes up to me and says, hey Mike, whatever happened to the Beat Generation? I look at this young person, say he's a young man, and he's got hair coming down to here on one side and the other side is shaved and he's got an earring and a nose ring, he's got on shorts and he has some tattoos, he doesn't salute me, he's not wearing a uniform, he doesn't say sir when speaks to me, he doesn't have a draft number and I know he believes in the environment and he's been active in it, I've seen him at the Mumia Abu Jamal demonstration—by the way there were about 20,000 people at that in San Francisco and 70% of them were twenty-five years or under—many new people were reading on the podium and speaking, from Angela Davis to Peter Coyote, I closed the rally with a poem by Shelley, which was appropriate, kind of like a blessing on the whole affair. I especially remember young hip-hop poets I'd never seen before who were cool, a guy named Michael Franti was good!

So, what happened to the Beat Generation? You're the Beat Generation, whether you want to accept it or not.

—June 21, 1999

KEROUAC'S SOUND

Clark Coolidge

I N MY OPINION SOUND IS THE KEY TO KEROUAC'S WORKS. I'M NOT SEPARATING sound from meaning. I don't think that's a useful distinction any more than form and content is a useful distinction. But sound is one of the two main ways that we apprehend the movement of language. And from the movement of language we get its meaning. You have to complete that syntax before you know what's happening. The other way is the visual, reading it off the page. I discovered a couple of years ago that you can probably divide the human race into people who natively, maybe from birth, hear subvocally, in the head, when they read off a page, they hear a voice; and some who don't do that, which sounds like a terrible gig for poets. I once was teaching a class of about sixty people and I asked how many of them did have the ability to hear right off the page and it was about fifty/fifty.

Kerouac was probably one of the greatest examples of an ear writer. He heard what he wrote and often at fantastic speeds. Everybody knows of his prodigious typing ability. Phil Whalen once told about how when he was in the house with Jack typing all you heard was the bell at the end of the carriage. Ding, ding, ding, ding, almost that fast. Jack had a terrific ability to hear and use vowel shapes and consonant shapes and string them out in lines. A vowel example might be, "gloom dooms"; and a consonantal one might be, "hotshot freight trains."

In about 1959 or '60 when a lot of his works were coming out, I used to lend them to friends; and I found that often they would bring the books back and they'd say, I really can't get into it, all these dashes and things, I lose the meaning. And then I had bought some of the records that came out in '59 that Kerouac made, and I would lend them or play them the record. I found that in almost every case when they heard his voice, reading his work, speaking his work, they had no more problem reading it by themselves. You almost have to read his works like a score of music, know how those long lines are supposed to be accented and articulated. Sometimes he doesn't punctuate them, just blows on and pauses, puts a dash. But once you have the sound down I think you have no problem with the sense of his work.

What I want to do now is give some specific examples of some of the rhythmic things, since I come to Kerouac directly from music, playing improvised music, bebop, jazz. That was the turn-on for me; I saw that here was the first writer I'd ever heard that was doing it in words. I'll try to give some specific examples from that direction.

One of the great qualities of Kerouac's writing of course is his long lines, very long stretches of words, with phrasing. He once said that he heard Lee Konitz, the great bebop alto saxophone player, in 1951, and he said that "Lee Konitz in 1951 inspired me to try to write the way he plays." Konitz was very much inspired by Charlie Parker and Lennie Tristano, particularly Tristano, who also had a very long line. For instance, from Kerouac's "Beginning of Bop," "Lester droopy porkpied hung his horn and blew bop lazy ideas inside jazz had everybody dreaming." That's one breath, one line. Sometimes in Kerouac's poems, because he was often writing in pocket notebooks which were very narrow, he would break the line; and some people have been confused about how that's supposed to sound. They think you're supposed to stop at the end of the line; but no. For instance, in *Mexico City Blues*, there's a poem [146th Chorus] that's broken up this way on the page: "The blazing chickaball –break—Whap-by –break– Extry special Super –break– High Job –break– Ole 169 be –break– floundering –break– down to Kill Roy." Now the way he would read that would be, [quickly,] "The blazing chickaball whap-by extry special super high job ole 169 be floundering down to Kill Roy." That's all one line. A favorite of mine is from *San Francisco Blues* [4th Chorus and 5th Chorus combined], which I see as broken up into lines like this, in terms of the music of it: "The rooftop of the beatup tenement on 3rd & Harrison has Belfast painted / black and yellow on the side the old Frisco wood is shown with weatherbeaten rainboards / & a washed out blue bottle once painted for wild commercial reasons by an excited seltzerite / as firemen came last afternoon and raised the ladder to a fruitless fire that was not there / so / is Belfast singin' in this time when brand's forgotten / taste washed in rain the gullies broadened & every body gone / and the acrobats of the tenement who dug bel fast divers all and the divers all dove /

ah / little girls make shadows on the sidewalk shorter than the shadow of death in this town—" Hear that beautiful arc in that last line: little girls make shadows in the sidewalk shorter than the shadow of death in this town. I think you can get some idea of that long, beautifully articulated, varying line. It's not just in the poems, it's even more so in the prose. It sometimes goes on for a whole page.

In 1959 in a letter to Don Allen, which was later published in his "Belief and Technique for Modern Prose," Kerouac said, "the rhythm of how you decide to rush your statement determines the rhythm of the poem." Rush your statement, in other words, actually accelerate, speed up the words. Here's an example of that from *Visions of Cody:* "There and there alone we'll find our chops and smoky talk of the most important dinner time in Denver." See how that last line picks up, it's almost like a bop player getting into a fast eighth note line. Another gig he got into, in the same letter to Don Allen, "add alluvials to the end of your line, when all is exhausted and something has to be said for some specific irrational reason." An alluvial is really a geological term for the sediment that gets spewed out at the mouth of a river, sort of like the river's afterthought, the dumping of its load. This example, from *Visions of Cody,* is from the beautiful long paragraph about Lester Young being like the river—I didn't realize that there was a river connection until now. He goes on, and then there's a point at which he seems to be done, and then suddenly he picks up again and gives you an incredible last, final splurt. It goes like this: "Lester is just like the river, the river starts in near Butte, Montana in frozen snow caps (Three Forks) and meanders down across states and entire territorial areas of dun bleak land with hawthorn crackling in the sleet, picks up rivers at Bismarck, Omaha and St. Louis just north, another at Kay-ro, another in Arkansas, Tennessee, comes deluging on New Orleans with muddy news from the land and a roar of subterranean excitement that is like the vibration of the entire land sucked of its gut in mad midnight, fevered, hot." And then he adds to the end of this, "the big mudhole rank clawpole old frogular pawed-soul titanic Mississippi from the north, full of wires, cold wood, and horn." Back to Lester at the end there.

Another thing he does sometimes is use a word as a punctuation mark, almost like a period—pop—to end a cadence, in other words a completion of a musical phrase. This, from *Dr. Sax:* "In the fall there were great sere brown sidefields sloping down to the Merrimac all rich with broken pines and browns, fall," set off by commas, and then "the whistle was just shrilled to end the third quarter in the wintry November field where crowds and me and Father stood watching scuffling uproars of semipro afternoons like in the days of old Indian Jim Thorpe, boom, touchdown." It's interesting, I noticed, reading this to prepare for today, that the first part, that ends with fall, is all color images and setting up the mood, and the second part is all sounds, the whistle, scuffling uproars, boom, touchdown. That's all one sentence too.

And another thing he does is extend his parentheses to an unbelievable extent, and then he'll sometimes get back to the original thought. This reminds me of, in music, a kind of chordal suspension, where in a standard tune that a jazz musician will play there's a set of chords that goes in exact, numerical rhythm and then repeats, and sometimes guys will, like they say, go outside and play way on one chord before they finally come back, as if the tune was elastic. In fact there's a beautiful description by Kerouac in this section of *Visions of Cody* called "Following Lee Konitz," where he talks about that and makes a figure for that in his own work. He's talking about following Lee Konitz around Manhattan, he saw him accidentally, so he says about Lee Konitz, "He can take care of himself even though he goofs and does 'April in Paris' from inside out as if the tune was the room he lived in and was going out at midnight with his coat on." This is the best description of that kind of bop improvisation that I know of.

I also wanted to mention that sometimes those parentheses don't ever get closed, he just never gets back to the thought, and that's somewhat like a jazz musician too. Sometimes a phrase or an idea will get dropped and just never get gone on with. Don't worry about it. If you hear the sound, you just get carried on and you'll forget it too unless he picks it up again. It's a principle of improvisation. You have to forget some things to improvise. It's also part of an excited talk, excited telling of a tale in a bar, you drop some things in favor of others spontaneously. It's almost like you're walking through a series of rooms. You walk in one room, turn on the light, walk in the next room, turn on the light, walk in the next room, turn on another light, maybe walk in one and turn on the light and it's a closet; but you don't stay there, you turn around and get back to another room.

—June 1, 1982

There's only one really good text, prepared also by David Erdman for Doubleday, *Complete Poems and Prose of William Blake.* The reason the text is important is if you don't use the Erdman text you'll wind up with a text that somebody else has punctuated and put capitals [in]—cleaned up Blake's capitalization and punctuation—so you miss Blake's original nervous system imprints. The Oxford Blake, the big book of complete Blake, Oxford Press, changes it and I don't know what they do [in the Norton anthology]. Let's take a look at "Tyger." You have "Tyger! Tyger! burning bright" in the first stanza and in the last stanza you have "Tyger! Tyger! burning bright." Now in the original manuscripts it's completely different. Blake has "Tyger tyger, burning bright," I think, as the first one. "Tyger tyger," or some mark, or a period, "burning bright," but not exclamation points and the two "tygers" are together as one breath. In the last stanza it's "tyger, tyger burning bright." And if you're singing it you realize you really need that extra breath.

So some dopey anthologist, not knowing the difference, has got "Tyger, tyger," another anthologist here as got "Tyger! Tyger!," and the original has "Tyger tyger, burning bright." It's [singing] "TY-ger Ty-ger BURNing Bright." That's how you'd follow the breathing. It's important to know the breathing. It's important to follow the punctuation, to know the punctuation in order to replicate or reproduce the breathing that Blake intended consciously, because he's as smart as any of these guys that punctuate. He knows what he's doing. And any great poet, you follow his punctuation, you'll get the cadence proper. Generally. Maybe the poets here at Naropa don't, are too sloppy to notice where they're slushing around their punctuations and commas and exclamation points, but after you graduate here you're supposed to know that if you've got a comma, you mean it, and if you don't have a comma you don't mean to have a comma and that you've got a blank space. Consciousness of punctuation is one of the bardic attributes, because consciousness of punctuation is consciousness of breath, and consciousness of breath is the substrate of the poetry.

—Allen Ginsberg
from "William Blake's 'Auguries of Innocence,' "
from a talk given April 19, 1991

BASIC DEFINITIONS

Gary Snyder

'D LIKE TO TAKE A LITTLE TIME TO GO BACK TO BASICS AND PROVIDE SOME definitions that I think will enable our dialogue to go forward. I don't work much with the contemporary or the modern, or even the Occidental for that matter. For many years I've been finding my greatest poetic sustenance and spiritual and intellectual challenge in working with a range of premodern poetries, many of them preliterate. These literatures are difficult because they are much more remote and it's easier to fool yourself into thinking that you understand what they are about, or think that you've learned a lesson. With remote texts you can be tempted to read into them what you will. But there is a chance, if you pay attention, to get some true information about the larger human consciousness of poetic practice with its depth, its antiquity, its richness. So this is an exercise in objectivity and clarity and in the illumination of twentieth-century subjectivity; to try to read and imagine our way into these unfamiliar poetries and learn from them.

So first to definitions. Beginning question is what is actually meant by the term *literature*? There is actually one perfect, complete, all-inclusive definition of literature. Would somebody like to throw out a definition of literature? Don't be afraid, you'll all be wrong anyway until we get it ironed out—and it's no big deal. Is literature limited to that which is written? And we'd have to say no, obviously, or we would be stuck with saying that ninety-nine percent of human beings in ninety-nine percent of human history never had any literature. It was only that one percent that was using writing systems in the overall human experience.

Literacy was not common until a hundred fifty years ago on any large scale. It's only in this century, really, that we have something approaching ninety percent literacy in the developed word. Much of the third world is still functionally nonliterate, but that doesn't mean the people don't have culture. Obviously a definition of literature has to cover the unwritten cases as well as the written. So now what do we say it is?

STUDENT: Information.

GARY SNYDER: But there's some we think of as "literature" that's not exactly information. True, a lot of literature is information, but some is not. Some is just mythical playfulness. And think of children's playground songs and verses—

> "Baby baby suck your toe, all the way to Mexico"

> "Kindergarten baby, wash your face in gravy"

> "It was not last night but the night before, that forty-eight robbers came to the door"—Those are all just magical and playful.

STUDENT: Expressions of thoughts and feelings.

SNYDER: That's definitely part of it too. But there are expressions of thoughts and feelings which are not literature. In fact we express our thoughts and feelings daily and yet we know it is not literature.

STUDENT: Transmission or communication.

SNYDER: Well, communication is a vast area, and it doesn't even require language. There's a lot of nonlinguistic communication that takes place.

STUDENT: Is there nonlinguistic literature?

SNYDER: That's a good question. What do you think? I think we'll have to keep literature within the sphere of language. Otherwise it becomes a metaphor for communication. Then we're into the larger area of communication and metalanguages. So let's say that we're still within the realm of language.

It certainly is true that literature is time binding, that it exists in a time scale that is larger than day-to-day verbal communication. But it's not limited to the aesthetic. There is scientific literature, which is not aesthetic, and there is technical literature—there are automobile and software manuals that are pure information, without any aesthetic component. You might be in the hardware store and ask "Do you have some literature on rototillers?"

Belle-lettres. [long pause] "Lovely Writings."

Well, I like the definition that Leonard Bloomfield proposed many years ago. Bloomfield was in an earlier generation of linguists previous to the structuralists, but the groundwork he did in his big book called *Language* is probably still the best overall introduction to language you'll pick up anywhere. I recommend it, because it covers everything. It starts out blocking out the major linguistic traditions of the world, giving you the number of mutually unintelligible languages as of the mid-twentieth-century, defining differences between what are dialects in different languages, and then he marches right on into phonetics, phonemics, morphologies, and so forth. Bloomfield was at the University of Pennsylvania, he's dead now, he started out as a rabbinical scholar, and then he went into Semitic languages as a Hebrew scholar, and then he went on to Semitic linguistics, and then he became a massive world linguist—an incredible fellow.

His definition of literature—the spare, elegant "scientific" definition is: "notable utterances." That covers the written and the unwritten and it covers all the possible genres that you might run across. Notable utterances.

So we're left with investigating the nature of "notability." Utterances have been going on for the last maybe hundred thousand years at a very great rate. In fact, much of the fabric of our daily life whenever we are in the company of others is a fabric of utterances, from dawn till dark.

The amount of linguistic activity that goes on in one human lifetime is staggering, and the overall total amount of linguistic activity, linguistic behavior in the world, would be virtually immeasurable. So notability, the matter of an utterance that gets saved, that is remembered, that is passed on, is a very rare occasion. It is most remarkable, very special, that somebody's use of language, some particular thing said, should be kept in memory and then passed along.

Another matter to consider is the time span of "notability." The shortest time span of a given piece of literature might be twelve or thirteen hours or even maybe three hours. That would be a case of somebody producing a good anecdote and somebody else hearing that anecdote, maybe laughing, and repeating it to another person three hours later. So it's been remembered for three hours. If the second person remembers it and repeats it to somebody else, its lifespan continues as long as that transmission takes place. If it is appreciated, retained, and resaid once, then it has had a short lifespan. But that lifespan puts it within the sphere of literature.

Jokes heard and repeated a week later, funny lines, proverbs, riddles, all could be a kind of literature and notability. In terms of long lifespan, it is those very same short phrases and interesting little turns of language that possibly have the longest lifespan in all of literature. Such are the now established anonymous proverbs and riddles.

Take an Arab proverb: "Take what you want, and pay for it" and imagine how that plays through centuries, from society to society. Or a Chinese proverb: "Be careful what you ask for, lest it be granted." These things have possibly several millennia of currency. There's no way of knowing. But certainly in the realm of folk literature, riddles, and proverbs, because of their very shortness and their instant impact, we are looking at some of the longest lived bytes of human lore and wit.

Otherwise, the long-lifers are basic folk tale and myth types that are performed over and over again, place to place with an almost vast range of small creative variations.

It's no secret what these are. There are certain elements in folk literature that crop up worldwide, such as the motif of someone being chased by an ogre or a demon, and as they flee they throw objects over their shoulder. They throw a comb over their shoulder, it becomes a forest and blocks the way to the pursuer. They throw a pencil or a piece of stone over their shoulder, it becomes a field of stones. This is the magic chase motif that's found so widely that we have to assume it represents a really archaic stratum of literary consciousness that gives it an antiquity, twenty thousand years maybe. Since these are found in North and South America as well as in Asia and Europe, this special number of globally distributed motifs—and since human beings have been in the western hemisphere for at least forty thousand years, and since we'll continue to think for the time being that they came from Asia, although that may be turned over eventually, then we'll have to say that by one way of transmission or another, these motifs go back to early Homo sapiens times. That's the longest span that you can hope for. And that implies that these tales and motifs have traveled through thousands of different languages.

If you stay within one language and there's no translation, what's the longest notability span that you can hope for in a piece of literature? How long can a piece of literature last in its own language? Only as long as the language lasts. The English culture goes on, but Chaucer's language is no longer easily available to us.

The language of *Beowulf* is really remote. Linguistic change as we can roughly figure it out goes on at about the rate of substantial change in any five-hundred-year period. That is to say, within any given five-hundred-year time-span, point A to point B, the language has become incomprehensible to itself. That's an estimate of the rate of change of spoken language, as a natural process, not dependent on invasions or trauma of various kinds, social revolutions and so forth, just working along the lines of a natural process within which syntax, pronunciation, and grammar seems to go through its own changes.

With writing systems, things change a bit. Spoken language goes on changing at about the same speed, but pieces of spoken literature that have been trapped or frozen into written language then become transmitted in another medium and become objects of study. And so it becomes possible to read in an archaic language. This was not possible in preliterate times.

So we have an additional element with writing on the scene, which is a long-range transmission of archaic languages or ancient or dead languages which then become sometimes enshrined as classic languages because of their association with religious hierarchy or an elite group of some earlier time. Thus Greek, Latin, Hebrew, Literary Chinese, and Sanskrit, which became frozen and established as hieratic, high culture languages that were later objects of special study.

STUDENT: I've noticed also the origins . . . what the basic word is, and then from that word we use . . . Why is Latin taught so early in schools?

SNYDER: It's not, they don't teach Latin anymore, except in parochial schools or special prep schools, like Horace Mann.

STUDENT: It was taught in the school I went to.

SNYDER: Public school? Where was that?

STUDENT: . . . Ohio.

SNYDER: Is that right? It sure isn't being taught in California anymore and it certainly is not getting very much play. Because people, when they do get a chance to study another language nowadays will go into Spanish or French or German. They should be having, of course, Russian and Chinese and Japanese in the schools, but they don't.

Your point is a good point. Why Latin? That's mostly the effect of the prestige of the Imperium, of imperial culture and imperial literature as a prestige item, and later its association with the Roman Catholic church, which was the carrier of the Imperium in the Middle Ages. The great city, the great empire. In actual linguistic fact, Latin is only a very moderate component in modern English. Most of that was filtered through French, which is a low-class dialect of Latin as spoken by the barbarians and soldiers out on the border. That's really how we get our Latinate words, our Frenchified words. The basic phonology, grammar, syntax, the guts of English are all from the Germanic family side. Much of the vernacular vocabulary is from the Germanic side.

That shows that English, *Anglais,* is a creolized language (meaning technically a language of mixed parentage in which the vocabulary of the dominant group was absorbed into the grammatical structure of the subordinate group and then stabilized). This adds to its vigor. But ancient languages are of historical and literary interest when you're zeroing in on a particular part of the cultural story. They don't contribute a great deal to the wealth or the vitality of the culture. And they tend to be oppressive, really, in the long run. If you think of literature as a matter of "Making it New," of continually refreshing consciousness and reviving cultural spirit, they may become oppressive and stultifying. Or, some great writer might find new excitement in a classic move and bring it again into our contemporary mind.

It should be remembered that without writing, a culture is perfectly able to have a full, aesthetic literary culture. Semi-professional raconteurs in a culture without writing have very well-developed memories. They can carry with them an enormous amount of lore and material. There was an old African that Melville Jacobs worked with in Dahomey in the thirties, who recited for him over three thousand different folk tales from memory. And that wasn't considered particularly extraordinary. In the village tradition of India, the great Indian classic, the *Mahabharata,* within which the "Bhagavad Gita" is just a chapter, is even today recited by professional raconteurs who know it by heart, out in the villages of India. It can be a five-day performance. The raconteur comes into the village, puts up her or his banners, makes the announcements that starting on a certain day we will have the full presentation of the *Mahabharata,* and the people, maybe mostly the kids and the old people who have the time, will be there for five days.

In Yugoslavia/Serbia, Croatia, Kosovo, and Albania, up until World War II there was a strong tradition of oral epic recitation, accompanied by a little stringed instrument. It was semi-prose semi-measured language, so you could call it a kind of poetry. These epic recitations were usually given in coffee shops, in the Muslim parts of the country, and they took four to five hours to recite. Examples of this could be multiplied considerably.

Knowing this helps to free ourselves from the notion that writing has been essential to the development of a high literary culture. It's not essential. We could perhaps find ways to argue that it destroys some of the creativity and spontaneity that is possible, and destroys some of the musicality that is always present in oral literary presentations.

So then, what does writing bring to literature? Classical languages, dead languages, the hieratic (meaning elite, top class, exceptionally valued), and a kind of literary pleasure associated with class structure. The two terms are hieratic and demotic: *demos,* democracy, *hieros,* hierarchy, the top and the bottom. Another set of terms is imperial and vernacular, referring to the two major cultural forces, namely the forces that come from the center of power, the government, the city, and the cultural tastes that are patronized by the city and by the ruling class, which is to say, opera, ballet, or whatever art form is being patronized and sponsored, as against the vernacular, which always remains the culture that is homemade without city-educated experts, in other words, folk culture.

I'll be returning to those terms, because vernacular is a very useful word, and vernacular culture is a very precise way of talking about what exists in opposition to mass culture. Mass culture is imperial culture, as against whatever vernacular we can keep going. In rooms like this, we're dealing with vernacular culture, because we're doing it ourselves, as against a mass produced and massively supported set of cultural activities. Vernacular culture is producing and reproducing itself always locally. A ten-watt radio station is a vernacular radio station. To the degree that it uses canned programming from outside, it becomes non-vernacular, it becomes "media."

A little more about writing. Writing may not be necessary, but it is a wonderfully useful tool. Now that we've got it, we'll probably keep on using it. There are certain, particular kinds of pleasures that are possible with writing that are not possible without it, like reading alone late at night. Written literature makes the literary experience more private, more solitary. For many people, it's a solitary experience. In preliterate times it was almost always a social experience, in the presence of others, someone is singing or telling a story, or, very occasionally, you're singing to yourself or telling a story to yourself.

A kind of solitary literary enjoyment, going on for hours and hours, is hard to imagine in a preliterate culture. With writing, a whole kind of experience becomes enshrined, which is the development of a solitary literary sensibility. This is exquisitely described in China, where that small percentage of people who knew how to read and write developed a considerable sensitivity to each other and the poems that had been composed within their class over the centuries. One of their pleasures was to sit in some remote village that they had been exiled to or assigned to as a public bureaucrat and read poems by the ancients, feeling slightly sorry for themselves, but also appreciating the fact that they could read.

So by being able to read they could share the minds of those of ancient times. This becomes an enshrined experience in Chinese culture. As Kenneth Rexroth once said, "One advantage of knowing the classics is that no matter what situation you might find yourself in, you'll remember that someone else was there before you."

STUDENT: Why are they feeling sorry for themselves?

SNYDER: Because they weren't in the capital, they weren't at the center of things. You go to school in the capital, you might even be raised in the capital, you know what's going on all the time, you're right at the center of all the literary gossip, you've gotten to know a lot of people, you're close to where the power is. Then you graduate from college or you pass your Jin-shi degree, you get assigned to a job and it takes you out to the provinces. It might be the Chinese provinces, it might be the Roman provinces. The same thing happened during the Roman empire. So out in the provinces, you've got employment and you've got a certain amount of respect, but you don't have any of your old drinking buddies or anybody you can talk with about Proust or Rilke or Shakespeare. So you console yourself by drinking wine and reading the classics late at night, feeling slightly sorry for yourself and also a bit superior. It's a classic literary experience. And then there are poems written about doing that, which becomes a type of Latin poem or Chinese poem, one small genre. This is all within the sphere of what writing does for us. I have enough pleasure myself on long winter nights living in a remote spot in the country, picking up books and reading from different times and places, to appreciate that.

That brings us down to our own work here and now, in the twentieth century. We've all been educated essentially out of books, we are people of the library. We haven't gotten our education by listening to a grandmother recite long stories by the fireplace, or having a grandfather sit with us for hours and hours, telling what he knows, perhaps in a measured verse form. That's not our education anymore. We are educated by the Imperium, not by the vernacular, as it happens. We have to make the best of that. There is place for our work in the culture, a place for free creative activity still. Nothing is ever finished, nothing is ever completely written. The story is never closed.

You arrive at the point where you say, what then is our task? What are we doing? The territory is still open. We will never reach the point where the literary tradition has finished itself and there's no work left to do; the power of the vernacular, which is like wild grass, is that it always comes up through the pavement and breaks through the asphalt. That means that we always have work to do.

More definitions, then.

The difference between prose and poetry: going back to basic definitions, we can't make our prose/poetry definition reliant on anything that is of necessity written, it has to embrace the oral and the written both. The difference is that between song and plain speech. Poetry is a variety of song, and throughout most of the world it still is. Throughout most of the nonliterate world, it clearly is song.

Folk songs, primarily. But folk songs have a lot of variety. We have to enlarge the notion of what song means enough to allow that it is not necessarily a finely crafted lyric or melody, but is in the territory of chanting, in the territory of any kind of rhythmic and measured language such is commonly practiced in the recitations of long epics. We think of epic literature as being prose sometimes. Unless you're clearly instructed in it, you might think that the *Odyssey* or the *Iliad* or the *Mahabharata* were all prose pieces. But that's not the case. In the broadest definition of poetry, they are poems. They are in measured lines or breath-pulses. The *Mahabharata* is in *slokas,* which is a verse, it is divided into verses. And the fact that they are in measured lines, rhythmic and to a degree set, is what makes them more easily memorable. In the oral tradition, to commit large quantities of material to memory, you are aided vastly by having it in a rhythmic form. So we can say that all poetic forms, meters, and types of structures owe their inception in some degree to the necessity of memorization, plus the pleasure people take in rhythm and structure.

When you observe children learning about song and poetry, and growing into language, you see them playing with rhythmic and repetitive language very early. Little chants, little verses that come to them as soon as they begin any kind of organized speech. Pure play, pure pleasure, language play. I remember when my younger son was about three, we were driving in a truck down to Marysville, California, and he had his arm out the window of the truck and was beating a little rhythm on the door and chanting to himself. Finally I got so I could hear what he was saying, it was "dirty dirty dump truck dri-ver, dirty dirty dump truck dri-ver," his own little poem. Another time the two boys, when one was about three and the other five, they were running around the open fire, white ashes, red coals, and black charcoal. They were singing something like, "the fire is a cake, the fire is a cake, the white is the frosting, the white is the frosting, the black is the chocolate, the black is the chocolate."

You can go right on from there into grade school and the playground— a whole world of playground rhymes and chants that are the origins of poetry for kids. The first poetic and literary experience that children have is playground rhyme. There's a book on that by a couple named Opie called *The Lore and Language of School Children.*

STUDENT: Do you think modern poetry is more effective than prose, because it really isn't rhymed?

SNYDER: Modern poetry is really anomalous. I puzzle over that. Since for forty thousand years of poetic experience in, shall we say offhand, four thousand different cultures and four thousand different languages, everything that we would call poetry has been rhythmic to one degree or another, in one way or another, so we need to ask ourselves, how does twentieth century poetics get away with it? and where does it come from?

Good question, although maybe not so difficult to see, if you allow as twentieth century poetics does have rhythm, does have music, does have measure, though not so tight as it was in earlier English language tradition.

Also when you investigate some other poetic traditions you'll find that their measure is looser than traditional English sometimes.

Everything is measured, everything is formal, but the range of form is quite broad from place to place. Dennis Tedlock, who translated a set of stories from the Zuni and also has worked with Mayan literature, points this out in his translations of Zuni tales. He has a way to break the lines as though they were twentieth century open poetics, both long lines and short. He says what he has done is to use devices from modern poetic line structure to represent the actual rhythms in the storytelling. Zuni is not highly metrical in a strict formal way like, say, a Sanskrit *sloka,* in the telling of the *Mahabharata,* would be. But the stories are measured, they are not prose as a prose telling would be; the tellings have an inherent set of rhythmic patterns that can be traced out over any given five minutes of utterance, that bring them close to what he says is twentieth century poetry. So Tedlock's suggestion is that what we're doing in a lot of modern poetry is catching the kind of use of language and the degree of periodicity and rhythm that is commonly practiced in preliterate storytelling. It's an interesting thought. This is all in his book called *Finding the Center.*

STUDENT: The conscious attempt in modern poetry is to imitate the rhythms of free speech.

SNYDER: To imitate the rhythms of free speech or natural speech—that's only a part of it. If that's all you were doing then you might as well write vernacular prose, full of colloquialisms. There are people who do that, who catch the rhythm of daily speech beautifully. So what does poetry add to that?

STUDENT: Poetry, if it doesn't add anything to that, just reflects the natural speech.

SNYDER: Is that true? Then why isn't it a nice, vernacular, colloquial piece of prose?

STUDENT: Maybe it can get called both. I don't see it being so cut and dry.

STUDENT: What you're saying is that making something poetry adds a certain music to it?

SNYDER: I'm saying that, yes. Otherwise we might as well not talk about poetry and prose. I think there is a working distinction that we are, in practice, all of us observing, all the time. Otherwise we wouldn't break our lines the way we break them. I remember when I was in college one of the English professors made the joke that is, modern free verse is just prose where the lines don't all come to the end of the page. If that's what we're writing, forget it. We might as well just block it out as prose then, and save paper.

In poetry you've already created a sound pattern, a rhythm, which is not evident in the prose block. If you take a piece of prose and you block it out differently on the page, then you'll read it differently, you'll read it according to the blocking.

STUDENT: [something about punctuation & prose poetry]

SNYDER: Of course all definitions break down at certain points. But let's stay with trying to make some definitions a little bit longer. The Latin root of prose is *prosa,* which means plain speech. Plain speech, then, is daily flow utterance. Any given language has rhythmic patterns that are inherent to that language, so there is a rhythm that you can say English has, just as there's a rhythm that French has or a rhythm that Japanese has. But the periodicities in that rhythm are so unstructured and work on such long loops that we neglect to make anything of them. A person who picks up prose writing will work with the natural language and will compress those periodicities to some point that we will say each prose writer begins to have a distinctive style. And part of that distinctive style may be certain kinds of rhythms that they have distilled out of the rhythms in the natural language. There is that possibility of rhythmic stylistics in prose. When we say prose poem, we generally think of something which is not too long and more frilly and more intensified rhythmically than a good, rhythmic piece of prose writing. So it gets boiled down farther. In fact, however, what most people mean when they say prose poetry is simply that it is to some degree an elaborated language, that is decorated and is perhaps emotive, just in sort of garden variety ways of talking about it.

But when you get into poetic form, when you jump into formal poetics, you have inherent characteristics of the language highly codified and highly distilled, made instantly recognizable. They are still part of what the natural language does, but it's been distilled to a point where it stands out strikingly. In, say, Zuni (because we'll come back to Tedlock), there is only moderately rhythmic daily Zuni language, which is their spoken prose. There is Zuni tale telling, which is very rhythmic and has identifiable structures within it, as tale telling, yet we might call it prose. And then there is Zuni song. Zuni song is very intense, very formal. What I'm saying is that our modern, twentieth century poetics puts us in a territory that can be identified in nonliterate cultures but can't quite be identified in our own culture, as a territory. And it's perfectly valid.

We don't have a rhythmic storytelling in our Anglic tradition anymore. We go straight from novelistic storytelling into poetry, a big jump. The territory in between, of what we might call prose poem, is not developed.

There are traditional narrative songs usually in ballad meter. They're quite formal. When I say storytelling I'm talking about prose storytelling. Of course narrative song, ballad or whatever, is truly poetic.

STUDENT: [something about Kerouac]

SNYDER: Kerouac's novels. He's a prose stylist bringing out rhythms that exist in natural English and intensifies them, he gives his own stylistic stamp to it.

STUDENT: [something about a prose poem, *Finnegans Wake*, genre]

SNYDER: *Finnegans Wake*. I would invent a category for *Finnegans Wake*. I think it's a variety of long, religious poem. It's a chant, actually, it's like a sutra, in that the intelligible and the unintelligible come together and the mantric rises and subsides; the overall effect is magical.

Poetry and prose, song and speech. Poetry, sacred and secular, two categories, sacred song and secular song. We don't have much to do with sacred song in the English-American tradition. We only have one category of sacred song, that's hymns, and one other category you wouldn't think of right off, the service in the Greek Orthodox church, that's sacred song. And the service in the Roman Catholic church, especially when they kept it in Latin. Because chanting is a variety of song, the roots are the same, to sing. So there are traditional, lengthy, sacred poetic structures.

The Buddhist sutras chanted in services. A chanted sutra is a sacred poetic performance. It's a performance that everyone does together and also it's a performance in that it is done regularly, in a ritual way, over and over again, using the same text over and over again. But it is also a variety of poetic usage according to this kind of looking at the largest scale. The chanting of sutras, and the chanting of dramatic texts, as in Noh drama of Japan or in the Chinese drama, much of which is sung or chanted, and in the recitation of the *Vedas* in an Indian Brahmin religious afternoon, are all varieties of sacred poetry.

Within varieties of sacred poetry you can say there's the intelligible and the unintelligible. The unintelligible has its own special magic and special reasons for existing. That brings us to mantras. Mantras, as used in Tibetan Buddhism or in Hinduism, are a variety of sacred poetry, an unintelligible variety sometimes. That's where *Finnegans Wake* fits in, in some funny way.

On the secular side we have all of these ballad and verse types, genres, forms, that we're acquainted with over the centuries, coming right down to modern times. In particular, with our modern poetics, the kind of highly self-conscious, searching, deliberateness, exploration of mind, exploration of perception that characterizes twentieth century poetry.

This probably belongs in the ancient category of song that we would call healing songs and vision-quest songs—songs composed for the occasion of making somebody well, or songs that come to you on the occasion of great personal questing and great personal seeking. That's the variety of poetic work that some of the greatest and most ambitious twentieth century poetry set itself to. Those two categories are part of the panoply of the poetic life of any culture.

The poetic life of any culture also includes lullabies, worksongs, hunting songs, fighting songs, drinking songs, marriage songs and post-marriage songs, and songs to die by; but we don't make much use of a lot of those possibilities. Our self-conscious literary intellectual culture of the twentieth century makes great use of the variety that is involved in personal quest and in the search for healing, because we live in troubled times. That's the way I see it.

STUDENT: Does prose fall into those same categories?

SNYDER: Not so clearly, I don't think so, except on the side and occasionally.

STUDENT: [something about vision quest?]

SNYDER: I would say Ezra Pound's *Cantos* is one great exemplar of a flawed and unsuccessful search for healing, of the attempt to find at least the beginnings of a way to achieve cultural and psychological integrity. I see James Joyce as attempting the same thing in another way and more in prose; and T. S. Eliot in a much quieter way. In fact it was the typical activity of early twentieth century poetics, anybody who launched into any kind of ambitious effort was essentially seeking wholeness—seeking to block out a way toward it—the effort of healing.

—August 8, 1983, © Gary Snyder 2009

PULLING IT DOWN
OR THE GOOD MANNERS OF VAMPIRES

Amiri Baraka

THE BOURGEOISIE OR THE RULING CLASS, WHOEVER YOU WANT TO CALL them, the big sticks, what they have done is eliminate the world of 1950 to 2000. So all the things of the people that we love and hold dear and the work that we did and struggled to complete, they have eliminated. So that aside from an occasional article about Allen Ginsberg, who you all love and who was crazier than you can ever appreciate and more brilliant than you can ever appreciate, still, aside from that, you're only a dit and a dot and a dit and a dot and a dit and a dot.

The names, if we look for names of the people who actually were part of the New York School, the O'Haras, the Ashberys, well Ashbery gets over more than anybody else, but the real leader of that is Frank O'Hara, the great poet of that period was Frank O'Hara. That's gone. We hear about Frank every once in a while, a funny aside, you know, or Ashbery gets another fellowship, which I'm not griping about, I'm just saying. But beneath that, the Barbara Guests in all the periods, people that came with the New York School—where is that?

We have those poetry readings at St. Mark's where we talk about the Black Mountain people. We talk about the Charlie Olsons, the six-foot-five behemoth that changed all our lives; Charles Olson who created a whole new poetics, the poetics of place, who took Pound's poem of history and converted it to humanism rather than the kind of elitism and fascism that Pound ended up with, may he rest in peace wherever he is. But where are the Charlie Olsons? Even the Bob Creeleys, the great living Bob Creeley poet, where are they? Not to mention the Joel Oppenheimers, the Gil Sorrentinos, the Joe Earlys, all the little poets that came under the Black Mountain poets. Where are the John

Weiners? the Michael Rumakers? great prose writers like that? Where are they? Covered up, covered up.

Then, we get the latest batch from the *Kenyon Review, Sewanee Review, Hudson Review, Partisan Review*—and I thought we had killed all those people. Because when I came to New York we tried to form a united front, that's what the magazine *Yugen* was. We tried to get all the poets together who were anti-academy. So we got the New York School, we got the Black Mountain School, and we had to listen to Fielding Dawson tell us endless stories about Black Mountain College, into the night over the eighty-eighth beer, we had to hear about it, but it was beautiful. It was beautiful because we found out about Franz Kline and de Kooning, we found out about the Bauhaus and how the Bauhaus was connected to Weimar in the last democratic thrust of Germany. We found out where modern art came from. The Philip Gustons and the Dan Rices, where are they? My old drinking buddy and boxing companion, Basil King, where is he? All these great people that I met as a young man in the Village, being artists, thinking that we would rule the world, thinking that we could kill all these little thugs from the *Partisan Review* and the *Sewanee Review* and the *Hudson Review,* we thought we could just beat them out of existence with our mouths. And Allen, of course, talking about the Beat Generation, of which there never was a Beat Generation except people who find out about it later. I mean, Allen Ginsberg was one of the most intelligent people you will ever meet in your life.

I came back from Puerto Rico after being in the service—first I got kicked out of college so I went to the Air Force and then I got kicked out of the Air Force, and finally they kicked me out of the Poet Laureate spot, I think it's something I said.* But coming back there to New York, 1957— you know how long ago that was?—looking for the world-class intellectuals, where are they? I know there are some bright guys. I had spent twelve hours a day for two years reading books, I was the night librarian

* "On September 19, Amiri Baraka, an influential beat poet and founder of the Black Arts Repertory Theatre in Harlem, read a recent poem, 'Somebody Blew Up America,' at the 2002 Geraldine R. Dodge Poetry Festival at Waterloo Village in Stanhope, New Jersey. . . . Since Baraka read his poem in September, popular news commentators and powerful political organizations have called for the revocation of his status as poet laureate of New Jersey. . . . Even though he wrote the poem last October, ten months before taking on the title as poet laureate, New Jersey Governor James E. McGreevey wants Baraka to resign and apologize." (Kurt Nimmo, in *CounterPunch*, October 3, 2002)

in Puerto Rico strategic air command under Curtis Lemay, who I once saw riding down the runway on a go-cart, and I said, that's the guy who controls the future of the world. So as my airman second-class two-stripe self, we formed a little group of people in that library and every night we taught ourselves the history of Western literature and the history of Western music. I knew nothing about that. We studied motets, Gregorian chants, Bach, all the way through every night. And we started with literature, the same thing. I read nineteenth-century literature, which I still hate, English literature. Even read Proust, stuff that you would not touch with a stick, I read. Why? Because I wanted to find out what was happening. I didn't understand that understanding and knowledge were important. I didn't understand that learning, that the raising of your consciousness is the most important thing that you can do. I was in my little Boy Scout suit, it wasn't a Boy Scout suit then, it was an Air Force uniform, in Chicago, and I came to this place called the Green Door. It was a bookstore. And I looked in the window there, I had just gotten thrown out of college, had just gone to basic training and set a new record for KP, twenty-two times in a row. But I didn't understand the importance of learning. All you would-be writers, you can never write if you don't learn, because you won't have anything to write about. So I stood there and it came to me and I said, I know, I should try to learn something every day. You know what a little boy I must have been, twenty years old, 'cause I looked at the names on these books and I didn't understand what they were saying. I didn't know what they meant. I didn't understand the language, I didn't know what Seven Types of Ambiguity—what did that mean? What did dissociation mean? I knew what a metaphor was, I had finished at least two years of college before I got kicked out. I had read James Joyce, Jesus, I knew something. I had even read a couple of poems of Pound. I had always read Langston Hughes, Langston Hughes was my man since I was a little boy. I'd read Richard Wright since I was twelve years old. I knew them, but out in the whole world—who was Baudelaire? what did he have to do with anything? what was *Fleurs du mal*? Who was Cézanne? What's the difference between Cézanne and Matisse? Those were the things I was grappling with in the aftermath. But the one great thing was that I was the librarian, so I could order anything. They would come up to me and say, Jonesy, airman second class Everett L. Jones, Jonesy, what's a Kafka? Geez, I don't know what a Kafka is, let's check it out. Hey, here it is, it's Franz Kafka, Austrian, the books: *Metamorphosis*,

The Trial. Order all of those, the whole box of old Kafka, and our boys, we'd just sit there and study.

So when I came to New York I was prepared then to be an intellectual. You know what I'm saying, oh, now I know things. But the only thing you don't know is what you'll have to face. You don't know the nature of the struggle that you have to get it. So I arrived and I was standing in San Juan one afternoon crying because I was reading a poem in the *New Yorker* and I said, I can never write a poem like that—about bird baths, trips to Connecticut, the 508 out of New York to Connecticut, I could never write like that. So I said, there must be something I can do with my life. I know what, I can write my own poetry. I can write it as it comes out of me, as messed up as that is, as broken down, as urbanly challenged, as ethnically squashed, that will be my poetry. And I will be so arrogant as to claim it and to say, this is my poetry, right here.

And that's what you all have got to do, you've got to be that mean, that arrogant, that bad. And so we took up the Beat Generation; someone would say are you in the Beat Generation? I'm in the generation that wants to pull all the great literature together and beat these thugs down into the ground, that's who I am. We jumped on all of it. We talked bad about every academic and they probably still hate us. . . . Then we had a magazine called *Kulchur* which was again the same thing, to put forward an avant-garde, an innovative, a new, a fresh culture, a new writing. We had met great writers, like Allen, like Charlie Olson, like Ed Dorn, who lived right here in Boulder and was a deep, old friend of mine. I loved Ed Dorn because he would rather hurt your feelings than lie to you, he'd rather box with you than not tell you the truth—he'd say, "I don't like that, that's no good, throw that away"—a lot of people can't stand that kind of criticism. If you want to read something of his, read *Abhorrences,* that's his last shot on the way out where he beats everybody to death, headed toward the coffin. He talks of "Chemo Sabe," chemotherapy and cancer. But between the Beats, so-called, the San Francisco School, that's an endless endless thing—not only Allen, but people like McClure, Whalen, fine poets like that, Robert Duncan.

But the point is that now it's time to come back to that. It's time to recreate a united front against the thugs that control the literary, political, and social world of this country and the world. In the last two years I've been in Caracas, Venezuela; Medellin, Columbia; Barcelona; Rome; Capo Verde; Africa; Pisa, Italy; Saint Martin's; Saint Thomas; Portugal;

Yugoslavia, all over the world. My poems are translated into Albanian. The point is this, "why are you all over the world, Baraka, and not here?" Because I cannot make a living in the United States. What's interesting, except for Anne [Waldman], when we went all over Latin America, the only two American poets that were invited to any of those festivals were my wife Amina and myself. Anne was invited to Caracas, to Venezuela, and couldn't come. But no American poets—and they know what they're doing. When we went to Medellin, Columbia, my wife and I came back from lunch and there was a letter to us from FARC, the revolutionary movement of Columbia, on our bed. "Welcome to Columbia, poet, we know you're in support of the people."

But the point is, ladies and gentlemen, comrades, brothers and sisters, that until we create an American revolutionary art, we will not be respected by the people of the world. Because we might go back through a particular tradition that upholds a Rexroth or a Ken Patchen or a Langston Hughes or a Henry Dumas, we might understand who a Zora Neale Hurston is or a Gertrude Stein, but that is not what America is being advertised as around the world. You're being advertised as the good manners of vampires—so, you don't kill, you write poems. You don't bring democracy to Iraq by blowing it up, by killing the children and starving them. You're the good manners of vampires. You will bite me in the neck, in a poem. If you value yourself as humanity, independent of nationality, ethnicity, race, creed, or color, but humanity in tune with the great majority of people who are not even in the working class—the great majority of the people in the world are still on the land, picking berries and potatoes and digging stuff, pulling wagons, in Africa, Latin America, Asia, they haven't even got to the city yet, they're out there in the countryside, trying to make a living. So that means we've got time.

But as the intellectual reserve of the greatest superpower in existence today, we have an obligation. That obligation is to pull this motherfucker down. Now how do you do that? You are a poet, well why don't you write some poetry, why don't you publish some books? I wish everybody here, whatever city they're in, would give a reading once a month. I wish you would get all the poets you know who are anti-imperialists or socialists or they just don't dig ugliness, to meet once a month and give a reading. You could spread out through the city, you could read in front of city hall, in front of the library, in front of museums, in front of the colleges. What I'm saying is you have to launch a movement again. What was the

Black Arts Movement? It was some black kids who'd been down with white people in the Village who knew nothing about Harlem but pretended they did 'cause they were black, and then found out when they got up there they didn't know anything about it at all. I had once said something ugly to two movie stars whose names I won't mention. That night there was a gangster sitting in front of me, a beautiful man, a great man—but that's how little I knew about Harlem. I didn't know that if I said something bad about Adam Clayton Powell that I'd have Bumpy Johnson looking me in the eye, talking about, are you LeRoi? I love your work, he said, everybody needs a friend. Because we did not know, we were just told we were black, black black black. The point is, we have to penetrate the minds of the people in this country, we have to bring them alternative visions.

When I said before, fight for a people's democracy, beat Bush, what is the common agitation? America needs a cultural revolution. And that's what you're in charge of—to change the culture of this country. How do we do that? By being insistent, as Creeley likes to say. By insisting. We say, beat Bush, and we all ought to do that propaganda fundamentally, that's fundamental, come in to a train station the least you can do is say "beat Bush." It's a fundamental address, the stance that we want.

—June 18, 2004

WOMEN AND THE BEATS

Hettie Jones, Joanne Kyger, Janine Pommy Vega, Anne Waldman

ANNE WALDMAN: I'M VERY PLEASED TO BE INTRODUCING THIS PANEL which is subtitled "Women Coming of Age in the Beat Generation, Being Writers and Being Women." I wanted to start off with a couple of ideas. Maybe some of you know the book, *Women of the Beat Generation.* It's a first in a sense, a landmark, yet it leaves a lot to be desired, especially in terms of some of the hagiographies and discussion of the overlapping lives: the intersections of how people came to do what they were doing. But it's important, it actually brings attention to women, some of whom had never been in print and never been acknowledged in terms of their role in the Beat literary historical period. It's interesting to use the term "Beat Generation" these days because it refers to an actual historical period, but many of the folks who were instrumental and important at that time have continued writing, have continued to go on with their lives and blossomed in voluminous, interesting ways. So from some point of view we're looking at a historical period and also what continues, and I hope the panel will touch on some of that history—that we'll hear about people's lives, about particular struggles, about gender issues, the relationship of the writers here in terms of work and life with many better-known members of that predominantly male generation. At the Kerouac School, even though we have invoked Kerouac's name, we caution people to avoid easy, facile labels, to avoid boxing writers in to one mode or condition. The artists you see here, the proponents and writers of that particular period, are often very different from one another in their work and ethos. One could speak about shared concerns, their being "consociates," which is a term I borrow from the ethnologist Clifford Geertz, which refers to people being alive at a particular period of time and experiencing many of the same things and intersecting in ways although they might not necessarily be intimate. As it turns out, of course, many of the people at that time were intimate in interesting and radical ways. It's an ever-expanding notion of community. You could talk about being "outside" the academy, being "outside" the mainstream, being economically in a different class, and even that gets mixed up, specific locations and sites of activity and intersection, shared interest in pursuing the "dérèglement des senses," the derangement of the senses which Rimbaud advocates for the poetic mind, finding outlets through means of hallucinogenics or other kinds of drugs, and interest in Eastern and Asian culture and religion, actually traveling to other places, traveling to the "fellaheen worlds," a phrase from Kerouac referring to so-called third worlds, that would be exotic but also having to do with an economic situation, worlds that represent very different emotional, cultural, and economic constructs from the ones people are coming from. In the case of women from that period, being very locked down—we're talking about the gray doldrums of the fifties for the most part, Eisenhower, post-World War II when everything was so-called rosy and you saw wonderful ads in *Life* magazine of women dancing around the kitchen with their dusters, opening their new Kelvinator refrigerators, toying with their appliances. Life was going to be easier with frozen food. Some of you were alive then, I was born in 1945 so I was in a slightly different position with all of this, a kind of younger sister. I did want to read a few lines from a foreword I wrote for *Women of the Beat Generation*.

"We benefited from the examples and trials of young women who had struggled to be creative and assertive before us, and we were certainly aware of the exciting artistic and liberal heritage of our New York City environs and yet many of us fell into the same retrograde traps. Being dominated by relationships with men—letting our own talents lag, following their lead—which could result in drug dependencies, painful abortions, alienation from family and friends. I remember my mother cautioning me not to be too 'easy' with men on the one hand, and on the other hand the advice to appease their egos! . . . I knew interesting creative women who became junkies for their boyfriends, who stole for their boyfriends, who concealed their poetry and artistic aspirations, who slept around to be popular, who had serious eating disorders, who concealed their unwanted pregnancies raising money for abortions on their own or who put their children up for adoption. Who never felt they owned or could appreciate their own bodies. I knew women leading secret or double lives because love and sexual desire for another woman was anathema. I knew women in daily therapy because their fathers had abused them or women who got sent away to mental hospitals or special schools because they'd taken a black lover. Some ran away from home. Some committed suicide. There were casualties among the men as well, but not, in my experience, as legion." And then I go on to talk about has that changed, how has that changed. And of course coming back to the work. It's been observed that the genre for the women of that period was primarily memoir and of course as we see there's poetry, some fiction, stories, and so on, but there is something to be said for the memoir genre which is powerful, generous, and often risky, but a way of articulating a lot of background, atmosphere, and details of quotidian reality. We have Hettie's *How I Became Hettie Jones* as one major example of that, and Joyce Johnson's *Minor Characters*.

Back to the notion of consociates, there were certainly a lot of intersections during this historical period. But the point is that people who survived went on with their lives. We're not trying to codify anything here but I think it's interesting for all of us, whatever our age or background or gender, to talk about these very real issues with the women who were "behind the scenes."

HETTIE JONES: Some years ago, before all this renewed interest in the Beats, a Columbia University student came to interview me. Her first question, as she arrived out of breath after hiking up the stairs to my apartment, was: "You weren't just Beat chicks, were ya?"

I like to tell that story because this girl's alarm seems to point in two directions: first to the idea that there were indeed Beat chicks, who would not be fit role-model foremothers, and then to its opposite, that the stories told by the men weren't true, that we were as savvy as they, and that in truth the Beat Generation was, if we get the story straight, "chickless." Even now the question and the qualifiers seem to persist. At the first conference on the Beats in 1994 I was on a panel titled "Women and the Beats." Then I got a letter from a publisher addressed to "Dear Beat Woman," which inquiry resulted in the book *Women of the Beat Generation*.

But while you're young and in the middle of living your life there are no labels. It's messy. How we laughed when people called us Beat-niks! The women with whom I was close were too busy struggling to give a damn about what they were called. And many of us, according to today's standards, would be considered failures. In the middle of being Beat, we did what the majority of fifties and sixties American women did—cooked, made beds, did dishes, and, most suspect of all, bore children.

One day during the eighties I was a guest in a class and found myself facing a rather hostile young woman who said, "Well, what really is different between then and now?" This was before I wrote my memoir and her question started a whole train of thought, a line of defense, really. What did we do, did we have a role in making things different for women, and what was it?

Well, I always like to start with underwear. I looked at that young woman, who was wearing a minimum of it plus jeans and an old shirt, and she was comfortable and therefore at her ease to speak her mind. To young people today I offer this: You know what Madonna used to wear on the outside? We wore it inside. This is not to trivialize the subject. Clothing, to shackle her or not, has been significant in the lives of women. It was no small thing to take off that girdle. We hadn't been loose since the twenties, and thirty years is a long time to be tied up. In this week's *New Yorker* I found the admonition "confine the body and shrink the spirit," a lesson everyone now seems to know. Giving that body its own space was critical. Those of you who have simply said, "I'm getting an apartment," can't imagine what courage that took and how suspect it made us in the prevailing social climate. Though my parents had reluctantly agreed to give me a mattress, they didn't want the neighbors to know I was moving out. So they tied the evidence to the top of their car and we left under cover of darkness. I had been planning that move ever since I was conscious, yet up to the time I did leave, in 1955, I had never known even one woman who lived independently.

Independence is a crucial word. How was a woman to achieve it? I wasn't brought up to believe that I couldn't take care of myself, but independence was never presented as an option. Every aspect of popular culture suggested that a self-determined woman's life was miserable and lonely and that sooner or later she'd "come to a bad end." This was very real advice. Women ended up selling themselves in lots of ways, as they still of course do. My first job paid thirty-five dollars a week. So you had to expect poverty as well as ostracism.

Just after my memoir came out I taught a semester at the New School in New York, where one of my women students presented me with a very interesting question. "You're the same age I am," she said, "so we grew up at the same time. I never did any of the things you did, although I wish I had. How did you know to rebel?"

Without thinking I answered, "Because if I hadn't, I'd have died."

Shocked silence greeted this, and I went home rather bemused, because I felt the truth of it profoundly. What I meant, probably, was that the person you're looking at wouldn't have existed, if you want to call me, her, a prototype. But throughout history this prototypical woman rebel has repeatedly died. Women are always under pressure to conform. So I think we have to look at why most of us "Babes" were even in that "Boyland," since being there was so risky.

Sex, naturally—but you could have sex anywhere back then, the couch, the back seat, the haystack. You just couldn't talk about it, couldn't live as if that were a part of your life. In leaving home we had at least escaped to where we could admit our desires. Of course in popular culture the fallen woman stereotype was still alive and well, and we were it, although most of us were hardworking and often supported the men we knew. Nevertheless, the picture of us that emerged on the lurid covers of so-called "Beat" paperbacks focused only on our sexual availability. There was no doubt in anyone's mind what we were doing in our own apartments because given half a chance they would have been doing it too. The difference between us and them was simply that question of death. The only "live" life that I could envision was one in which I functioned as a sexual human being. Yet I never thought of myself or my women friends as "bad." We were merely reinventing a more satisfying, more real woman's life.

I suppose this brings me to the relationships with the men of the Beat Generation, since those were the ones I had sex with. And here I'd want to include not only the writers but the entire downtown Bohemia of the fifties and sixties, though I promise I didn't sleep with every one of them—although that might have been nice. But recently another woman my age, who had not been a Beat chick, said to me, "You had all the luck because you slept with all the right guys." Well, as you can imagine I smarted over that one, because naturally our time with these men included a lot more than bedtime, and as a subset included of course the struggle to maintain one's integrity in the life they defined, all the while trying to create new definitions for ourselves. I don't know that I'd say it was luck. Instead I like to think that strong women require strong men or at least noisy ones.

Still, you had to have more than just sex to keep you in Boyland with your pride intact, because it was a man's world, no lie. As a woman you had to believe that stirring things up in general would eventually define a new life for you in particular; you had to believe in the transformative power of art and the word; and you had to believe yourself part of that process. I think it's common knowledge now that back then very few women managed to work as artists, or their efforts were overlooked or at best underserved. Some of us did other things, editing magazines and books for example, as I did. Logistically it often wasn't possible to be the breadwinner and the editor and the wife and the mother and the writer. But—a very important but—I have also come to see that sometimes women's silences back then were due to the verboten nature of the subject matter we wished to cover—a woman's life. Some of us were less afraid to tackle that, others were better educated to make the attempt.

I'm sometimes asked to consider the question, "How did women get published back then?" and I'm afraid the answer to that is, with some notable exceptions, if men wanted to include them. Yet in defense of these men, there weren't that many women demanding. Don't forget that forty years ago most women were still depicted petting their washing machines and their avocado-green refrigerators. Their real lives, the real lives of women, barely existed in the public mind. A lot of us didn't know what we thought or how bad off we were. Myself, I stuck the poems from that time in a drawer, but because I at least had a life of my own and a direction, I knew enough to save them for later. And when later finally came, I'm pleased to report they won a prize.

JOANNE KYGER: I always felt the Beat Generation belonged somewhere around the late forties and ended in 1962. Recently the tendency to label this midcentury San Francisco writing as "Beat" has been an annoying simplification. I never considered myself a Beat writer, nor did the so-called Beat writers of the time consider me one. And I never thought I was coming of age in the Beat Generation. I was aware that there was a group of writers that were starting to be described as Beat through the media. There's an interview that Kerouac did in 1967 with Ted Berrigan that was published in the *Paris Review,* and he says, "We [Ginsberg, Burroughs, and Kerouac] were just three interested characters, in the interesting big city of New York, around campuses, libraries, cafeterias. . . . So here comes Snyder with a bottle of wine . . . and here comes Whalen, and here comes what's his name, Rexroth, and everybody, . . . and we had the poetry renaissance of San Francisco. . . . That community feeling was largely inspired by the same characters I mentioned, like Ferlinghetti, Ginsberg; they are very socialistically minded . . . I was a loner." So, the Beat Generation, he says, "was just a term I used in 1951 in *On the*

Road to describe guys who run around in the country in cars, looking for odd jobs, girlfriends, and kicks." That was his very simple definition of the Beat Generation.

These writers were published and known poets, albeit by a small group, by the time I arrived in San Francisco from Santa Barbara in 1957. Ginsberg was rapidly achieving notoriety through the publication of his *Howl,* and the subsequent bust of the book at City Lights bookstore, and the subsequent trial. This was the beginning of a kind of worldwide awareness of this "Beat" voice, which was essentially a writing of what became known as disaffiliation. It was a writing of disaffiliation and it was becoming ragingly successful and notorious. It was of course comparing itself culturally to the writing and the culture in existence during the forties and fifties. Mark Green talks about this in his small photography book. (*A Kind of Beatness: Photographs of a North Beach Era. 1950-1965.* Focus Gallery Booklet, 1975) "When *On the Road* was finally published and the *Howl* obscenity trial started, people began associating what was happening in North Beach with Kerouac's writing of *On the Road.* Although the writing of *On the Road* was what was really happening to his circle of friends in New York City in the forties and fifties. And then reporters started coming to North Beach to get the Beatnik story. And people in North Beach would tell them fantastic put-on stories about what was going on. Which they printed. And that would bring more newsmen and more tourists, all with preconceived ideas. And as these reporters increased in number, their stories became more distorted. It made it even harder for outsiders to find out what was really going on. So Beatnik became a kind of dirty word to the people that were in North Beach, who mostly considered themselves pre-Beat bohemian, because San Francisco has a long history of artists and poets and musicians."

Lawrence Ferlinghetti in the *Chicago Review,* Spring 1958, talks about the writing of the time. "San Francisco poetry is not a school. There are all kinds of poets here writing very dissimilar types of poetry, but the poetry which has been making itself heard here, is what should be called street poetry. It makes it aloud. In fact off the printed page. It is using its eyes and ears as they have not been used before. It is the Resocialization of Poetry."

So poetry at that point was alive and in the air, very exciting. And poetry and jazz together was a phenomenon happening at The Cellar; poetry on stage, monster poetry readings with a thousand people coming.

Prior to this time, there was Dylan Thomas and a few other people that could go on the road and make a happening of poetry, but it wasn't a cultural activity.

As for myself, poetry was just part of a youthful quest for meaning and self-awareness that every young person has. The three years I spent in San Francisco, from 1957 to January of 1960, was a major university time. I was out of school, but what was happening to me in my life was my real schooling. Then I went to Japan. After four years in Japan, the San Francisco I returned to was past the Beat era, and an emerging counterculture had started to appear, using many of the ideas of the Beats, freedom, disaffiliation from this crass capital culture that was going on. It was the beginning of the so called Hippie counterculture movement. By '64 it was well on its way. By the time of the San Francisco Be-In in 1966, a major cultural change was going on. So the so-called Beat era didn't last a long time.

I came to San Francisco in 1957 from Santa Barbara with some years of religious and philosophic search behind me. I was twenty-three and I had dropped out of organized Christian religion. In the late fifties it was a little more unusual maybe. I remember I was working in the Santa Barbara public library and this guy came up to me, I was nineteen, and he showed me this book called *Existentialism* by Jean Paul Sartre, and he said, but don't show it to anybody else. It was a little, slim volume, and I devoured it, I had to read it over and over again because I hadn't a clue what Sartre was talking about, but I knew this was another kind of thinking. I'd go to the Santa Barbara Mission and want to argue the existence of God with these poor priests that were there. They said, you have to take this as a matter of faith. Anyway, I was very young and vigorously challenging all these preconceived existences as you can do when you're really young. Also at the university I was interested in philosophy so I read the work of Ludwig Wittgenstein and Heidegger and tried to understand this direction of a general history of Western philosophy. And during this time also the work of D. T. Suzuki became available for the first time. His writing was published first in England and then in the United States as an Anchor paperback. I became aware that you could go from Western philosophic thinking like Wittgenstein who wanted to go beyond concepts and language so that problems would just disappear—over this bridge from Western ideas into Buddhist ideas as expressed by Suzuki, a state of mind beyond thinking. And I also read Freud and Jung and Joseph Campbell's *Hero with a Thousand Faces* which used as source common mythical themes.

My teacher in English at UC–Santa Barbara, Hugh Kenner, had introduced his class to Ezra Pound, W. C. Williams, Yeats. So I had some background of information before I came to San Francisco in 1957.

In 1958 I was given peyote, which certainly showed an alternate reality. I met poets and wrote and saw artists crash and burn on speed and alcohol. I felt I needed some kind of daily practice in order not to go truly nuts, so I went to Japan for four years and learned how to practice meditation. I also got married. Few women were writing in the late fifties, at the time I was coming of age, at least among the groups of writers I was interested in. There was Denise Levertov and there was Diane di Prima, whom I didn't hear about until I was in Japan. But the self I was interested in wasn't concerned at that point with a male-female identity so much as what was this human self, how could I get rid of these horrible anxieties of existence. So I used a lot of classic mythic identity patterns to find a larger cultural context in which to place myself as a person, a persona. Through Homer's *Odyssey* I found a lot of that. I read books, the *Prolegoma to the Study of Greek Religion,* by Jane Ellen Harrison, and other books on Greek religion that spoke about Penelope, Persephone as living entities in a great historic time of Greece. My informal but real teachers in '57, '58, '59 were Robert Duncan and Jack Spicer, who kind of represented the mythic person and the truth of the voice. They did not consider themselves "Beats" of course.

The Beats were a really male-bonded clique, but that's not to say that the muse wasn't used by them, in her persona as a female. So that was kind of the inspiration of poetry, the muse as a female. The only trouble with that, according to Robert Graves, if you are a woman, you couldn't take on the muse yourself, so you had to be a muse. This was repeated to me as gospel truth by my husband at the time, "you're just going to have to be the muse, because you're female and you can't use yourself as the muse." Or something like that. . . . This sounds like a real bit of nonsense but it was reiterated, so it was a warning that any writing I might do might not be really inspirational. The only role really for an inspired woman to act in, as the muse, was to inspire your male companion, and do things like dressing and cooking and being the midwife for any great writing that might come along and be delivered by the men; but not having the facility to make any great poetry yourself. I labored under these conceptual restraints for a while until I realized it was really idiotic, and went on with my own practice of writing—although it's always great to feel that you're inspiring someone with your beautiful behavior.

As I continued to write in Japan I used the lineage of the poet-story-teller Homer, so I kind of wove my own life and experiences through his particular odyssey. This was during the time of my first book of poems. I went to India during that time for six months with Gary Snyder and Ginsberg and Orlovsky, and kept a journal, later published as the *Japan and India Journals*. Gary kept a journal as a series of letters, and Allen wrote a journal. I would go over and look at Allen's journal to see if he was writing anything about me, but he never was, so I copied down a few of the little things he had to say and put them in my journal, which was about his own dreams and aspirations.

Living and breathing in Japan, acquiring the practice of paying attention to the details of daily life became a part of what I perceived as Zen. Paying attention to the details of daily life, they didn't become the mundane thing of the "housewife," they became the things of what your daily life is made up of. You pay attention to those details. The independent and Western attitudes that I carried, however, were not helpful, especially for a woman in Japan, where women were expected to play a subservient and supportive role in relationship to men. I with my Western outspokenness—an older Japanese woman lived with us and I really knew what she thought of me—but there was of course no way I could stop being myself. But as they say in Japan also, by saying nothing the woman runs the house. In other words she has a large authority—the man doesn't know where to find his underwear and socks in the morning unless they're put out for him, doesn't know what to eat unless he's cooked for. So at that point the so-called subservient role is really one of control. Ego was something that I had tried very hard to hold onto and cultivate in order to have a good, strong ego to stand up to the various personalities that I was around. . . . Then I was informed in Japan, ego was what you were supposed to lose. And I thought, well that's just akin to insanity, for god's sake, I've spent all this time trying to get a really good, strong ego going and now I hear that this is just a difficult illusion.

So I continued to practice my own poetic voice, trying to find my voice in writing in my notebook/journal. And I understood that the brotherhood of the Beat writers had their own particular voices. I was never discouraged from writing, ever, but there wasn't any place there for me among them. I was essentially on my own, and when I returned to San Francisco in 1964, Don Allen wanted to publish my first book of poems, *The Tapestry and the Web.* He was a well-known editor, of, among other books, *The New American Poetry.* There was also a lot of activity that was going on in the North Beach community with a magazine that was being published by Stan Persky called *Open Space.* So I was immediately taken back into a very energetic writing environment that went on for the next three years.

JANINE POMMY VEGA: The impetus for my voice as a writer began in elementary school when in fifth grade I wrote a horror story. The writing engaged me, I got an A and some comments from my fifth-grade teacher. The idea of creating something out of nothing, and creating it with words, appealed tremendously to me. I wrote more stories, thought about likely and unlikely plots, names for protagonists. I also wrote rhyming, spiritual poems and read voraciously.

My seeking out the people of the Beat movement, when I was a sophomore in high school was, for me, the closest I could come to politics at that time. The people I met were living their lives according to their beliefs. I had just read *On the Road.* This was at the end of the fifties, during a period of relative affluence but of straight-laced mores, and no one seemed to be having as much fun in Union City, New Jersey as the people in *On the Road.* And the persona that one was expected to inhabit at that time as a woman of relative intelligence was, you had to be the dumb blonde. There was a certain blandness which I could accomplish very easily by taking off my glasses. I'm totally nearsighted, so it's very easy for me not to know what's going on without my glasses. But I didn't find anything there, it was all fluff.

So I went to New York, and the first person I met in New York was Gregory Corso, who took me down to meet Peter Orlovsky. So—wow, he was bringing me down to meet Jack Kerouac and Allen Ginsberg, he was calling them by their first names, and I was thrilled. And I also was very eager to get rid of my virginity, it was becoming a stumbling block, from further growth. So I made an appointment with Peter Orlovksy, we were going to meet on Sunday. My friend Barbara was going to fuck Gregory and I was going to fuck Peter. We did. We became instantly non-virgins, but of course we couldn't let the kids in high school know. We still lived there, we still lived in Union City.

Allen and Peter went to San Francisco at that time, so I got to know other people in the Beat Generation through Barbara's relation with Gregory and then John [Rapanick of the Seven Arts] and Arnie Levin and Irving Rosenthal. And I got a job in the Village, I was a waitress. Being working class has its real value, in terms of my mother's reaction, which is you can come home at any time, as long as you're working. So I got a job. I'd come home at three in the morning, "it's O.K., you're working." So I was in the Village and that's where I first heard, "so you want to be hip little girl, so you really want to swing." Ted Joans, Hugh Romney, and various others were on that scene.

There was a two-year period where I was meeting everyone. I met Ray and Bonnie [Bremser] in a coffee shop, and I met Jack Kerouac, and then Herbert Huncke got out of prison and I instantly loved this man. He wasn't interested in women, but he had a large outlook which wasn't sexist and which was constant. He was totally devoted to drugs, he was a junkie for fifty years. He died at eighty-two and he'd been a junkie all that time, he was very clear about that. If you had anything, it was gone, cause Huncke sold it—your typewriter, your TV. But he had a capacity for including anyone, including me, a young kid with relatively nothing to say, into his life, his sense of who was worthwhile thinking about.

When I left New Jersey I was still underage, and I struck a deal with my mother. This was, I would go to her party and after that I'd leave and I'd go to New York and she would never again ask me where I was going. So right after that graduation I went to Huncke's house, and I moved in with him. Where I moved to was 170 E. Second Street. That's where Allen and Peter lived on the second floor, Bobbie Kaufman lived on the third floor, Stella, from the picture on the cover of City Lights, she lived on the fourth floor, Carol Bergé says she was there, though I don't recall, and Elise Cowan lived on the next floor, and Huncke lived on the top floor. So I moved in with Huncke and then from there I moved in with Elise and became part of the life of what was going on in the world there, at large, and with the Living Theatre, very political. They were the first people I ever saw committed to putting their beliefs on the line.

In the middle of this, in this expansion of awareness through a political point of view and through the arts, the painting, the plays, the writing and all the reading I did—the development of my own voice was a private affair, which I showed to no one. I remember Peter reading me his first poem, a beautiful poem. But I wouldn't consider reading him a poem,

I guess I didn't feel it was worthy or I wasn't sure of my voice. So I showed it to no one with the exception of Elise Cowan. She always managed to live just about half a block or so from Allen, who she really loved. I lived with her for a year and I showed her maybe two poems that entire time. She showed me nothing, I didn't even know she wrote, I was never even aware of her as a writer, in fact, until this book [Women of the Beat Generation] came out.

Then Allen and Peter left for India. Allen had been living in South America writing The Yage Letters, and I was living with Peter and his brother Lafcadio, and Allen came back and just announced that he and Peter were going to India. There wasn't any mention of anything like, hey why don't you save your money and come join us, or, maybe you'd like to come along. It was just, you're going to stay here and take care of Lafcadio, Peter's brother.

So I thought, well, shit, is this the way it is with the poets? This is my first lover and this is the way it goes? Fuck those people, man, I don't want to know about the writers, I'd rather meet the painters, the musicians, the magicians, let's get to the street, I want to know the real stuff. So, there were lots of drugs, tremendous amounts of amphetamine, seventeen times a day, in the arm, constant vision of God somehow propelling you down the street, your eyes weeping crystals and rainbows around all the lights. This went on for two years. I was talking to Huncke about this before he died, and I said, Jesus that was a really heroic time we lived through, and he said, it's a time you can live through only once, you can never do it again. First of all, what would you chew with—everybody's teeth are gone, they're bones. Amphetamine, imagine, two years.

But in the middle of this big drug-taking foray there were many women. I don't know any of their last names. Many of them that I knew were artists, Inez comes to mind, fantastic woman, Ayesha, with a pinwheel hat, Michelle, and that other woman with the dog. The thing that Allen is talking about, the changing of consciousness, in "Howl," all those episodes he mentions are actually real episodes. That's Tuli Kupferberg jumping from the Brooklyn Bridge. There's a totemic act, it seems, in this busting through of walls and trying to get to the other side. So in the context of that time, like Alex Trocchi, Cain's Book, a tremendous junkie, we were all of us taking a tremendous amount of drugs. When I was sixteen or so the first drug I ever took was peyote and then mescaline. There's no drug that you can mention that I didn't take. I was living with Huncke, you know, he tried everything.

There were long love letters that I was writing to Herbert Huncke—because all of these drugs are of course counterposed with a certain amount of jail time, routine jail time, and a lot of that jail time accepted by them as part of the deal. So I spent a long time writing to Huncke in the Tombs, six months here, four months there. I've read the notebooks that I kept at that time. They were written in a calligraphic pen with black india ink with run-on sentences for an entire book. I can attest to the fact that they are absolutely illegible, I don't know what anything of it is saying. But I know I was very sincere and it was all one vision.

In the middle of this, I met this painter, Fernando Vega, who was very attractive. He seemed to have a center for his seeking, a spiritual base of some kind that I gravitated toward. He knew who he was in terms of being a painter and we started to relate and the drug use accelerated until it became pretty clear that we would have to wind up in jail or dead. There's just no way you can go on with that kind of intensity, you just can't. You look at those kids, the crack kids, they're kids, twenty-one years old and my god, they look so ancient, they've been through the wringer. So his father, a Peruvian Jew, was properly thinking, "how can I save my son?" and he decided to send him to Israel. So he changed one ticket into two tickets, and in the summer of 1962 I began living with Fernando Vega, and he began introducing me as his friend and afterward his wife, the poet, which made me cringe because I didn't want to own it to that degree. But he supported the idea that I had a voice and I had something to say.

So in Israel I began to seriously address the idea of my own work. First of all, the drugs were gone, so you actually had time stretching out. And I began to have in my walks—you couldn't go anywhere at that time in Jerusalem but you would run upon a border—my walks went further and further afield. And I would bring back, in my poems, the things that I was witnessing on those walks. We were there for about a year and a half and by the time we were ready to leave I had a small body of poems that I was satisfied with, that I felt was close to something I felt was me.

After Jerusalem, we went to Paris, and my first public reading was in Paris, in an Armenian church. I began to learn French and read the French poets. And then we also went to Ibiza, where I did my second performance in a cafe. There was a writer there at the time, Thomas McGrath, who was the first writer to actually sit down with me and say specifics—this line for instance. He was totally encouraging, totally giving in that mammalian way of him and his work. He really spent time with me; I was pretty willful, and he was able to couch his comments in such a way that I could accept what he had to say, and use his eye for honing down my message.

At that time, then, Fernando died, right there in Ibiza. Fernando died in November of 1965. I returned to the United States with his paintings and there I had more work published in small magazines. I moved in on the Lower East Side and I began work on a body of poems which would then become *Poems to Fernando,* published by City Lights. Now at that time also there was a great interchange with other writers but I wasn't using speed— but I was using junk, I was using junk heavily, I was always into drugs. Perhaps because it came up in a time when a woman writer was not as encouraged or seriously read as a young man would be, and I saw this time and again, perhaps because for the years outside the country I had developed my own style, or perhaps for other reasons long lost to this memory bank, my poems, though straightforward in text, had unusual, to say the least, punctuation. Slashes everywhere, periods at the front of a line, commas in the middle of the line relating to nothing; and when I read it years later, I didn't know what I was doing. I don't know what I had been thinking when I did it. I can only assume that the nonconforming punctuation mirrored my trying to punch my way through the paper bag of my own thought process and spill it onto the page. Between that first book and the next one that was published when I was in Bolivia in 1974, called *Journal of a Hermit,* I lost three complete manuscripts. So I really don't know if that whole process continued or not, obfuscating the issue via your way of putting it on the page, the craft you invent for yourself. But the challenge to make the work as clear as possible, for the reader as well as myself, has become an ongoing process. It's not an easy matter. It's so easy to go aside, to things that perhaps one part of you thinks is necessary but really isn't to the ongoing momentum of the story.

In relation to the women of the Beat Generation, I think of this quote from Jacob Lawrence, the painter who recently died. "We all like headlines and that type of thing. But this shouldn't be confused with the real meaning of your work. In fact, I think an artist is most fortunate when he doesn't get too much attention. The so-called art movements usually come after the fact. If you're unfortunate enough to get swept up in a movement then you'll find yourself following yourself." The first thing I thought of when I read that was Jack Kerouac, who I only knew as a drunk under the tables. I came to New York City to meet this person who really was a hero to me, and he really was only drunk all the time, beautiful, sweet, and very drunk, then I can only say that perhaps, had fate been kinder, he might have just gone on writing in relative, just relative success so that he could maybe have said more than he did.

The literary path as I see it has several components. There's the writing, for which time is usually at a premium. That's the first love, the losing of self in the process of creation, the poem, the short story, the children's story, the novel. Then there's the research and considered work of book reviews, essays, commissioned articles, translations, editing, where as a writer one performs part of the weave of intellectual thought of one's time. And there's the teaching, the kids, the adults, the prisoners. What all the components share is the idea of service, of serving something other than the ego, serving as the glue of a civilization, serving clarity of thought, the specific vision of your truth.

—June 15, 2000

When I read these passages [of *On the Road*] in late August of 1957, I thought of my mother and her sisters, but Kerouac's lost girls did not remind me of myself—it was Sal, passionately impatient with the status quo, with whom I identified.

By then I had begun my relationship with Kerouac, but even before that, I'd had my immersion in real life. I'd defied my parents to have a painful affair with Donald Cook, left home, broken with my family, found jobs, had an abortion and had my first taste of despair. Still, I wouldn't have turned back if given the choice. At twenty-one I felt I'd gone to the bottom and floated up; I had the lightness of feeling there was nothing left to lose, so I'd let Kerouac come home with me the first night I met him. Quite the little existentialist, as my Barnard professor once wrote. Or perhaps my state of mind approached the original definition of Beat.

"Come on down, I'm waiting for you," Jack had written to me from Mexico City that July. "Don't go to silly Frisco. First place, I have this fine earthquake-proof room for 85¢ a night for both of us, it's an Arabic magic room with tiles on the walls and many big round whorehouse sex-orgy mirrors (it's an old 1910 whorehouse, solid with marble floors)—we can sleep on the big clean double bed, have our private bath . . . it's right downtown, we can enjoy city life to the hilt then when we get tired of our Magian inwardness sultan's room we can go off to the country and rent a cottage with flowerpots in the window—Your money will last you 5 times longer & in Frisco you wouldn't be seeing anything new & foreign and strange—Take the plane to Mexico City (bus too long, almost as expensive too), then take a cab to my hotel, knock my door, we'll be gay friends wandering arm-in-arm . . ."

How could I resist such an invitation? I immediately quit my secretarial job at Farrar, Straus and Cudahy and gave up my apartment. Jack and I were going to live forever on the five-hundred-dollar advance I had just gotten from an editor at Random House for my first novel, but unfortunately I didn't move fast enough. By the time I was ready to leave for Mexico City, Jack, too depressed and shaky to stay alone in that sultan's room, was on his way to his mother's house in Florida. From there he wrote me asking for a loan of thirty dollars, so that he could take a bus to New York in time for the publication of *On the Road.* Being a witness to Jack's collision with sudden, unexpected fame would soon turn into one of the most profoundly educational experiences of my life.

—Joyce Johnson
from a talk given June 24, 1998

ALLEN GINSBERG'S LANGUAGE GAMES: A WITTGENSTEINIAN PERSPECTIVE

Marjorie Perloff

Do not forget that a poem, although it is composed in the language of information, is not used in the language-game of giving information.

—LUDWIG WITTGENSTEIN, *ZETTEL*

IN 1952, WILLIAM CARLOS WILLIAMS BEGGED MARIANNE MOORE TO HAVE A look at the work of a then unknown young poet named Allen Ginsberg, whose clean, rigorously unrelenting mind he found appealing, without being able quite to say why. He begged her, he wrote her a note (which can be found in Lewis Hyde's *On the Poetry of Allen Ginsberg* [Michigan, 1985]), asking her if she wouldn't let the young poet come to meet her. Moore read the manuscript in question, which was *Empty Mirror*, and wrote Ginsberg a kind but very disapproving letter in which she declares that *Empty Mirror* is too literal. "You don't get behind it," she complains. "in the opening piece you say 'I wandered off in search of a toilet,' and I go with you, remember. Do I have to? I do, if you take me with you in your book." Of the poem "Paterson," Moore says, "slobs and dumbbells hardly sustain the crucifixion metaphor." And from "The Night-Apple" she singles out the line "sweat skin eyes feces urine sperm saliva all one odor" and complains, "the poem begins with 'Last night I dreamed of one I loved.' Why did you not go on with it in that way? You betray us with a taunt, with an I fooled you." This is the taunt Moore is referring to:

Last night I dreamed
of one I loved
for seven long years,

but I saw no face,
only the familiar
presence of the body;
sweat skin eyes
feces urine sperm
saliva all one
odor and mortal taste (*Collected Poems*, 52)

Here one could respond that the deflationary turn in lines 5-6, the "presence of the body and its sweat skin eyes," is, of course, intentional. A dream of one's lover, Ginsberg is suggesting, even in this very early poem, is by no means necessarily pretty. It is what it is, the mix of sweat, skin, eyes, feces, urine, sperm that the poet has known in reality. The interest of this particular poem depends, I think, on precisely that mix, that romantic opening—those seven long years of desire for the loved one—versus the reality of what it is that one is actually desiring.

In a similar vein, the crucifixion metaphor in "Paterson," which Moore took to be inappropriately related to "slobs and dumbbells," is, on closer inspection, a metaphor almost comic in its bombastic recital of different Calvary sites. The part about crucifixion goes like this:

I would rather go mad, gone down the dark road to Mexico,
    heroin dripping in my veins. . . .
rather drag a rotten railroad tie to a Golgotha in the Rockies;
rather, crowned with thorns in Galveston, nailed hand and foot in
    Los Angeles, raised up to die in Denver,
pierced in the side in Chicago, perished and tombed in New
    Orleans and resurrected in 1958 somewhere on Garrett Mountain . . .
    (CP, 40)

The question, of course, is why there is such intense longing to criss-cross the United States. Why does one have to go to Denver to die or to New Orleans to be buried? Can't one's suffering take place in a single locale? In Williams's *Paterson*, after all, such fantastic and absurd shifts do not occur. On the contrary, Williams's epic stays grounded geographically. Its furthest movement away from Paterson, New Jersey is probably to the Cloisters museum in Manhattan, right across the river. But Ginsberg's "Paterson," however much Williams's epic may have been its model, is a very different sort of poem, and that's what Marianne Moore didn't like. She wanted him to be like Williams.

Consider the relation of "Paterson" to another early poem, "The Bricklayer's Lunch Hour." This is the one poem in *Empty Mirror* that Marianne Moore praises as fine work, as accurate and contagious, no doubt because it does have the air of a Williams poem. "The Bricklayer's Lunch Hour" (CP, 4) begins like this:

> Two bricklayers are setting the walls
> of a cellar in a new dug out patch
> of dirt behind an old house of wood
> with brown gables grown over with ivy
> on a shady street in Denver. It is noon
> and one of them wanders off. The young
> subordinate bricklayer sits idly for
> a few minutes after eating a sandwich
> and throwing away the paper bag.

No wonder Moore liked this particular poem, whose simple, declarative, present tense, indicative sentences present a series of concrete images without authorial commentary. The short, fairly uniform free verse lines, many of them run over, are reminiscent of Williams's poems. The language is colloquial, "natural," unpretentious. The incident described further along in the poem, is that the subordinate bricklayer eats the sandwich, drops the bag on the ground, stares into space, vaguely flexes his muscles, and finally, in a chilling gesture, picks up a kitten and smothers it in his cap.

But "The Bricklayer's Lunch Hour" is rather atypical for the early Ginsberg. Let's compare it to the opening of "Paterson," which was written in Berkeley in 1949.

> What do I want in these rooms papered with visions of money?
> How much can I make by cutting my hair? If I put new heels on
>   my shoes bathe my body reeking of masturbation and sweat,
>   layer upon layer of excrement
> dried in employment bureaus, magazine hallways, statistical
>   cubicles, factory stairways,
> cloakrooms of the smiling gods of psychiatry;
> if in antechambers I face the presumption of department store

supervisory employees,
old clerks in their asylums of fat, the slobs and dumbbells of the
   ego with money and power
to hire and fire and make and break and fart and justify their
   reality of wrath and rumor of wrath to wrath-weary man,
what war I enter and for what a prize! the dead prick of
   commonplace obsession,
harridan visions of electricity at night and daylight misery of
   thumb-sucking rage. (CP, 40)

Now, suppose we read this passage in terms of what Wittgenstein called the "language game." What Wittgenstein meant by the language game is the situation or context within which the participants are using their words and locutions. The words "king" and "queen" for example, mean something different in a game of chess than they do in an article about British politics. Chess players know how these pieces are to be used, and it is use, not some sort of essence, that counts. In his famous example, at the beginning of *The Investigations*, Wittgenstein describes the relationship between a builder, who asks for a slab, hammer, brick, and so on, and the workman who brings it to him. In that particular language game, when the order comes, the voice rises with an exclamation point, and the other person will bring the thing that's being asked for. You don't have to say, please bring me this. In other language games, the same words would work very differently. If you look at the way children learn how to speak, you'll see exactly how it works. What Wittgenstein is countering is the Augustinian view of language, which is that the way one learns how to speak is by learning the names of things, and the name of something points to an object in the real world. Wittgenstein understood, more clearly, perhaps, than had any other philosopher, that most of language does not consist of names or nouns that refer to things, but consists of all kinds of other, smaller words and phrases. What, after all, does the word "the" point to? What does the word "is" point to?

If you think of the particular idiom in Ginsberg's "Paterson" as constituting a language game, the first question you ask yourself is, why would anyone say these things? Who is speaking in this poem and to whom? Marianne Moore, we recall, was quite offended by all the references to masturbation and dumbbells. But consider line 2, "How much can I make by cutting my hair?" If someone had just entered a hairdresser's that had an ad in the window saying, "we buy hair," and he asked, "how much can I make by cutting my hair?," then that would mean one thing. But that is obviously, in the context of the poem, not what the poet means. He means, if I cut my hair and look bourgeois and wore a coat and tie and went to various employment agencies, how much money would I be able to make? So you have to understand the whole usage of "make" in this poem.

Ginsberg's emphasis is by no means Williams's emphasis on "no ideas but in things"; rather, he wants to define a state of the mind. His is a subjective, fantastic, bombastic poem of a very young man who has to get a job and cringes at the need to conform to the norms. Here are these hyperbolic images of his own excrement dried in employment bureaus, magazine hallways, statistical cubicles, factory stairways, cloakrooms of the smiling gods of psychiatry—which looks ahead to "Howl"—it's absolutely literal and makes perfectly good sense. He's talking about the values of this period, especially the early fifties, when the standard route for the Columbia BA was to pound the pavements hunting for a job, sitting for hours cooling his heels in employment agencies run by "slobs and dumbbells" who never seemed to have any job you wanted; or maybe there was one available job for *Time* magazine, that might be waiting in the magazine hallways; or maybe a market research firm. That, in the days Ginsberg described, was the big prize. When you graduated from college, you didn't mess around, you had to go right out and get a job. That's what you did. And it wasn't a day job, it was your job. So, statistical cubicles and, God forbid, perhaps a routine factory job, and the letdown of this search, after the heady days of having fun with his friends at Columbia and elsewhere around the country, was enough to send anyone to the "cloakroom of the smiling gods of psychiatry."

Let's remember too that psychoanalysis was ubiquitous in those days: it was just par for the course, especially in New York. Everyone had a shrink and therefore he or she had to have a job so as to pay for the shrink, and so on. No wonder then that this "I" / "eye" conjures up an alternate vision as wild and excessive as that of "rooms papered with visions of money." Look how interestingly the word "visions" is used here, for money is precisely what involves no "vision" at all. In the context, the urge to "crawl on my naked belly over the tin cans of Cincinnati," far from being an image of suffering, of Calvary, of crucifixion, has a comic book absurdist quality. Ginsberg doesn't want to cut his naked belly on a bunch of tin cans, and what's so attractive about Cincinnati anyway? But the poet is using extravagant images to express his overpowering desire.

"Paterson" is thus a poem about desire, the desire to escape, to go places, to do everything, to experience everything; and that means when you've finished experiencing everything, you're going to explode, you're going to die—in Denver, or wherever. Therefore, the notion of being crowned with thorns in Galveston, nailed hand and foot in Los Angeles, and raised up to die in Denver—an image that recurs in "Howl"—is designed to give the reader an incredible sense of space and possibility. Imagine, the poet seems to say, what a huge country this is, how much is possible, how rich those names are—Los Angeles, Galveston, Denver—rich because they're very far away from Paterson, New Jersey. Notice he doesn't use any words in that poem of those places nearby, until you come back to Garrett Mountain. If we think of Ginsberg's catalogs, here and in "Howl," in this way, there's nothing at all bizarre or in "bad taste" about them, as was originally thought. Like Keats in the "Ode to a Nightingale," which is a poem Ginsberg cites frequently, the poet wants to shed his body—"Already with thee, tender is the night"—to enter the "bayous and forests and derricks leaving my flesh and my bones hanging on the trees." That's the way the poem ends: now his soul and spirit can take off.

In this sense, the roll call of places in "Paterson," as in Ginsberg's later poems, is very important. If the meaning of a word is its use in the language, it matters that the poet wants to die in Denver rather than in Trenton, because Denver becomes the emblem of the other, the strange, the unknown. Ginsberg has been criticized, notably by Helen Vendler, for being too much of a geographer. Writing of *The Fall of America*, Vendler says, "the trouble with the present book is that the minute particulars of mankind seem to be vanishing from Ginsberg's latest verse in favor of the minute particulars of geography." But, if you approach Ginsberg's geography in a Wittgensteinian frame of mind, the first question you ask is, what are the minute particulars of mankind, and why can't they participate in geography, or vice versa? Aren't the minute particulars of mankind related to the minute particulars of geography? Why not? When we stop to ponder that, we realize how much more difficult, how much more subtle Ginsberg is than is often thought by his critics. Despite the apocalyptic tone, the prophetic energy of his most famous poems—and that's what he's usually praised for—Ginsberg could be said to follow Wittgenstein even as he follows Eastern philosophy, believing that philosophy is not a choice between different theories, that it's wrong to say there is any one theory of truth, for truth is not a concept. As Wittgenstein puts it, there is no such thing as an ethical proposition (it can always be countered), but it is possible to perform an ethical action. And that axiom is very close to Eastern thought.

Even in his early poetry, then, Ginsberg is devising a language more complex and subtle than is usually thought. Let me close with "Four Haiku," written by Ginsberg in Berkeley in 1955. In the *Journals* they were called the "Winter Haiku."

Looking over my shoulder
my behind was covered
with cherry blossoms.

Lying on my side
in the void:
the breath in my nose.

I didn't know the names
of the flowers—now
my garden is gone.

On the porch
in my shorts—
auto lights in the rain. (CP, 137)

What one might well ask, if one approaches these haiku from a conventional perspective, is the significance of having one's behind covered with cherry blossoms? Why should we care that Allen lying on his side feels the breath in his nose? or that he's standing on the porch in shorts watching the auto lights in the rain? On re-reading these accounts of everyday incidents, they are charged with meaning. Cherry blossoms are the ultimate tourist cliché for everything Japanese. Ernest Fenollosa, for example, makes much of them in his essay on the Chinese written character, and Ezra Pound picks up on it. But Allen doesn't contemplate their grace and beauty; he sits in the cherry blossoms, by mistake as it were, while he's looking over his shoulder.

Again, this is the Allen who thinks he loves nature, but he really doesn't know the names of the most ordinary flowers in the garden, with

the result that he doesn't take care of them and—"my garden is gone"—
they die. The other two haiku capture the extreme loneliness of this par-
ticular Berkeley moment. It's a novelty to be outside in the porch in one's
shorts, so unlike the New York scene which is Allen's habitat, but then
there's nothing to do but watch the auto lights in the rain. And "lying on
my side" is not lying with anyone, there's only the void filled with the
breath in my nose, the sounds of silence.

These four haiku add up to a very specific image of the poet as one
who has sought solitude in nature only to find that it makes him very
nervous. The "lost America of love," as he calls it in "A Supermarket in
California," is not to be found merely by traveling west, nor in the neon
fruit supermarket with "aisles full of husbands, wives in the avocados,
babies in the tomatoes." You always, in the end, take yourself with you.
So you try to see it for what it is, but without the kind of fanfare
Wittgenstein hated, the transcendental gossip his philosopher friends
engaged in. You do it by taking nothing for granted and by looking care-
fully at every word and how it's used in the language. In the third haiku,
the sound structure is incredibly intricate, suggesting that although Allen
doesn't know flowers too well, he certainly does know how to make the
word "flowers" grow, both semantically and orally. So these little haiku
provide a good illustration of the Wittgensteinian aphorism that there is
nothing contiguous to language. "The limits of my language mean the lim-
its of my world."

—July 7, 1994

RECOLLECTIONS AND GOSSIP: FIRST MEETINGS WITH JACK KEROUAC

David Amram, Gregory Corso, Allen Ginsberg, John Clellon Holmes, Edie Parker Kerouac

ALLEN GINSBERG: OUR IDEA WAS TO GO THROUGH AND EACH ONE TELL how we first met Kerouac (in chronological order).

Edie Parker knew Lucien Carr from drinking at the West End. I was living across the hall on the seventh floor of the Union Theological Seminary in New York City, near Columbia. During the war, 1944, the dormitories were filled with young navy trainees, so the college students were bumped and had to go live at the Union Theological Seminary dorm. I heard Brahms's "Trio no. 1" coming outside of Lucien's door, so I knocked and saw Lucien Carr looking like an angel and made friends. A few days later he had met Edie Parker at the West End bar at 13th Street on Broadway, where all the college kids drank. Lucien told me about this guy he had met who had just come back from the ocean; he was a sailor who wore a black leather jacket and was a poet and novelist. That was the first time I ever ran into somebody that was a writer. I was going to Columbia University and there were no writers there. Nobody boasted of being a writer in 1944. There was nobody that claimed being a writer or poet.

So I found out where he lived—I think it was an apartment that Edie Parker's mentioned somewhere, right off Columbia University down 118th Street—climbed up, knocked on the door. I think Edie or Jack opened the door, and he was sitting there eating breakfast, wearing a T-shirt and chino pants. He was amazingly handsome, really young, he would have been twenty-two years old, really sharp looking, dark, handsome, deep eyes. Beautiful in the way that Jan Kerouac* is quite now. I remember eyes, handsome, straight nose. So I immediately dug him . . . I'd never been laid anyways, I was a virgin and completely innocent and scared and nobody

---

* Jan Kerouac, 1952–1996, was the daughter of Joan Haverty and Jack Kerouac.

knew I was queer to begin with. So I was there under false pretenses, as some kind of studious, intelligent, interested student going up to meet him for what reason? Well, he couldn't figure it out and I couldn't figure it out; and he was eating his eggs. So I said something, he said something. Then I said, well, discretion is the better part of valor, which was something I heard from my father, and I hardly knew what it meant except that it was something I would drop into a conversation when I couldn't think of anything to say in order to appear smart, because I felt like a complete fool. So he gave me this funny look that I've seen in movies, like a side twist grimace of the mouth, meaning what is that? I guess he must have decided that I was a New York Jewish intellectual.

That day, or another within the same week, I had to move from Union Theological Seminary, following Lucien Carr, who had moved to a hotel on 115th Street. So I decided I'd move out and go to the hotel, and I asked Jack to help me move. So we had to walk down to Columbia campus from 118th to 125th Street, through the campus, and up seven flights, down a long wooden corridor in the Theological Seminary setting to an arched brown oaken door, where I brought out my valise. I took my valise out and turned to the door, closed the door, and said, good-bye door. And Jack said, ooh. Then we walked down the rest of the corridor and I said, good-bye corridor. He said, mmm. Then I said, good-bye step number one, good-bye step number two, and we had seven flights of steps to go down. He said, what do you mean? I said, well I know I'll never see it again in the same body, or if I'm in the same body it'll be twenty-five years later or forty years later and so it'll be like walking back into an ancient, interesting, classical dream. And he said, do you think like that all the time? And I said, I always think like that, nobody else does but me I think, maybe. Or does anybody else ever think of those thoughts? Like, one day I remember when I was walking home from the Fabian theater in Paterson, I was passing by the hedges near the church on Broadway and Paterson, and I thought, gee, I wonder how big the universe is? And at the end of the universe, is there a wall? And what would the wall be made out of, rubber? But if it was a wall made out of rubber, wouldn't then the rubber go on for another billion miles? And what would come after the rubber? So what is the end of the universe?

GREGORY CORSO: [interrupting] I know, Al, I can tell you. It's spherical like a bubble, but there's another bubble that's attached to it. Water bubbles.

GINSBERG: Well I didn't think of that at that age. So those were the kind of questions that Kerouac and I both thought about. Our first rapport was over the fact that both of us said good-bye all the time to the space where we were at that moment, realizing that the space was floating in the infinite universe and the universe was changing and that we were transient, interesting, charming phantoms, appreciating the space around, and that we were only there for that hour or two, so we were constantly saying good-bye.

JOHN CLELLON HOLMES: In the late spring of 1948 I heard about somebody called Jack Kerouac. A friend of mine, who was then working for, of all places, the *New Yorker* magazine, knew Allen—Ed Stringham. And through Allen he heard about somebody called Jack Kerouac who had written and almost completed an enormous novel that weighed something like forty pounds. So Stringham told me and another friend of mine, both of whom were aspiring novelists, about this and we were eager to meet this guy. The long weekend of July 4th that year, my wife was out of town visiting her family and Harrington, the other guy, came to me and said, Ginsberg called and he and somebody else are throwing a party up in Russell Durgan's apartment. That sounded good, and also I think Allen had told Harrington that Kerouac would be there. So up we went. It was hot, sweltery. Got into Spanish Harlem, the streets were full of the great smell of beans and there was plenty of music coming out of all the windows. We hit a building that was just like every other building and up we went to the fourth or fifth floor, and the closer we got to it the noisier it became. The music was not Latin music, it was jazz. In we went and I met Allen first, who was hosting it, at least he acted like a host. There were a lot of people, I didn't know any of them. Lucien was there. The others were kind of a conglomeration of Columbia students, I don't think John Hollander was there but he was part of that crowd. Allen, as you probably all know, is extremely generous and saw that we had beer and introduced us to a few people. It was one of those typical poverty-stricken tenement houses. All the rooms butted up on one another, there was no hall, you entered into the kitchen. All the windows were open because it was a hot night and the beer was flying. I went into what was probably the living room, where Russell had his books, and I did what I often do when I'm in a place I don't know or I don't know anybody, I kind of stood around and I checked out the guy's books. They were primarily seventeenth- and eighteenth-century English poets, and very fine editions as I recall. And then I looked over, there was a couch against one wall and there was a guy I'd never met, who turned out to be Jack. Just as Allen has recounted, I was struck by his looks immediately, undoubtedly for many of the same reasons; he was an arresting man to see. He was incredibly handsome. But beyond that there was something in his face that you couldn't take your eyes off. (There are certain movie stars that are like that, they're not necessarily good actors but the camera loves them and you look at them.) So I went over and he was very shy and withdrawn until he learned that I was a writer too. Then he opened up a bit, but both of us didn't quite know what to make of one another. Allen hustled in and did what he so often kindly does, which is to make two strangers to each other feel at home.

So that's how I met Jack Kerouac. A week or two later he gave his novel (*The Town and the City*) to me. It was in a huge doctor's bag and it did weigh about forty pounds. And I read it with some interest but I knew nothing really about the man except that he had struck me as being somebody I wanted to know. Of course reading the book astounded me. And almost immediately thereafter he came by my apartment for something and we saw one another from then on.

GINSBERG: I'd completely forgotten about that party till you mentioned it.

CORSO: It could be 1950 or 1949, cause I had come out of prison towards the end of '49 and that's when I met Allen Ginsberg. And through Ginsberg I met Kerouac. I met Allen in a lesbian bar in Greenwich Village. I was about nineteen and I was in this lesbian bar because a friend of mine was doing caricatures of people there, an artist, first artist I ever met, his name was [Emanuel Diaz]. Anyway, one night Allen came in. I don't know if at this time he was out of the closet, because he just said when he met Kerouac he was virginal—were you virginal when you met me?

GINSBERG: 1950, no.

CORSO: All right. So I had a good looking young Italian face, so I figure that's why he came up and spoke with me. But I mentioned I was a poet

and I had my prison poems with me, and Allen said, I've got to intro-
duce you to the Chinaman then. The Chinaman in his head at that time
was a good minded poet, Mark Van Doren, who was his teacher at
Columbia. So he first brought me to Mark Van Doren, and after Mark Van
Doren was Dusty Moreland, this is how it worked. I told them I was liv-
ing on Ninth Street and Sixth Avenue and there was this girl I'd watch
go to the bathroom and have sex with a guy and all that and I'd jerk off
to it. And he said, where, what apartment. I told him and he said, well
I'm the guy that's going to bed with that girl. So I said, wow, then you
can bring me up there and introduce me. So he did. That was a beauti-
ful coincidence, right, Dusty Moreland.

I think maybe a month after that, a man in a white CIO cap—did he
wear CIO for the Merchant Marine?—white shirt, white pants; what house
did I meet him at? It wasn't Dusty's house.

GINSBERG: Henri Cru, maybe?

CORSO: It was someone's house, it wasn't yours. It was in New York City
and it was Allen and him alone. Allen introduced me to him.

GINSBERG: Henri Cru was a friend of Jack who had a place—

CORSO: Could you go out the window on a little roof? Anyway, we hit
it off right away, Kerouac and I. There was some kind of warmth that
Ginsberg and Holmes both hit on, which was his features. I had him in
a poem once with "Clark Gable hands." That was the best way I could
describe him, that way like a movie actor and very strong, you know
Clark Gable had hairy hands, so did Jack. But I told him I wrote poetry,
that was the ball game. He had to ask me what poetry was and I told him
it was everything. So that's the first encounter with Mr. Kerouac. It could
have been late '49 or early '50.

GINSBERG: I don't remember your meeting with Kerouac. Do you
remember the conversation?

CORSO: You brought me there. Yeah, the conversation was, what's
poetry. And I told him it was everything.

GINSBERG: What did he say?

CORSO: He looked at me.

GINSBERG: We called earlier for Edie Parker Kerouac . . . Edie was the catalyst for a meeting with me and Jack and William Burroughs and Lucien Carr.

EDIE PARKER KEROUAC: I first met with Henri Cru, who lived in my grandmother's apartment, 438 West 116th Street. His mother and my grandmother were friends and Henri Cru and I liked each other. He was going to Horace Mann with Jack and he wanted me to meet his best friend. So he took us out to lunch, we went to a New York delicatessen, which I'm not used to; I sat down immediately and had six sauerkraut hot dogs and from that time on he fell in love with me. This was 1940.

I'll tell you what he did. He liked me, so the next day he wrote me a love letter and he delivered it by hand, he gave it to the bellboy who brought it up to me. It was gorgeous. He called me his bird note. He always called me his bird note. And he talked about when he first met me, that I walked on Amsterdam Avenue and I fed a junk man's horse, he talked about that; and then he talked about, if I went into the deepest part of the forest and I lifted up a rock, there I would find his heart.

GINSBERG: Do you remember what book he was writing then?

PARKER KEROUAC: I think it was *The Sea Is My Brother.*

GINSBERG: Do you remember anything about that book?

PARKER KEROUAC: I'm really not kidding you Allen, I think it's in the attic of my house. When we moved from one house, it was on the top of a shelf, and my sister and I recall reading it—but it did go on and on.

GINSBERG: That was his first novel, which he was writing when he was a sailor, sailing around Greenland. That was his big symbolic novel while he was reading Thomas Mann, *The Magic Mountain.* But *The Sea Is My Brother* is a sort of classic title, and it was his first really romantic prose and it was the first extended work before *The Town and the City.*

PARKER KEROUAC: As long as I knew him he never stopped writing.

GINSBERG: How did you get that manuscript?

PARKER KEROUAC: He lived with me in Grosse Pointe and he had it there.

GINSBERG: Oh, when you got married—he left it there when he left?

PARKER KEROUAC: That's right, he left it there. And that's where the picture is in my book, of the Merchant Marine with the white hat, it's in my little book.

CORSO: I remembered another thing. When I had come out of prison—in prison it's rough to make friends, it took a while before you made any friend in prison—but when I came out of prison, and I said I was a poet—quick friends. Kerouac and I were immediately fast friends, but actually just an acquaintance. That's why when I went to bed with his girlfriend, Arlene Lee—he wrote *The Subterraneans* and has me pretty heavyweight in that book, that I was disloyal, that I went to bed with his girlfriend. Now, I didn't know him that well; and I don't know who came on with whom—me or the girl—I think she came on to me a lot too. So anyway, we had just one sex shot. But he wrote *The Subterraneans* and he had the manuscript done and he showed it to me. And at the end he had himself picking up a table, about to kill me. And I said, don't do that, don't have it end like that because it did not happen that way. And he did, he changed it—so he picks it up and his whole mind changes and he suddenly realizes that everything is beautiful and I'm all right and all that. Yeah.

I got to be friends with him maybe about two years later.

DAVID AMRAM: I met Jack first in 1956 when I attended a bring your own bottle party at a painter's loft on the Lower East Side in NYC. A stranger in a black and red lumberjack shirt came over to me, handed me a piece of paper and said "play for me," then he took back the paper before I could see what it was.

I had my french horn and penny whistles with me. There was no piano there so I started playing the horn as he read. Playing with him that first time was the same feeling of instant connection I had as when I played with Dizzy Gillespie, jammed with Charlie Parker, Thelonious Monk and the great Latin, Native American, Middle Eastern, folk and classical artists I had already played with. There was instant rapport.

I later found out, as we kept running into each other and spontaneously doing words and music together that we had a lot in common. He spoke French before he spoke English and I learned French at home from my mother, who translated it. I had been a gym teacher while working my way through college and he had been a football player. I was brought up on a farm in Feasterville, Pennsylvania (pop. 200) until I was twelve years old and he was brought up in the mill town of Lowell, Massachusetts. He loved Bach, Mozart, Berlioz, as well as the masters of jazz and what we now call world music and so did I. Both my uncles spent a good deal of their lives with Indian people and so did Jack. My uncle David, whom I was named after, was a merchant seaman and traveler free spirit as was Jack. He came from a strong religious background with Catholicism as his base as I also had as a Jew. And he, like myself, always was a people person and liked to hang out with anybody and everybody, eat good meals, have fun and work endless hours writing work no one was interested in at the time (his novels, my symphonies).

January third, the week before he sailed to Tangiers after learning that his "road book" as he called it was finally going to get published in the coming fall season, I was playing at a place called the Five Spot on Third Avenue between Third Street and the next street down. It was a place where the painters and poets, musicians, everyone used to come in New York City during that time. I brought Cecil Taylor down there in the fall of 1956 and all the painters loved his music. He played there five weeks, January third I began playing there, and Jack came in.

When you're playing at a place, especially at what would be considered to be a rugged environment, usually part of the way that you learn how to survive each night is to try to be aware on some kind of a psychic level of who's there, whether you make eye contact with them, which sometimes could be dangerous, or whether you just feel. Mostly you look and feel for someone who is listening, if there was one person listening, since there was no microphone then and most of the people who you've heard of, the fantissimo rappers here at this festival, were all there in force; so there might be two hundred people having a hundred and eighty conversations, drawing pictures, painting, while the music was going on.

We were the foreground and the background; the music was just part of the whole happening. But I could feel Jack's presence. I looked over and I saw him sitting there, listening. I said wow, man, we got one person listening tonight.

A few months later I was at my place on Christopher Street—I moved from the Lower East Side between Avenue B and C in two trips in a Volkswagen—I had all my earthly belongings. Less is definitely more, if you have to climb six and a half flights of stairs two times to move to a five-flight walk-up, which was a big step upward that time. 114 Christopher Street. Howard Hart, who was a fine drummer and a struggling poet came over with Philip Lamantia and Jack to my place, because they wanted to do some jazz poetry readings. Jack came up and Howard sat down and started playing the drums on the table with his hands, Philip read some of his fantastic poetry, then Jack started reading and I was playing the piano behind him. We didn't say anything, but in backing him up, he was so musical, so sensitive to the music, that it was just like playing with a great saxophone player or a great musician.

Even though we had the material, the way he interpreted it and the way he timed it was like a true musician. After about the third poem that we were messing around with, I took out the French horn and started playing that. At the end of one of the poems, he started improvising and scat singing, making up melodies. [Sings a bit] I said, wow, here's a man from the literary world that can sing.

That was the only jazz poetry rehearsal we ever had, about forty-five minutes. Then we hung out for about three hours. We were rapping away in French, he started talking about Céline and Baudelaire, and baseball. He began to tell me about his baseball games and the way he had his own little league of teams and games that he made up which I saw later at Dody Mueller's apartment when I visited Jack there.

I'd still never read anything by him but I was so impressed by the expanse of his mind and by his kindness. We left my place on Christopher Street and we started walking down the street towards Macdougal Street, saying, let's go hang out, go from Christopher Street to Macdougal Street and Bleecker Street to the Cafe Figaro and see what was happening.

Of course there was always something, twenty-four hours a day, on the street, happening. We were walking and didn't say anything for about half an hour when suddenly he turned to me and said, sometimes, he said, you know, you meet somebody and you feel you've known them forever. That was exactly the same feeling I had felt with him, but I never would have been able to articulate it that way. "You didn't have to say it," he said.

We continued walking around and finally when we got to Macdougal Street, which is about four blocks long, there were a lot of lights, bright lights, over on one side where they have all these little dinky shops, and on the left-hand side, where they had the Gaslight, the Kettle of Fish, all these great places where people would get together and hang out, it was very dark by then. I said, man, let's go on the sunny side of the street. And he said no, he said, this side. I said, how come? and he said, because a writer should always be in the shadow.

That was something I never forgot and that's why I think he was such a beautiful observer, such a beautiful person to be with, such a sympathetic, modest, humble, warm, giving, caring, and sharing person—because he always saw himself as being part of the situation. Even when he became so well-known later on, he never would barge in and take over. He would go to the most insecure person in the room and consciously go to hang out with them. If anyone was a writer, poet, painter, musician, carpenter, plumber, whatever, he'd try to find out what they were doing and encourage them to feel good.

Ever since that time, up until a few months before he passed, I would always see him when he came to New York City, and very often talk to him on the phone. We worked on the film *Pull My Daisy* together in 1959 and my cantata *A Year in Our Land* in 1964–65, where I set his words from *Lonesome Traveler* for chorus, soloist, and orchestra as well as other texts he suggested. We had plans for other pieces to write together. I feel blessed to have known him.

I'd just like to add one thing: the last two days I've been here, I've seen and felt more attention and respect and love for his work than I think he ever had in his own lifetime. I think that's a beautiful, beautiful thing, for all you people who came here, if you're writers, whatever you do, to know that if you have one person listening, one person reading it, you have the beginning of your audience.

The rest of your life, you can write, even for that one person. Eventually if you keep on, and you're true to what you believe and what you feel, and keep developing, then it will never stop. Jack's flame is very much alive. I think a major thing about it is that all of us are able to be here. What he did is really just beginning to be appreciated; twenty-some years later, to see that happen is a very beautiful, moving experience and a cause for rejoicing.

—July 28, 1982

The difference between prose and poetry . . . It all has to do with the music. And Jack Kerouac's poems are poems, and his—the passages in his novels which read so beautifully just like poetry, are not poems. And how you know that is you can hear it. And the way that most of us have been influenced by Jack is how to take what he could do in prose, with that music, in the way he could do his voice, and make use of it in our poems, which we wanted to make.

. . . Jack could write about prose writing and I don't even know, yet, the names of what kinds of things he was making. Jack was a teller of tales. Most of the tales of the tales have more tales. He was not a writer of autobiography. If he wanted to be, he would have written autobiography. But, rather, he had seen this other thing to do that was the thing he had to do, given what he could do. So, that's what he did, and it's—it's changed everything, just as Allen changed everything with "Howl."

—Ted Berrigan, from a workshop at
the Jack Kerouac Conference, 1982

READING, WRITING, AND TEACHING KEROUAC IN 1982

Ann Charters

AST NIGHT ALLEN ASKED THE PARTICIPANTS IN THE *ON THE ROAD* conference to talk about how we were influenced as writers by Kerouac, so I'll start my workshop today by telling you a little about that. That subject will take me to how I read *On the Road* in a larger literary context as an important American novel. After I make my comments, I'd like to open the rest of the workshop to include your thoughts about the book as a literary work. For example, yesterday someone in the audience said that when she first read *On the Road* it struck her as a sad book rather than as the riotous odyssey of two American dropouts.

Tomorrow in my workshop I thought we could look more closely at *On the Road,* in terms of how it was written. We'll compare the various versions of *On the Road* that have been published and are available, for example the version of it in *Visions of Cody* and the section of it published as *Jazz of the Beat Generation* many years ago; and we'll see how they compare with the book published in 1957, which is the true subject of the conference.

Today I'll begin with how I was influenced as a writer by reading Jack Kerouac. I first mentioned this in the introduction to my biography of Kerouac, published in 1973. By profession, I am a college professor; I teach at the University of Connecticut, and I took my doctorate in American Literature. I received my basic undergraduate education at the University of California in Berkeley in 1953-1957, the period so beautifully described in *The Dharma Bums.*

Although I had good professors at Berkeley in those years, the most significant event influencing the direction I took in my professional life was not learning about literature from my distinguished professors, and I had very distinguished professors—for example I remember Charles Muscatine who gave very elegant lectures on the work of Geoffrey Chaucer, and I remember Travis Bogard who lectured brilliantly on Elizabethan and Jacobean revenge tragedy, and if you took his class in the right semester he went on to talk about Eugene O'Neill. I didn't study with the poet Josephine Miles, the only woman on the faculty of the English department in those years. Later I discovered that Josephine Miles, an excellent Berkeley poet, part of the Berkeley Renaissance group of writers in the 1940s, was also an authority on how to teach Freshman English. She wrote some very useful essays revealing the secrets of expository prose, which enlightened me.

But in the early 1950s the emphasis in the English department at Berkeley was not on contemporary writers, and so none of these distinguished professors changed my life.

My most significant learning experience there, as far as literature was concerned, happened in March 1956 when I attended a poetry reading in a downtown Berkeley movie theater where several poets came over from San Francisco and repeated the "Howl" reading that they had done at the Gallery Six the previous fall. I hadn't been there the previous fall, but I went to the 1956 re-run in this movie theater, where Allen Ginsberg read the entire, recently completed "Howl for Carl Solomon" for the first time, and where Kenneth Rexroth was the master of ceremonies. Ginsberg was last on the program: Snyder, McClure, Lamantia, Phil Whalen, all these San Francisco poets read first.

I also remember that Jack Kerouac was in the audience that night, but I could be wrong. I could be confusing my memory of the March 1956 reading that I actually attended with Jack's description of the October 1955 reading in *The Dharma Bums*. Kerouac didn't read with the poets on the stage at the Gallery Six. He stayed in the aisle, distributing wine and passing the hat. Five months later I can't give you an exact analysis of what turned me on about the poetry reading I attended in Berkeley, because it did change the whole course of my life, but I could suggest the feeling of excitement that I felt at the time by playing you a short tape of Jack reading.

What you're going to hear is a snippet of Jack talking about the history of bop and the Beat Generation. The poetry reading I attended in March 1956 was before I knew about *On the Road*, the book wasn't published until a year and a half later, so the whole uproar over the Beat Generation was yet to come. I certainly hadn't encountered the term "Beat Generation" when I listened to the poets reading on the stage in Berkeley in 1956. But the tape will give you a sense of Kerouac's presence, when he was in that San Francisco audience where Ginsberg read the early part of "Howl," and Jack shouted "go, go" to the poets. Jack's voice will give you a hint of what was to me an unforgettable experience. Listen to it. [plays tape]

In the tape Kerouac describes himself as being on the sidelines in the jazz club, partly because he doesn't want to be noticed by the bartender and forced to pay for another beer, but also because he generally hung around the sidelines. At the Gallery Six he didn't want to be part of the reading, he was invited but he said no thanks. This is at the end of the summer of 1955, right after he'd arrived at Ginsberg's Milvia cottage from Mexico City, where he'd written *Mexico City Blues*. Jack preferred to remain on the sidelines, often scribbling in his notebooks when he'd put down the bottle of beer or the glass of wine in his hand.

Besides Kerouac's presence, that tape also gives you a sense of what the scene was like in the East Bay in the middle fifties. In March 1956 the poetry reading in Berkeley was my first encounter with this scene, and the person who introduced me to it was Peter Orlovsky, who took me to the poetry reading on a blind date arranged for me by my college roommate. The day afterwards Peter mentioned our date in a letter to his mother—he was very pleased that he'd met a girl who was a student at Berkeley.

Soon afterwards, Sam Charters continued my education. He drove me across the Bay Bridge to the City Lights bookstore, the first paperback bookstore in this country—we don't often think of Ferlinghetti as an entrepreneur, but that he was—and a center also for the local literary life. The shelves of the bookstore displayed small press publications sent to City Lights from all over the country. People drove over from Berkeley and Marin County in old jalopies just to read what they discovered on the store's bookshelves, because most often we couldn't afford to buy anything. Sam also introduced me to a jazz and folk music scene, both in Berkeley and in San Francisco. His interest in African-American music sparked my interest. I didn't know much about it, all I knew about from the time I was in high school was Bix Beiderbecke. I did know about ragtime, and through Sam's encouragement, I became the ragtime pianist I am now. All of these things, the jazz, the music, the poetry, the books, made up the scene for me. What you get in Kerouac's books is not the creation of a scene but the recording, the chronicling of a scene. There were a lot of people on the same road, but Jack was the one who wrote about it the best.

After the Berkeley reading in March 1956, I knew I had to become more knowledgeable about the poetry of Walt Whitman, because those poets on the stage were part of what was later called an outlaw tradition that my professors weren't talking about. Walking me back to my co-op dormitory on Forest Avenue after the reading, Peter Orlovsky tried to convince me that Ginsberg was at least as good a poet as Walt Whitman. Listening to Ginsberg read "Howl for Carl Solomon" had been an unforgettable experience, so I agreed that he was a powerful poet, but as important as Whitman? It took another couple of years for me to decide that Peter was right. Reading Kerouac's books convinced me.

I stayed in college for another year and earned my bachelor's degree. Then I took a job teaching English in a high school in Oakland. *On the Road* was published in the fall of 1957, but I didn't pay much attention to it twenty-five years ago because at that time I was floundering on a heavy trip of my own. I had found out that I could not discipline the rambunctious San Lorenzo high school students who ran riot in my crowded classroom. I barely made it through my first semester, resigned from the job, and let Sam take me to Sausalito and put me quietly to rest. After this experience I knew I'd have to go on to graduate school, because although I realized I wanted to teach, I'd learned that my career was going to be in literature, not in teaching. There really is a difference. I was fortunate enough to be awarded a Woodrow Wilson fellowship and became a graduate student at Columbia University, so I was in New York City just at the time *The Dharma Bums* was published in 1958.

Of all my professors at Columbia, I will tell you only about William York Tindall, because it was Professor Tindall who got me involved in the Beat writers through a negative experience. After *The Dharma Bums* was given a sneering review in the *New York Times,* Tindall took a moment during a lecture on William Butler Yeats to tell the class that he didn't think that Kerouac was much of a writer: he was a Columbia dropout who couldn't play football any better than he could write. I was surprised that my professor had attacked a writer, not his book. I had read *The Dharma Bums* and thought it was a brilliant account of the life I'd also led in Berkeley. After Kerouac had been put down by a snobbish Ivy League intellectual, he rose higher in my estimation. Professor Tindall didn't take the trouble to put down any other contemporary writers in his classroom. I was hooked. That's probably when I decided to become a Beat scholar.

Twenty years ago at Columbia if you were getting a doctorate in contemporary American Literature (this was the Dark Ages), you had a choice of Shakespeare, Chaucer, or Milton as your major author. I remember looking in complete disbelief at the professor who told me this, and asking him what about Emerson? what about Melville? what about Hawthorne? (Notice I didn't say what about Kerouac.) I made a vow that I would do my own work on the contemporary writers I admired as soon as I had completed the requirements for the PhD. Chaucer, Shakespeare, and Milton didn't need me to write scholarly books about them.

My first independent project was a Kerouac bibliography. By this point it was 1965, there were a lot of Kerouac books published, and I'd become an avid collector. In Greenwich Village Robert A. Wilson, owner of the Phoenix Bookshop, was publishing a series of bibliographies on contemporary authors—this is something you shouldn't take lightly. Of course today there are bibliographies of McClure and Corso and Ginsberg and Kerouac, but in 1965 these were really just recently published writers, and it was something of a courageous venture for the Phoenix to undertake these contemporary bibliographies. So I signed aboard for the Kerouac one, and that's how I spent two days together with Jack Kerouac and his mother Gabrielle in their home in Hyannis in August 1966.

Before I met Jack I had spent nearly a year on the project. I had done most of the work compiling the bibliography, but I wanted to check what I had done. I had heard that Kerouac's personal collection was nearly complete, that he kept copies of everything. Now of course I had imagined him living out of suitcases, being on the road all the time. The impression I'd gotten from reading his books was all I had. I couldn't believe that he'd own more than a tattered copy of On the Road along with perhaps a couple of scattered manuscripts. But I decided to check it out. I got my invitation to visit Jack's home by writing to his mother. This was the early summer of 1966. Bob Wilson at the Phoenix Bookshop told me that Kerouac was a drunken recluse, so I wrote his mother asking if I could come and look at the books. She gave my letter to Jack, of course, and Jack must have been intrigued by the idea of a woman professor working on his bibliography so he invited me to Hyannis.

I climbed into my Volkswagen Beetle and drove there with my edgy Irish setter, and Jack and I spent two days working on his books. It turned out, much to my amazement, that he had beautifully organized his archive. In every house where he lived with his mother, he had a bedroom, and in every bedroom was a bureau, though he owned very few clothes. He kept his manuscripts in his bureau drawers, everything gathered together with rubber bands or tied up in string. On the last day I was there, Jack posed for twelve photos, including one with his mother, and later we corresponded, he looked at the various galleys and was kind enough to revise the first edition of the bibliography. This was my first independent scholarly project. I am very proud of it. With it I became a Kerouac scholar.

After compiling the biblio, I wanted to write a history of the Beat writers. Kerouac's death in October 1969 shocked me terribly. No one had the faintest notion he would die so soon. I was living in an apartment in Brooklyn Heights, and I found out about it by hearing from my upstairs neighbor who always listened to the radio in the morning, that Jack Kerouac had died in Florida. She knew of my interest in Kerouac and so she came down and knocked on my door. I was getting ready to go to teach an English class at New York City Community College, and she said hey, did you hear that? And I said what? She said, Kerouac's dead. I said, you're kidding. He was only 47. She said no, no, it's on the radio. And indeed it was true. Ironically enough that day when I met my class, I had assigned *On the Road,* and it was a very weird experience, with the knowledge in my head that the man was no longer living in Florida, yet the spiritual presence of the man was alive on the desks of all my students, since everybody had a copy of the book right in front of them when I came into the classroom. It was a strange moment, as you can well imagine.

After Jack's death, Lawrence Ferlinghetti asked me to compile and edit Kerouac's *Scattered Poems* as a volume in the City Lights Pocket Poets series. Sam and I had started a small press of our own called Portents, and in the late 1960s Ginsberg encouraged us to publish a small book titled *Scenes Along the Road* using his early photographs. Allen did the wise thing in his lifetime of depositing his literary archives in a university. His earliest materials went to Columbia, a sale arranged by Andreas Brown at the Gotham Book Mart. Andy saw Allen's marvelous photographs taken first with his Brownie and then later on with his 35MM camera. Andy knew that I was a photographer too and asked if I wanted to see these photographs. I said yes, I did want to. I went up to Columbia when it was still a very disorganized archive. Now it's meticulously indexed and stored, but at the time Ginsberg had put his photographs in cardboard boxes. They were on the floor of the Rare Book and Manuscript Room at the Butler Library, and I first saw them there when I selected images for *Scenes Along the Road.* It was a wonderful experience.

At the end of 1970 I moved to Stockholm with my husband and daughter Mallay as our personal anti-Vietnam War protest, and I wrote the first biography of Kerouac there. All the interviews and tapes and materials for my projected history of the Beat writers were sent in two black trunks to Sweden. Once I started, I found that it was easier to focus on Kerouac as a biographer than to attempt covering the entire subject as a literary historian. About six years of research notes went with me to Stockholm. I spent a year writing the rough draft of the biography and then learned that Aaron Latham had been signed by Sterling Lord to do the authorized biography for Random House.

Sam said, well, let's write this book. It's either that or give it up. So with his help I revised it, and several months later it was ready in manuscript when Snyder and McClure came to visit us. They were in Stockholm for an ecology conference during the summer of 1972. They came over to our house for lunch and a swim, and I said, hey you guys, I've been working on a book. They looked at it, and McClure went back to San Francisco and sold it for me with Straight Arrow. I had sent my prospectus and a sample chapter of the biography around for a year, getting nowhere, because everyone knew that Random House had contracted for the authorized life, and who needed two books on Kerouac? Only Straight Arrow and *Rolling Stone* had the commercial instinct to publish the manuscript, on McClure's recommendation.

Kerouac: A Biography was published in 1973. The *New York Times* listed it as one of the year's hundred most important books, and today it's a mass-market paperback. Ten years ago I was in San Francisco editing the final manuscript at the Straight Arrow office. I did my final research there and interviewed Carolyn Cassady, whom I had not met before. She was very generous in letting me look at her unpublished memoir, she played me tapes of Neal, and she was perfectly marvelous. All the rest is history, right?

That's my account of Kerouac's influence on me as a reader and a writer. As a biographer and an editor I'm still working on books about the Beat writers. In the last two years I've been the editor of a very large project, returning to my original concept of writing about the Beats as a group of writers. This is an encyclopedia of Beat Generation writers to be published in 1983 by Gale Research in two volumes in their Dictionary of

Literary Biography series. It's titled *The Beats: Literary Bohemians in Postwar America*. There are sixty-six authors and fifty contributors; different scholars throughout the country, including many of the people here at this conference, have contributed articles on different writers.

Now let me go on to something else. What was the effect on me and my career of taking Kerouac as a subject for research? I think you know the answer from Tim Hunt's lecture—academically, very difficult. It's always difficult forming judgments of contemporary writers, but the situation with contemporary writers is even more complicated because of what we call literary politics. There are special difficulties working in the field of Beat writers. Academics aren't much interested, frankly, except in some very narrow circumstances, in the poetry of Ginsberg and Snyder, and in the prose experiments of William Burroughs. There is very little mainline academic interest and no one teaches in this field in any of the major universities. However, if you'd like to read literary studies of Saul Bellow or Flannery O'Connor, there are many of them, while in 1982 there's just one literary study of Kerouac's work, Tim Hunt's excellent *Kerouac's Crooked Road.*

Kerouac is a difficult writer for academics to research because, to date, the manuscripts aren't available. That's one reason why we have so many biographies, as well as the fact that his life is legendary and has heavy cultural ramifications. The manuscripts of Gertrude Stein, Ernest Hemingway, Katherine Ann Porter, to give a few examples, are readily available, and if you are a literary scholar, you know where to go. They're accessible within certain permissions situations and you can do any literary study you like.

What I'll try to do tomorrow will be the most tentative kind of reconstruction of the stages of *On the Road* as a literary experiment. With Kerouac there's no straight line in his development as a writer. He followed what Tim Hunt called a crooked road—that crooked road business is taken from a quotation from William Blake. Jack was influenced in his early years, as you know, by Thomas Wolfe, by Hemingway, by Saroyan, there are masses of influences as a youth and a young writer. After he met Burroughs and Ginsberg, there was a period of factualism, in the early drafts of *On the Road.* Then, with the letters from Neal Cassady, which started to arrive in the fifties, there was an awareness on Kerouac's part that he could use Neal Cassady's way of telling a story about his personal adventure in the first person, and that's when *On the Road* got started in the version we have it here. There are excerpts from the letters in *On the Road* verbatim, from Neal's letters. I'll talk about that tomorrow.

Then after getting turned on totally by the letters as a way of solving this problem as a writer, the problem of narrative, Kerouac went even further, and went into trying to capture, in sketching or spontaneous prose, the kind of rhythms that were related to the speech patterns of Neal Cassady, not only the writing of Cassady but also the talking of Cassady, you could hear this kind of energy which was Cassady's energy too. And then drawing back, after the radical experiments of *Cody* and *Dr. Sax,* into what he called picaresque narration.

Kerouac didn't stay with spontaneous prose all his life with his novels, as he did with his poetry. He modified the picaresque narrative technique in *Maggie Cassidy, Desolation Angels, Big Sur,* and *Satori in Paris.* It's very complicated to trace this out. People want instant formulas—ah spontaneous prose, that's what his greatness is. You can't do that with Kerouac. His work didn't evolve in the straightforward way of, say James Joyce, from *The Dubliners* all the way to *Finnegans Wake.* Kerouac is more unpredictable, and it's impossible to make final judgments until the manuscript versions are available.

Then, to further complicate Kerouac's writing as a subject for research, it's very hard to judge *On the Road* because it is, of course, a work about people who are still present in our midst. Kerouac uses the name Huncke, he drops it in, you'll remember, in the text, on the tape that I played. And immediately I think of the gentle, courtly man on the porch at breakfast this morning where I'm staying during this conference. I get distracted from the work as a work of literature and I think of the actual person himself.

Then Kerouac mentions the name Dean. He invents a name for the character who was Neal Cassady to prevent a libel suit, but otherwise Kerouac insists that he's portraying his characters exactly as he saw them. Which is another problem. The way Kerouac portrays the people in his books isn't necessarily the way other people saw them, or the way the characters saw themselves. So we are very handicapped in one way, reading Kerouac in 1982, because fortunately many of the people whom he wrote about are still with us.

There never was a novelist who trusted his imagination so little. Jack didn't fictionalize. He put the events of his life down as he remembered them. He used his imagination in his haikus, but in the prose works he insisted he was writing picturesque narrative, not novels. He went back to models who are totally out of fashion—another reason why Kerouac challenges the critics. It isn't so much that books such as *Cody* are experimental works of fiction, because academics enjoy analyzing anti-novels or anti-stories, anti-narrative in other words. For many readers the difficulty with Kerouac is his casual use of picaresque techniques. Jack really did think of himself as an old tea-head of time. His choice of picaresque narration reminds us not of the latest hip contemporary writers but ancient novelists such as Henry Fielding or Lawrence Sterne. It takes academics a while to catch up. They aren't always the sharpest people in the room.

Another reason why academics find Kerouac difficult, besides all of the reasons I've given, is because Jack himself made it so hard. Unlike Ginsberg, Jack couldn't deal with the media. You've seen Jack on the Steve Allen videotape, where Steve Allen was so condescending to him. These old telecasts are terrible. I was in Nashville recently and saw young Elvis Presley on the Steve Allen show and the Milton Berle show, and the contempt of the emcees for a young popular artist is hard to watch.

On the videotape Steve Allen tells the television audience, "We made this record together"—and then he throws it on the piano as if it's garbage. He turns to Kerouac in a very belittling way, "You're nervous, come on Jack, don't be nervous, I'm only going to chew your head off if I can." It's definitely a confrontation rather than a mellow exchange. He asks Kerouac, "Well, I hear that you were on the road for seven years and you took only three weeks to write this bestseller," with a contemptuous curl of the lip. And Kerouac answers shyly "Yes, that's true, three weeks." Steve Allen crows, "Well I would have gone on the road for three weeks and taken seven years to write the book!" People watching the program saw Jack Kerouac looking incredibly intense and sort of crazy, and they thought, who writes bestsellers in three weeks? "Wouldn't revise a word," Jack says. "When this hand writes, it doesn't go back. God directs it." You just don't say things like this on television and impress academics. There's a problem, because not only are academics not impressed but the rare reader interested in fine literature also isn't impressed, thinking of Jack's writing as "just typing," to quote Truman Capote's famous rebuke.

A hundred years from now, when Naropa gives a conference to celebrate the 125th anniversary of *On the Road*, there won't be this kind of trouble. Jack's book will have become an American classic, and nobody will be around to remember Allen Ginsberg or Jack Kerouac or William Burroughs or Herbert Huncke personally. There will be no windy, cloying reminiscences by wordy old-timers. Unfortunately here I am in 1982 trying to function as a literary historian with all these difficulties, plus the personal bias of having been there myself.

Of course, no matter how much the formalist or the modernist critics look at literature just as something on the page, there will always be people wanting to know what Dickens was like, or who Shakespeare really was. There is a greater possibility of achieving distance from the text after the writer is long dead—there is a vast difference in evaluating the work, especially when it tells stories about contemporary people who are still going strong. Also, needless to say, what will happen in the evaluation of Kerouac's writing will depend on the subsequent careers of the people in the books, and we're not finished yet. I hope all the Beat authors live to be at least a healthy hundred years old and continue to create masterpieces.

As a literary historian I feel that *On the Road* is an extraordinary work of literature. I'd rate it as one of the four most important American novels of all time. If you have been to college you know that academics who write about American literature agree on three early prose masterpieces: *The Scarlet Letter* and *Moby-Dick*, written in the 1850s, and *Huckleberry Finn*, written in 1884. And then they stop. They say, now what? Nearly a century has gone by since *Huckleberry Finn* was published—and what has happened? I'd say that *On the Road* is the fourth masterpiece. Just as we pair *Scarlet Letter* and *Moby-Dick*, I think we should pair *Huck Finn* and *On the Road*. There's a time warp there to be sure, it's almost seventy years later, but there are significant parallels to be drawn.

In the 1850s, America was a new country. Hawthorne, whose tendency was to look back on the Puritan heritage, looked back to the forces that shaped America as a new continent, especially the civilizing forces. And these in his book, *The Scarlet Letter*, are given a fictional shape. Specifically, of course, it's about the relationship of the new settlers of America, the Puritans, to God, and, something else Hawthorne is very concerned about, the basic hypocrisy of their relationship to God. The hypocrisy of their being there on Indian territory, leaving England for a religious reason and going over to the New World to set up what they consider a more godly society. *The Scarlet Letter* tests this notion.

Herman Melville, in *Moby-Dick*, is not interested so much as Hawthorne was in the Puritan heritage or the founding of America, although he was actually much more obsessed with God than Hawthorne. Melville, in *Moby-Dick*, was writing about his contemporary America, where it had come. He was judging the civilization which had as its design the conquering of nature through industry, specifically in his case the white whale in the whaling industry, and Ahab's diabolical pride attempting to conquer nature in his hunt for Moby-Dick.

Now we jump ahead and we have God, nature, and Huck Finn. In 1884 Mark Twain was testing the American ideal of freedom, how human beings functioned in the most progressive society on earth at that time. We had existed for over a hundred years as an independent nation, yet during the post-Civil War period our so-called democracy completely failed to live up to the American ideals of freedom, equality, and brotherhood. *Huckleberry Finn* is indeed a very dark look at the limits of our supposedly democratic society.

Huck Finn in the last section, lighting off for the territory ahead, brings us right up to Sal Paradise in 1947, heading west for the first time on the road to join his buddy Dean Moriarty. After World War II, this brotherhood is seen in much narrower terms. Rather than a democratic ideal, as it had been in *Huckleberry Finn* with the black slave and the white outcast boy, we have in *On the Road* two feckless, fatherless white deadbeats, Sal and Dean. By the end of the book they should have learned that there's nothing waiting for them in the territory ahead.

On the Road is the fourth book in this sequence of great American novels. I'm a firm believer in the richness of American literature being strongly rooted in its geographical base. Charles Olson pointed this out to me, and he's absolutely right to look at it closely. Reading *On the Road* again, you marvel at Kerouac's accurate description of America, the landscape of America, the size of America. The vigor of Jack's prose suggests the vitality of America. The character Sal Paradise epitomizes the open-heartedness of America, the promise of America, perhaps even the fatal sentimentality of America. *The Scarlet Letter, Moby-Dick, Huck Finn,* and *On the Road* are great books because they're all involved in an exploration of the promise of America, the dream that is still alive in many of us, even if it seems to be receding rapidly. I think that if it weren't still alive, we wouldn't be in this room celebrating Kerouac's book.

It is true that some people reading *On the Road* for the first time find it a darker book than someone who is revering it as a glorification of the two cultural heroes Dean and Sal. Then it's a very dark book indeed. But on the other hand, Sal Paradise wants to go on that road, the road is life, just as it was life on the river to Huckleberry Finn. Kerouac is aware of the irony that all the Indians in Mexico along the road want something from him, but he wouldn't be on the road if he had it. Close to the beginning of the novel, this theme is beautifully dramatized when Sal is on the road hoping to thumb a ride west with Eddy, another hitchhiker, and they're approached by a carnival man who wants one of them to come work for him, take a little job. This carnival man says to Sal Paradise, "Are you boys goin' somewhere? or just goin'?" Kerouac's novel is testing "just going." As such it answers something very deep within us as Americans. I wonder, do any of you here today in this workshop read it the same way?

—July 26, 1982

KEROUAC, CATHOLICISM, BUDDHISM

Gregory Corso,
Allen Ginsberg, John Clellon Holmes

ALLEN GINSBERG: FELLOW CELEBRANTS, FELLOW POETS, FELLOW SENTIENT beings, welcome to the discussion of Kerouac, Catholicism, and Buddhism.

GREGORY CORSO: About this picture, I've been asked many times, on the crucifix: Jack was posing for *Mademoiselle* with Allen, myself, Philip Whalen, Peter Orlovsky, I don't remember who else. A woman had given me this beautiful silver cross, and Jack and I had thoughts in common with talks of Catholicism. The first shot I did to make him Beat was his hair. His hair was always well combed back. Before they took the photograph, I mussed up his hair. That's what I did. Then I gave him the crucifix, I came on like a John the Baptist in a sense to this man. I said here, put this on; and he put it on. He loved that cross. The big deal about it of course is it was wiped out many times in newspapers and whatnot. But not the hair, the hair remained. I think that answers that one.

The second one was in his household. I was invited with my first wife, before my eighteen-year-old daughter, who was here and left today, was born. And I was allowed to sleep in the bed with my wife because I was married to her. No one else who went to that house, if they weren't married, could sleep together in that house. Mother had it so. I don't know if my daughter was conceived while I was there or not, but that's a good shot. Over the bed was a crucifix.

Those are the only two shots I think I can mention—the clarification of that, the addition of the hair being mussed up, and the invitation to his home. When I left I received a nice postcard from him, saying, thank you for blessing our home. That's it.

GINSBERG: I might as well supplement what Gregory said about the mussed hair and the crucifix. "That nutty picture of me on the cover of *On the Road* resulted from the fact that I had just gotten down from a high mountain where I'd been for two months completely alone. Usually I was in the habit of combing my hair of course, because you have to get rides on the highway and all that, and you usually want girls to look at you as though you were a man and not a wild beast. But my friend Gregory Corso opened his shirt and took out a silver crucifix that was hanging from a chain and said, wear this and wear it outside your shirt but don't comb your hair. So I spent several days around San Francisco going around with him and others like that to parties, arties, parks, jam sessions, bars, poetry readings, churches, walking talking poetry in the streets, walking talking God in the streets, and at one point a strange gang of hoodlums got mad and said, what right does he have to wear that, and my own gang of musicians and poets told them to cool it, and finally on the third day, *Mademoiselle* magazine wanted to take pictures of us all, so I posed just like that, wild hair, crucifix and all, with Gregory Corso, Allen Ginsberg, and Philip Whalen, and the only publication which later did not erase the crucifix from my breast from that plaid cotton sleeveless shirt front, was the *New York Times*, therefore the *New York Times* is as beat as I am and I'm glad I've got a friend."

Letters from Kerouac in 1954, when he was first beginning to absorb Buddhist texts and Buddhist ideas and ideas of meditation and transform them into his own personal vehicle. December 1954, writing from New York: I had written him from Mexico about a dream I'd had of seeing a hero on a cross with a gorgeous Catholic-looking ceremonial drapes all around. He said, "wealth of drapes and dark lapped colors and Rembrandt splendor can't make up . . . for the simple line of clarity as elicited by a near naked Indian whose crown of glory far exceeds messianic hung-up maniacs . . . and whose main ambition is always political and terrestrial, otherwise there would be no reason for multitudes of pharisees to give them political crucifixion. . . . Jesus got in everybody's hair, face it. Edgar Cayce is nothing but a Jesus Christ hillbilly who pretended to be ignorant of medicine, pretended to go into trances, was just apparently extremely intuitional and classic physician who however had a mystic streak and wanted to prophetize and so cooked up this bed trance medicine." That's an early take. "I accused Lucien of being proud of suffering, which incidentally is what Neal is, because the only reason why I couldn't make any impression on his intelligence with the doctors of the East was because he, being a life proud American like Burroughs or Lucien, wouldn't accept the number one truth of Buddha, the first of the four great truths, all life is sorrowful. Thinking that misery is grand ruptures their rapture, life is suffering, this you've got to understand. If you think it is anything but suffering you've lost completely the significance of even the need for emancipation. And of course, for your beginning studies in Buddhism, you must listen to me carefully and implicitly, as though I was Einstein teaching you relativity or Eliot teaching the formulas of objective correlation on a blackboard in Princeton." Then he prescribes a reading list from the Lankavatara Sutra to begin with. This is for any of you who are curious about his entry into Buddhism or your own parallel inquisitiveness into that field: the *Buddhacarita* or *Life of Buddha,* by Asvaghosa the patriarch, which is a book used popularly around Boulder incidentally, Paul Carus's *Gospel of Buddha,* which is a more nineteenth-century shot, *Buddhism in Translation* by Henry Clarke Warren, also in the Harvard Classics, those were texts used by T. S. Eliot previously; *The Buddhist Bible* by Dwight Goddard, which was his main source—he says of that, "this is by far the best book because it contains the Surangama Sutra and the Lankavatara Sutra, not to mention the eleven-page Diamond Sutra, which is the last word, and Asvaghosa's *Awakening of Faith and the Tao.*" *The Buddhist Bible* uses sources from the Pali, Sanskrit, Tibetan, Chinese, Burmese, and modern, and from *The Buddhist Bible* he got *Songs of Milarepa* and a lot of talk about Marpa's wife, Damema, whose name constantly recurs in *Mexico City Blues,* Damema, mother of Buddhas, whom he identified with his own mother. The list continues with the Digha Nikaya, the dialogues of Buddha, and the *Visuddhimagga* by Buddhagosa, path of purity—the *Visuddhimagga* is the exposition of Abhidhamma, that would be precise instructions for how to eat, how to sit, the systematic scientific analysis of the psychology of consciousness while sitting—and *Sacred Books* and *Early Literature of the East.*

"Now, Allen, as Neal or Carr can tell you, last February I topped up a hundred-page account of Buddhism for you, gleaned from my notes, and you'll see proof of that in several allusions and appeals to [Allen]. And I have that here, if you really want to see it I'll send it importantly stamped. It's the only copy, we must take special care with it, right? *Some of the Dharma* I called it and it was intended for you to read in the jungle. Some of it is now, I see, useless because mistaken or written on grass or other faults, but it may really give you a send off into the above tomes, which is my wish. Listen, you must begin with *The Life of the Buddha* by Asvaghosa, then if you can read the Surangama Sutra next, this is how I found path, but the paths of the many are many to the one path . . . I don't have to write, I may write to teach. I suppose I gotta teach, but like Joe McCarthy I'm getting awfully sick of being reprimanded for losing my hold on life's attaching apparatuses. It's like I committed some crime. Nirvana means snapping a relationship, so naturally nobody'll like me any mo. Close your eyes, cross your legs under you, practice slow in breathing and out breathing, think 'I am breathing in, I am breathing out,' then you think, 'there is the breathing in, there is the breathing out,' and soon essential mind will begin to shine in you and you will begin to experience your first samadhi."

So those were his instructions to me, and I immediately wrote him back and said, o.k., you be my guru. So then he wrote me back a long letter and said, well I don't know enough about it, I can't be your guru, however, listen to me and do this and that, and read the Diamond Sutra. My first reaction, actually, it's something I've mentioned before but it's really interesting because it's something I think that Kesey would understand and most of you will understand, there is a resentment that I felt instantly at being told that existence is suffering, the first noble truth that Kerouac talks about. Because as a high school kid from New Jersey I was looking forward to a career and getting on in life and having a successful happy whatever, either a career or a marriage or a house or an American future, and then Kerouac was coming in and saying existence is suffering. And he did it with a slight edge of aggression, which I think turned me off for the first couple years, thinking that I was going to submit to some horrible doctrine from the East which turned the universe into an inhuman dog-eat-dog affair, not realizing that it's actually sort of a neutral descriptive statement. I found it easier to understand in terms which I've heard around Boulder, existence contains suffering. Because obviously, being born in a body there's a slight not insecurity but discomfort, having a body and having to sit in a body, and the discomfort obviously of the body falling apart.

Well that was Jack's first take on Buddhism. I hadn't realized but he apparently had some idea of sitting, probably from reading. The difficulty was that there was no Zen master or meditation teacher that we knew of until Suzuki Roshi came in 1958 to San Francisco. I don't think Jack met Suzuki Roshi. In the period of 1954–56 when we were all hanging around together with Philip Whalen and Gary Snyder, which totally turned him on to the texts, the Lankavatara Sutra and Surangama Sutra that he was reading with them, I don't think Gary ever showed me how to sit. Gary, I found out recently, didn't know either except from books, he hadn't actually met a sitting or meditation teacher. So Gary had learned the postures from statues, he said, statues and books. And so there was no transmission of exact precise information on how to sit; so Kerouac sitting as it's described in the *Scripture of Golden Eternity* is more of a force feed fast instant squeeze tight ass kundalini shot of holding your breath, at least at that point, by the year he wrote the *Scripture of Golden Eternity* at Snyder's recommendation that he explain what he knew.

JOHN CLELLON HOLMES: I'm here on this panel I suppose for two reasons. The first is that I was asked some months ago, after looking over the topics that were to be taken up in this conference, if I had any suggestions, and I said that I thought there should be a panel on Catholicism and Buddhism as they related to Jack Kerouac. I later discovered that I was to be a member of that panel, which is interesting because I am neither Catholic nor a Buddhist. Knowing Jack as I did and corresponding with him regularly in the twenty-two years that we were friends, it was inevitable that I would be a witness to his spiritual travels, which were continuous and endless. He was that way when I met him, he was that way when he died. He saw spirit in everything. At various times in my relationship with him he explained it in terms related to or borrowed from various religions, primarily the oldest sort of Christianity and later what I took to be, and it has not been proved opposite since then, a profound and penetrating understanding of the Buddhist view of life and of reality. As a man without a faith then, I observed this because I could not feel that anything that this man was interested in was insignificant. I was an atheist when I met him; I studied religion primarily because I wanted to understand what he was talking about. The Catholicism was instinctive to him when I met him. When he spoke of spiritual matters, he talked usually in terms borrowed from one aspect of Christian theology or another. This changed. In my experience with him, I noticed it changing in letters, but when he came back from the mountain, it was almost a year before *On the Road* finally got published, he and Allen and Peter were on their way hopefully they thought to Europe or North Africa, which is where they did end up, and Jack seemed to me different than he had been before. He was still the same man, but he seemed to have achieved a kind of peace that was at first puzzling to me but eventually made me extremely happy for him.

Something had happened to him on the mountain where he was compelled to be by himself. And in that setting which was awesome and magnificent he looked, as I think he always looked, for God's footprint, God's plan. And I felt he had seen beyond that. The plan or purpose he had looked for had been only partial. In my experience with him, Buddhism was sincere, it wasn't faddish to be a Buddhist then. I'm not saying that it is now, but more people know about it than certainly knew about it then. I also felt that it had provided him, for that period of his life, I didn't know the uproar to come, with a serenity that I had never seen in him before. The question has come up many times, as to whether he reconverted to Catholicism or what have you. I don't think it's important particularly. Jack often fell back on instinctive knowledge or knowledge that he had achieved very early. On that trip that he did make, a few months after I saw him for a week up there, he wrote me a funny letter when he got to Tangier. He was traveling on a tramp steamer and they got into a terrible storm. Jack had been to sea, this should not have been unusual to him, but I gather this was a really bad storm that went on for three or four days. The way he described it, and he was being somewhat facetious, was, "all my Buddhism evaporated in a green crap of fear." This of course was a sign of Jack's essential honesty about himself, because when I saw him again, later, he was Buddhist again. But the point to be made, from my experience as a religious man myself without a creed, is that Jack saw in religion an artistic expression of man's spiritual striving, both to know the truth and to be reconciled with reality. He did not invite suffering upon himself, he did not take suffering upon himself consciously in my opinion. But he realized that suffering was innate to life, distinct to life, that one couldn't get through life without being hurt, disappointed, rejected, baffled, and sometimes in despair. I think that he believed that the last despair, if you can call it that—this is where the Catholicism perhaps still remained—the last despair was a mortal sin. That to give in to despair was to violate your nature, and to use it cheaply. He did not try to avoid despair, but he did not invite it. And I think through despair, going through despair and coming out on the other side, thereby all the suffering that goes along with that, that was the only way to achieve peace. And I think that Jack, in his calmest moments and the moments when he was alone, it was peace of spirit that he wanted to find inside himself so that he could speak with more authority in his writings to all of us. I think he profoundly believed that he had to experience what everyone experiences and go through it and come out the other side. However I must add, I think probably towards the very end of his life he was relying on the rituals and attitudes of his boyhood religion. But I think if he was here listening to us he would say all this doesn't matter. As long as we keep open to faith, it may come. He remained open to belief and to hope for the world and for all of you, to the end of his life. You know what this must have cost him because you have all felt it, a little at least, yourselves. If we despair of the world, if we grow bleak and cynical and angry, then that is where no hope lies. We can make the future and we can save ourselves, no matter how we do it or where we end up, and that endeavor is the highest thing that human beings can achieve. He lived in that belief, he wrote in that belief, and only when he became so tired did he long for sleep, and find it.

—June 1, 1982

I've been meaning to talk to Francesco [Clemente] about this, to tell him about my recent stay in Rome where I was doing some collaboration at the press where Mimmo Palladino is producing a beautiful, large book called *Dogana. Dogana* is a huge size art book with about a dozen different graphic artists with poems facing the illustrations. I did four stone lithographs in that book.

The other collaboration I've done in Italy was with Sandro Veronesi. Sandro is an editor of *Nuovi Argomenti,* which was a great literary magazine founded by Alberto Moravia and is still going. I think it's published by Mondadori now. I did a painting of a man in an electric chair at Sing Sing. It happens I did a photo silk screen of a photograph that was found among one of my brother's papers. My brother had been an assistant warden at Sing Sing for twenty-five years, and as assistant warden had to witness the executions. After thirty years of service in the New York State penitentiary system he retired and flipped out. Among his papers was found this old sepia photograph of a man in the electric chair, a wooden electric chair at Sing Sing. And on the back written in hand, in pencil, were the instructions to the executioner, written in this very crude handwriting, saying "two electrodes attached to head, one to leg, 5,000 volts, first jolt knocks man unconscious, pronounced dead in two minutes." So I took this and silkscreened, large silkscreen positive, onto the silkscreen, I did four prints on artists' paper, six-foot sheets, and one on canvas. Each one is different, you know how it is with silkscreen prints or with lithography prints, each one can be worked on afterward. On several I wrote, in several languages—"Ceci n'est pas une pipe," you remember that from Magritte? I wrote "Ceci n'est pas un homme," on another one I wrote "Questa non è un uomo," and then another one "This is not a man." Sandro Veronesi is using this in an international campaign to abolish the death penalty by the year 2000. *[applause]*

—Gregory Corso: That's a nice painting, I saw it.
  "This is not a man." It certainly didn't look like a man . . .

—Lawrence Ferlinghetti, from "The Third Mind," a panel on collabora-
  tion, July 9, 1994

COMMONPLACE DISCOVERIES:
LEW WELCH

Philip Whalen

I DON'T KNOW WHAT WAS HAPPENING AT THE TIME LEW WROTE THIS POEM, "Springtime in the Rockies, Lichen"; I presume it must have been around the time that he was down here at Greeley. They asked him to do a summer poetry thing at the University of Northern Colorado; he seems to have manufactured this poem around that time. I don't know how it got into its present position in *Ring of Bone*, I'll have to ask Donald Allen that. "The Song Mt. Tamalpais Sings" comes first, then there's the "Olema Satori" poem, then there's the "Sausalito Trash Prayer" . . .

Tamalpais is the mountain that's just across the Golden Gate Bridge from San Francisco as you're going north. The old road went through Sausalito and then on up to Mill Valley and Santa Rosa and so on, going north toward Oregon. But now a big freeway just continues as you come off the Golden Gate Bridge, you zoom on this big freeway and across overpasses and you don't go through Mill Valley or a hundred other small places. After you go through the tunnel that goes through the little mountains directly above Sausalito, you come out the other side of the Waldo tunnel at the top of the Waldo Grade and you can start seeing Mt. Tamalpais, which dominates the center of Marin county. It's only about 2,300 feet high, it's not a high mountain, but since it's coming up right off the coastal plain it looks quite imposing. The Indians thought that it looked like a sleeping lady, I think that's what Tamalpais means.

It's been of interest to us to construct it very slowly into a magic mountain or to restore its magic by very traditional means—not black magic, but magic magic. We started this process around 1959 by performing circumambulation of it and reciting sutras at various points around it. Actually Locke McCorkle started and then the rest of us continued from time to time. There was one time when Ginsberg and Snyder and I actually set up specific altar spots around the mountain. It's funny, that sort of formal trip was done first in maybe 1964 and we all wrote poems on that occasion, at each of those places. It wasn't until much later that the Zen Center was given, at a greatly reduced price, the Green Gulch Farm, which is right at the bottom of Mt. Tamalpais and more or less includes Muir Beach where the wobbly rock is that Lew writes a long poem about in here. It was a place where we had gone in the early fifties to collect mussels and roast them on the seashore, drink wine, and laugh a lot, before Gary went to Japan the first time in 1956.

Marin County is very interesting, you've probably read a lot of nonsense about it in the press; it's even been satirized by the comic strip called Farley—and it's very funny. It is, to a large extent, ridiculous what happens there. But physically it's quite beautiful, it's an extremely varied landscape. In places where there are little valleys, little gulches, or little canyons, there will usually be water and redwood trees. Then you come out of the little gulch or canyon and up onto a ridge or a meadow and there's a sudden change of vegetation, there are California live oaks and brush, grass, more typical California hot and dry quasi-desert. If you get over right on the ocean side, again there is a mixture of live oaks and cypresses and meadows; and then in among the rocks you'll find kinds of succulent plants growing, kinds of sedum and what are popularly called "hen and chicks," things people usually see in someone's cactus collection. So you have all these kinds of things going on within a very short distance from each other, a strange feeling. There's one open hillside in the village of Tiburon which is now protected by the state, it has more kinds of California wildflowers than almost any place else in the state, and nobody knows why. If you visit there in the spring season, you can see kinds of plants that you can't see anyplace else; it's a very strange botanical phenomenon.

If you live outdoors enough and stay alone enough and walk around enough, you tune in on landscape and it becomes important to you; and you like places, you like the way things go together. When Lewie wasn't too distracted with dope and alcohol and problems of all kinds about money, he always enjoyed himself out of doors and spent a lot of time out of doors. He was always making wonderful commonplace discoveries that made it possible for him to write poems like this one. But the time between the discovery and the manufacture of the poem, I don't know how long that would be. He tended to work things over mentally for a long time before he ever actually wrote anything down. He would have it in his head, and be adjusting it and thinking about it and then getting new ideas about it and rearranging it in his head some more and adding to it maybe, before he ever set down even a fragmentary version on paper. Then that in turn would be altered considerably before he finally would have a typewritten version, that he would tell you was no good. Then somebody would ask him for a poem and he would finally recopy that typewritten version with maybe another change or so and send it out. That's what would appear in print.

I first saw this poem in the shape of a printed broadside by Clifford Burke (Cranium Press). It's quite a handsome broadside. What we've got now is "Springtime in the Rockies, Lichen:"

All the years I overlooked them in the
racket of the rest,
this symbiotic splash of plant and fungus feeding
on rock, on sun, a little moisture, air—
tiny acid-factories, dissolving
salt from living rocks and
eating them.

Here they are blooming!
Trail rock, talus and scree, all dusted with it:
rust, ivory, brilliant yellow-green, and
cliffs like murals!
Huge panels streaked and patched, quietly
with shooting-stars and lupine at the base.

Closer, with the glass, a city of cups!
Clumps of mushrooms and where do the
plants begin? Why are they doing this?
In this big sky and all around me peaks &
the melting glaciers, why am I made to
kneel and peer at Tiny?

These are the stamps on the final envelope.

How can the poisons reach them?
In such thin air, how can they care for the

loss of a million breaths?
What, possibly, could make their ground more bare?

Let it all die.

The hushed globe will wait and wait for
what is now so small and slow to
open it again.

As now, indeed, it opens it again, this
scentless velvet,
crumbler-of-the-rocks,

this Lichen!

In this poem he's got a whole complicated set of notions going on. Does everybody know what lichen looks like, what lichen is? It's flat, you look at it and you just see flat, sometimes it looks like a splash of paint, and you don't think about it, you see color and you say oh, that's lichen. Actually they're quite primitive plants and they grow in the most untoward-appearing places. They grow in the Arctic and in the desert; all sorts of places where you wouldn't expect to find anything, there are lichen happening. They go through phases of dormancy when they turn all kind of black and dusty and look like they're totally dead. Then if the seasons change and a certain amount of moisture comes around they start lighting up again and opening up and functioning. They're able to survive quite severe changes in climate and seasonal changes without perishing. They really are very successful creatures. They are successful perhaps, we're told in biology class, because of the fact that they are a symbiotic arrangement; they are two things that live together to make one apparent organism. In this case it is a fungus and a kind of algae; an algae and a fungus mixed up together make a lichen. Goodness knows how that got started. If you have any interest in the start of such phenomena, incidentally, there's a marvelous book written by a very smart woman [Lynn Margulis] at Yale University, called *Symbiosis in Cell Evolution: Life and Its Environment on the Early Earth*. It's all about how at first there was undifferentiated protoplasm rolling around in the ocean, organizing itself out of the chemicals in the water. Nobody knows why yet, but for some reason protoplasm started building up out of amino acids rolling around in the water, perhaps because of an electrical discharge. After a while they learned to clump together and make what we think of as protein molecules; of course protein molecules are what living material is made out of. Presently I think, according to this lady's theory, there became different kinds of protein molecules; some of them were more complicated than others and at some point these two different kinds of viable protoplasms got together to make a symbiote. The first known symbiote was a nuclear cell. The animal or creature, whatever you want to call it, that became the nucleus joined up with this hitherto unnucleated but growing undifferentiated protoplasm; so you began having a cell that was distinguishable, it acquired a wall and the nucleus had the function of conveying the genes and so on, so that the thing reproduced itself as such, as an amoeba for example. And everything continued on from there. Among the kinds of amino acids and whatnot in various protoplasm, supposedly the materials we now know as RNA and DNA started going at some point; maybe they were responsible for the symbiosis of the first primitive nucleated cells. Anyway, it's an interesting book to look at.

(A curious literary manifestation of this rather complicated book is a play by Michael McClure called *The Feather* which has been produced in Berkeley. I saw a performance late in 1971. It's one of the more entertaining of his Gargoyle Cartoons, you'll find it in the book called *Gargoyle Cartoons.*)

So, lichen go back a long time in the history of the development of plants; they are quite ancient ones that are still around. Usually things develop and then fade away; but we have other curious hangovers, like cockroaches, for example, which have been the same for a good many million of years. They seem to be perfectly adapted to doing anything and everything. I think in the mammalian order things like rats have succeeded where many others have failed.

So Lew Welch says, "all these years I overlooked them in the / racket of the rest, / this symbiotic splash of plant and fungus feeding / on rock on sun, a little moisture, air, / tiny acid-factories, dissolving / salt from living rocks / and eating them." I think that there might be a mistake there, he might have written "salts." That's one of the things that happens if you have a lichen sitting on something. In the process of its taking in moisture and carbon dioxide it excretes acid, which attacks the rock it's sitting on; the acid in turn breaks down the goody and makes it into something else.

So he sees them as tiny acid factories dissolving salts from living rocks and eating them. It isn't usually fashionable to think of rocks as being alive. We like to think of the planet, we like to think of nature as being controllable and as being dead—it's just matter, you can treat it any way you want to; rocks are simply stuff you can throw around. He says they're alive and they're being devoured by these little plants. He doesn't say what the rocks think about it, he just says this is happening. I do remember "living rock" as a phrase, something I carved from the living rock; somebody was talking about the city of Petra in Arabia, or maybe they were talking about the caves at Ajanta, carved from the living rock in India. It's a literary phrase, insofar as the rocks at Ajanta were all carved into relief statues, so they looked alive. But Lew is talking about the rocks being alive, being devoured just like animals eat each other. So it's a life process, it's not simply a chemical process, it's life going on.

"Here they are blooming! / Trail rock, talus and scree, all dusted with it:" What is the difference between talus and scree? I don't know where we get that word, *talus* means something like field, I think, in Latin; and *scree*, I don't know where we get that either. It might be a funny English word, maybe borrowed from Welsh, like many mountain climbing terms are. If you read books about mountain climbing, you find people talking about cwms for example, [pronounced "cooms"], meaning a little valley. Because many English people who became celebrated mountain climbers practiced or learned some of their basic techniques on the mountains in Wales where they do rock climbing—which is quite as dangerous and difficult as any in the world, partly because of the nature of the rock and partly because of the foggy climate, which makes it impossible for you to see where you're going a lot of the time and makes the rocks wet. Then of course they would go on to climb in the Alps and end up in the Himalayas.

So he says these colors are there, "cliffs like murals!" I can't remember seeing an entire cliff painted by lichen quite that elaborately, but Lewie says he did, and there it is. "Huge panels streaked and patched, quietly / with shooting-stars and lupine at the base." The shooting-star is the flower that I was taught to call "bird bill" up in Oregon. Actually it's a kind of native cyclamen which grows in Europe and the United States. Lupine is a kind of a thatch plant that has very handsome spikes of blue and white flowers, yellow sometimes.

"Closer, with the glass, a city of cups!" If you look at lichen under a magnifying glass quite often you'll see they have a kind of cup shape where they grow quite closely together; you might see that if you have a small pocket glass. You see a whole raft of them, he says you see a city. "City of cups" is quite a lovely phrase. It brings to my mind the tarot deck, one of the suits of the tarot is cups. I don't know whether he had that in the back of his mind or not, he was never terribly interested in all that kind of stuff.

"Clumps of mushrooms and where do the / plants begin? Why are they doing this? / In this big sky and all around me peaks & / the melting glaciers, why am I made to / kneel and peer at Tiny?" This is something that's quite unusual in contemporary American English, to have an object be given a pet name; people used to do it in more sentimental poetry in the nineteenth century. I don't think there's a sentimentality here, but there certainly is an affection.

What do you think are the answers to these questions? Do you think that Lewie knew what the answers were? Where do the plants begin? That is to say, you can't see when you're looking down with your hand glass at it, where they start and leave off and if there are other mosses and mushrooms and things mixed in with them, you can't tell where things begin and end. And, as I was saying, the beginning of anything is floating around in some ocean a long time ago. We all begin together, actually, although we never remember that. "Where do the plants begin, why are they doing this?" Well, they're doing this for the same reason that everybody else does everything, they're all full of those curious chemicals, that double helix unwinding itself to make what we think of as life and death and history.

"In this big sky and all around me peaks & / the melting glaciers, why am I made to / kneel and peer at Tiny?" Human and otherwise, we like to look at things. This of course is part of our training when we're quite small; we're told, look at that, isn't that pretty. I can remember distinctly seeing a number of things that were pointed out to me as pretty which I could not for the life of me connect with that word or with the emotion of the person who was explaining to me that it was "pretty," meaning that it was of value and that it was nice and they liked it a whole lot and that I ought to, etc. Well, if you say so. We'd be driving someplace and people would point out the window and say, look at that view over there, it's just gorgeous. I would look out the window—you look out a window and what do you see out of it? Traveling in the window, when you're in a car, you see the fence posts speeding past, the telegraph posts, or you might suddenly see a cow standing in a field. The way of looking out a window and seeing it composed as a landscape was a faculty which I had to develop much later, I certainly didn't possess it when I was small. It wasn't until much later that my eyes began failing, so I don't think it could have been nearsightedness at that age. It was a simple disconnection between language and experience, between what was real and what wasn't, some lapse in communication on my part or on the part of my parents. In any case it was very difficult to indoctrinate me with proper feelings. Many proper feelings I have never been able to acquire, I'm sorry to say. So in many ways I'm a failure. The habit of going to pieces at Christmas time, for example, I have a great deal of trouble with that; I cannot be terribly interested in the joy that you're supposed to have. Various other things of that kind, especially the public examples that everyone is supposed to participate in, have always been difficult. Things like, let's all sing now; I'm just sitting there, fuck. Sing, schming. I love to sing, I'll sing in the bathtub or if I'm by myself or with two or three other people, sometimes I include some song in a poem; but not if somebody says, all right now we're all going to, because we're glad or because it's fun, aren't we having fun? This of course was usually accompanied, when I was with my family, when I was small, with threats and accusations of ingratitude, which were very hard to live down.

So the reason we look at things is we're told that things are pretty or ugly or certain things are to be looked at and certain things are not to be looked at; we're programmed to respond to things in a certain way. Why am I made to kneel and peer at Tiny? Ideally, I suppose, as far as I'm concerned, because Lewie was a friend of mine, I think that he was looking because he was interested, and because he was attracted by the color and, ultimately, because he was always, like all of us, looking for himself. We never look for ourselves in the middle, we always look outside for everything, because outside is where reality is, we think, and that's what we're told we ought to have and we ought to go for it: it's outside there, it's better, it's wonderful, it's expensive, it's hard to get, and everybody ought to have it. I think that in this case—Lewie being a poet and being excited by seeing this cluster, this city of cups that doesn't start or stop anywhere—what's happening is all of a sudden he's really turned on, really excited, and so he's looking, looking to see out there and always, because he doesn't understand himself too well, looking for himself.

Then he says, "These are the stamps on the final envelope." That's a great piece of news and I think at that point the poem should have stopped (just between you and me; you're not supposed to listen, Lewie, in heaven). But I think that he has delivered his whole message right there. He could have moved that line, maybe, to where it says "Let it all die," and moved that line down at the bottom. In any case, that's the poem almost, in that one line. Like the title, "These are the stamps on the final envelope." is a splendid poem. But he's telling you why—it's interesting. And suggesting of course that it would be a good idea if you went out and looked at some lichen once in a while, and found out that it was possible to be turned on by looking at these otherwise ignoble or who cares kind of creatures. The thing is, if you do, you'll find out more than you bargained for. These are the stamps on the final envelope.

Of course he explains about the final envelope, "How can the poisons reach them? / In such thin air, how can they care for the / loss of a million breaths? / What, possibly, could make their ground more bare?" which is quite beautiful, an interesting way of arranging sounds. And of course it's talking about the air that's killing us all; the lichens are likely to survive is what he's saying, I suppose. How can the poisons reach them? they'll just turn them into more lichens, likely, something we're not able to do to ourselves. "How can they care for the / loss of a million breaths?" That is to say, if a whole lot of animals and people died, they would just continue to operate anyway. "What, possibly, could make their ground more bare?" That is to say, their ground being bare rock, which he suddenly forgets is living; what possibly could make their ground more bare is the disappearance of themselves, I suppose. What could make it more bare? Well, of course, being burnt and disintegrated by the forces of a fusion bomb would make it barer for a while, certainly if it turned into glass. "The hushed globe will wait," that is, hushed because there's no more breathing going on, "the hushed globe will wait and wait for / what is now so small and slow to / open it again." Although if the places where the rocks are all fused into glass in spots, as quite often happens where there's that intense kind of heat that is produced by a hydrogen bomb or a nuclear explosion, it's unlikely that a lichen is going to attach itself to a piece of glass—it hasn't happened yet and the possibilities of its happening are slim, unless there's some mutation in which a lichen decides that it would like to go into the business of dissolving silicon salts out of glass and living on that. "The hushed globe will wait and wait for / what is now so small and slow to / open it again." Lichens grow at a very low rate. They're small, as he says, and it takes years for them to get into a patch big enough for you to notice. The globe of the world will break down again, crack open, by this stuff as ". . . indeed, it opens it again, this / scentless velvet, crumbler-of-the-rocks, / this Lichen!"

As you know, when the lichens break down the rocks, part of the salts they eat and then the silicon parts and other bits that are indigestible simply become what we call sand. Then eventually the body of the lichen plant itself dissolves away into humus, eventually that's the basis of where other things can grow. Even while the lichen is still alive quite often fern spores and other seeds get involved with it and start growing because there's that moisture there and there's a hole, a spot for them to grab onto in the actual body of the lichen. So a lot of other plants get started from that patch of lichen on otherwise bare stone. "It opens it again, this / scentless velvet, crumbler-of-the-rocks." If you touch some kinds of lichen it feels quite soft. The thing that's interesting is, it comes up about how the rocks are breaking up and even with the phrase, "this Lichen!"—there's a poem that is doing very much the same thing, written by a dear friend of Lewie. Not me and not Allen Ginsberg, somebody older. There's a trip that William Carlos Williams goes into about saxifrage, about the stone crop, the one that breaks the rocks. Maybe Lew was remembering Williams's poem, but I kind of doubt it. He knew the poem of course, but this one is a kind of grandchild of that saxifrage poem, which is rather short.

So on the one hand he foresees some eventual catastrophe that is going to take away a million breaths and then he says, "Let it all die." because it'll all start over supposedly, in some way. The idea of the destruction and renewal of the universe is an ancient religious notion we still are stuck with to a certain degree. It means more or less to anybody. Just at this point, please remember all the roaring I was doing recently about how things are alive and people ought to realize it and take care of them, and not think of ourselves as masters of all we survey or as controllers of this dead matter we can push around any way we want to. The rocks are alive; everything is alive. The final envelope, the last message, is please turn around and don't drop those things. Although something will survive, it ain't going to be you. It might be these lichen, which are very nice things and are going to make a new start, probably, after you're gone. But what is it that lichen are doing? They're sitting there very quietly growing, very slowly, and not bothering anybody. They don't even get involved in the whole bee and flower business. They're just sitting there, spreading out and being pretty. Maybe as far as Lew was concerned—like he says, they make these murals—maybe I'm straining at a gnat to swallow the camel again about how the whole poem is metaphorical, being about art, being about people who are creative like they say nowadays, people who paint and write poems, by being quiet and working slowly and turning purple, will last, will endure, will do something when everything else is gone. That may be an extrapolation, which Lewie wouldn't allow, he might at that point say, oh come on. But when somebody leaves a cryptic note* and walks off into the wilderness and leaves you all his poetry to handle, it's his own tough luck if people extrapolate.

—July 28, 1980

---

* "I could never make anything work out right and now I'm betraying my friends. I can't make anything out of it, never could. I had great visions but never could bring them together with reality. I used it all up. It's all gone. Don Allen is to be my literary executor, use mss. at Gary's and at Grove Press. I have $2,000 in Nevada City Bank of America, use it to cover my affairs and debts. I don't owe Allen G. anything yet nor my Mother. I went Southwest. Goodbye."

THE BEATS AND BEYOND

Lorna Dee Cervantes

W E MIGHT AS WELL BEGIN WITH "BEYOND." REALLY I KNOW
that my roots come out of the Beat movement. My roots
come out of there in the way that all of our roots are
intertwined, there, not so much in New York but in San
Francisco, where I was born, in the Mission District. I
grew up in San Jose, California, in a place that was incredibly liberating
in that—what? what's poetry from San Jose? It defied definition; it wasn't
a school, it wasn't a certain way of writing. It was this incredible freedom
to do and sound like anything you want. To me this idea, this linking to
the Beats is much like the use of one of those Tibetan meditation gongs
that you take up to the top of the mountain, you sound it like you sound
this poetry. Not that I write like that, or anyone else writes like each other;
but instead this tone dissolves the language and you travel out on it. You
send your soul out in this thing, this gong. So this is how I connect my
coming out of the Beat movement.

As I said in terms of how our roots are intertwined, I am a Chicana
poet, I'm an indigenous American, I'm a California native from Santa
Barbara, from the Chumash nation, and the Californios. Whenever any-
one asks me "what part of Mexico are you from?" I always answer
"California."

One thing that I want to bring up is how so many Mexican and Latin
American poets and Latino poets had influenced what was going on, par-
ticularly in San Francisco. Margaret Randall and Sergio Mondragon were
editing, along with others, a magazine that was trilingual, English, Spanish,
and Portuguese, called *El Corno Emplumado*. My first book was called
Emplumada. El Corno Emplumado is sort of like The Feathered Horn,
corno is like a horn but it's also like cornucopia. This was where the first
poetry of Pablo Neruda, César Vallejo, and of course Paz and others, García

Lorca translations, were published. It had an incredible influence, there's always been this connection between the Latin American sensibility or what Robert Bly called Spanish leaping poetry and what was coming out of some of these writers. There's a connection between writers like Kerouac and Ginsberg and Duncan and others that come out of these poles, beginning with Rubén Dario and reaching to Roque Dalton, a poet from El Salvador, from César Vallejo to Fernando Pessoa, from Pablo Neruda to Borges, from Paz to Ernesto Cardenal, from Nicanor Parra to García Lorca. Also there were what I call the Second Wave Beats, the women who began publishing after. I can remember hearing Anne Waldman come to Berkeley, to the poetry festival, and reading that incredible woman poem, "Fast Speaking Woman," that's a take-off again from María Sabina, a Mexican shaman-poet; again that interconnection, that indigenous and Spanish leaping. There are poets as well like Diane di Prima, Joanne Kyger, Diane Wakoski, who's often not talked about in terms of the Beats but was very much a part of that early movement, more in New York than in San Francisco—being born in San Francisco, I used to say the San Francisco poets are really New York poets—Wakoski was one of the ones who grew up in California and ended up in New York; and also feminist poets like Alta and her small press and the sorts of poetry being published at that time. There's a direct lineage that I see, that I come out of through my poetry, again as a Chicana poet, as I identify myself, as a Chicanao poet—I like to dissolve that gender distinction, chicana/chicano poetry, so Chicanao, let's turn it into Portuguese—that finds itself somehow wedged between *Howl* and *Reality Sandwiches*.

When I first discovered the poetry of Allen Ginsberg, my first thought was "at last, here it is, Chicano poetry." Now what I mean by that is, consider the aesthetic, consider the poetics of Ginsberg. First of all there's the notion of suffering, the acceptance of suffering or, as one of my favorite philosophers, Rickie Lee Jones, used to say, "you don't have to suffer to create art, you will suffer (period)." And there is, as was quoted earlier, the sense of no self but in other selves, for to be a Chicanao poet is to be dealing with the politics of identity as irony. No self but in other selves. No multiples selves, no individual self, no universal self. It's a very Chicano sensibility, to know that you are in the intersection or are sometimes the target of all of these multiple subjectivizations, which is beyond stereotype. Also there is an attention to minute particulars that you find in this poetry, which comes out of William Carlos Williams, another Chicano poet. His mother was Puerto Rican, his first language was Spanish, hearing the crooning of his mother—very interesting when he writes about that. To me he's Chicano. There's the sense of the line as a breath unit, which is the legacy of Allen Ginsberg via William Carlos Williams, again via these indigenous Latino sensibilities. The line as a breath unit, form in poetry being pure rhythm. And certainly in *Reality Sandwiches* there's this denouncing of American bourgeois values—very Chicano. Ginsberg is the first American pachuco. There's also the technique of listing, the intricate cataloging of the everyday, of things as they present themselves. This goes along with what [Edward] Sanders has talked about, this questioning of Ginsberg's, these constant questions along with this cataloging. It's not just cataloging for the sake of cataloging, but a strategy of multiplying the conditions of possibility in order to break out of oppression, to break the tyranny, including the tyranny of a single idea. This rejection of the abstract and symbolic. I go back again to that Robert Bly essay on Spanish leaping, he contrasts it with French Surrealism and French Symbolism. There's a rejection of that in favor of presenting life, presenting material as it has presented itself—this is the sort of thing you find in Pablo Neruda's *Elemental Odes*. Also there's this technique, this strategy of what I call the rasquache poetic. Rasquache is—for example, I was a small press person. I printed a magazine out of my kitchen, published the first books of Gary Soto, Sandra Cisneros, Jimmy Santiago Baca, Alberto Ríos, Ray Gonzales, all of the early Chicana/Chicano writers. But I did it out of my kitchen on a little multilith press, which is sort of a pre-offset press. And it came out all smudgy pages and everything. But there was this explosion of this sort of literature being published and it didn't matter, it was anti-slick, it was the anti-aesthetic, you work with what you have, and you make good with what you have, you make it damn good, even though it looks rasquache. "Yeah, yeah, my shoes are all scuffed and everything, but man, I have style when I walk." This is the rasquache sensibility. And this is the sort of poetic you find in writers like Ginsberg, like Kerouac, and others. This is how I was reading them, as Chicanao poets.

Also a very interesting connection is the voice of the Bible that you find in Ginsberg, in particular in "Howl." Of course it's from another angle, coming out of a Jewish tradition in "Kaddish" and all of that, but it's that voice that so permeates Chicanao writing and Latino writing today, that influence from the other end, from Catholicism. And there's a recognition of the division or rather, finding a creative resolution to the supposed opposition of the spiritual versus the profane world. This is all tied up in that poetic aesthetic of rasquache as well as, again, that attention to minute particulars, all the dirty little details of daily life that you can raise to the level of poetry. The work in particular of Ginsberg is a poetry that's stripped of artifice, so that it becomes spoken word. Again, back to that idea of the line not just as a breath unit, but spoken word and how it moves into beyond—there's very much a connection between Beat poetry and Chicano and what we used to call Third World poetry back then and now the spoken word movement, to take it off the page, to take poetry off the intimidation of the book. This is certainly something Chicanao poets have always dealt with and experienced.

There's also the fact that Beat poetry is what I've always considered "bomb poetry," coming out of that sense, as Ginsberg said, of poets confronting the destruction of the entire world. As he said, no other poets have ever experienced that. I have to say, we have to consider the conquest, and this sense of Chicanismo, of being conquered by the sword and the book, had become universalized, globalized, through globalized threat, beginning with the atomic bomb, now with extreme ecological destruction, the destruction of our entire world. And how do you create poetry out of that, how do you write about that? How do you not write about that? All of these things are very much connected to the Chicanao sensibility. Also there are the Buddhist tenets, or non-tenets I guess I should say, which to me are indigenous, indigenous American, that I see and draw from my indigenous side. This erasure of self, of the self and other split, and this notion of poetry and the body being in service to others. Going from the body into the body politic, through the magic of spirit inspiration. Poetry, breath—back to breath, spirit, etymologically has to do with breath, inspiration. This is the magic of poetry.

And there is the reliance upon jazz and the African-American aesthetic, through poets like Amiri Baraka (who was LeRoi Jones then, and in the Bay Area) and in particular Bob Kaufman. This book of Bob Kaufman's just came out a couple years ago, *Cranial Guitar*. He's a very underrated poet; if you do not know Bob Kaufman, pick up this book. This is the poetry that I was exposed to growing up in California.

—June 21, 1999

BOB KAUFMAN: BEAT, SURREAL, BUDDHIST, AND BLACK

David Henderson

KAUFMAN WAS A STEADY PRESENCE IN THE BEAT LITERARY movement for most of his life. Neeli Cherkovski, the San Francisco-based poet and biographer of Lawrence Ferlinghetti, says about Kaufman in Aldon Lynn Nielsen's fine scholarly study *Black Chant: Languages of African American Postmodernism,* "Both in his poetry and because of his presence in the community of poets, he has left a legacy unequalled by others." Cherkovski speaks for a plethora of younger poets who, through the personage of Kaufman were able to personally receive a direct transmission of the Beat poetic. He was a constant on the scene who listened to their poetry at a great many poetry readings in the San Francisco community, and rather than offer literary criticism, would offer a Zen nod, smile, or toast as acknowledgment of the continuity.

Cherkovski also speaks volumes about the levels of fame visited upon the early Beats. Ginsberg had become an international celebrity who was sought after to appear at various functions all over the world. Certainly, to a lesser extent, but no less intense, the same could be said for Gary Snyder. Also in great demand, Corso and Kerouac were not necessarily happy campers in their celebrity status as they struggled to continue their poetic missions. Anchored to political activism, Ginsberg was able to elude the delusion of celebrity and use his influence for the benefit of international human progress. But Kaufman was the main man on the San Francisco scene who would spend long hours with the local poets at readings, at parties, and in the coffeehouses and bars, just as he had done in the late 1950s with the original Beats, up until his death from emphysema in 1986.

Kaufman provided Beat poetic continuity also through his strict adherence to the mission of *Beatitudes,* a magazine that he had co-founded at

Cassandra's Coffeehouse in San Francisco with Ginsberg and others in 1959 and that continued the message into the 1990s.

Kaufman's central role in the continuity of the Beat Generation cannot be minimized. He actively helped foster an entirely new community, a new generation of San Francisco Bay poets: Jack Micheline, Jack Hirschman, Simon Alexander, Paul Landry, Marty Matz, and an entire roster of poets who would then be joined by local Black poets such as Conyus Calhoun, Al Young (who was a recent Poet Laureate of California), Q. R. Hand, Reginald Lockett, Devorah Major, (who would become the poet Laureate of San Francisco—to be succeeded by Jack Hirschman), Buriel Clay, Ntozake Shange, Ishmael Reed, and others; to be also joined by Latino poets such as Roberto Vargas and Alejandro Murgia, who would lead a delegation of Mission poets and others to Nicaragua where they helped comprise the Sandinista Movement that overthrew the oppressive dictator, Somoza, and created a new government there.

Vargas, as Nicaragua's cultural minister, would host a visitation of American poets led by Ginsberg and the important Nuyorican poet Pedro Pietri and the Native American writer and poet Diane Burns both from New York. That u.s. delegation interacted with Nicaraguan poet Ernesto Cardenal in essential meetings that helped to legitimize the new government in 1986.

Kaufman may have been too ill to be a member of that delegation. He died in San Francisco that same year. But his presence was the nexus to that large community of poets who, unlike the Beats, achieved a viable diverse community. Asian poets and writers like Frank Chin and Kathleen Chang, Kitty Tsiu, Janice Mirikitani; Philipina poets Jessica Hagedorn and Genny Lim joined Latino poets like José Montoya, Fernando Alegría, Victor Hernández Cruz, and other local African Americans such as Buriel Clay, formed an American Third World configuration that was not limited by economic considerations but celebrated an original spiritual trinity where those who by being steadily conscious in both their native lands and the new America developed a third level of consciousness. Kaufman, as a bridge between the diverse communities, also represented not only the original spirit of the Beats but also the older incarnations of the hipster and leftist political activist.

Lynne Wildey, a working-class white woman who while studying poetics at New College became Kaufman's active partner, reinforced his essential links to the poets' community with hard work. She was his explicator, whose five-foot-seven height was a couple of inches above Kaufman's often downturned head and his thin body's shuffling gait, sometimes visited with palsy. Attention to his various health challenges became crucial to his continuity and Wildey understood, to a deep degree, the importance of her role she tirelessly worked at. She helped to keep Kaufman together physically and emotionally, took care of the organization of his writings, and made sure he stayed well connected to those who sought out his relationship to the poetry scene.

Lynne Wildey became Kaufman's main relationship up until his death, and Ferlinghetti remained a true and constant colleague and supporter. Jack Hirschman, Jack Micheline, Q. R. Hand, and a host of others were his buddies to the core. Kaufman had the major league record for being 86-ed from North Beach bars. He was known to act up on occasion, but his buddies never put him down. Neeli Cherkovski had Kaufman live in his home for an extended period of time. The African-American photographer Andre Lewis, as a local resident, documented Kaufman's North Beach peregrinations.

The community recognized Kaufman's dedication to be the living link of the Beat Generation of poets and with his involvement, if only as a participant or on an honorary level, organized in a continuous series of large rostered poetry readings, often at Glide Memorial Church, where poet Janice Murakitani was the active link between the community and the church. There were readings in support of Nicaragua, for disinvestments in South Africa towards an end to apartheid, in support of Native American issues, disaster relief, and any number of causes to which the poets lent their support and in which Bob Kaufman was an important participant. His presence was key and he could always be counted on to be there.

Former wife Eileen Kaufman and his son Parker, with Kaufman's many brothers and sisters were his official family even though he had married and separated from Eileen twice. She was dedicated to his life and his poetry. Kaufman's poem to his son Parker (named after famed bebop jazz saxophonist Charlie Parker) is a monument to the age-old strength of vision any father would want to impart to his son.

TO MY SON PARKER ASLEEP IN THE NEXT ROOM

On ochre walls in ice-formed caves shaggy Neanderthals
    marked their place in time.
On germinal trees in equatorial stands embryonic giants
    carved beginnings.
On Tasmanian flatlands mud-clothed first men hacked rock,
    still soft.
On Melanesian mountain peaks barked heads were reared
    in pride and beauty.
On steamy Java's cooling lava stooped humans raised stones
    to altar height.
*****

On this shore, we shall raise our monuments of stones,
    of wood, of mud, of color, of labor, of belief, of being,
    of life, of love, of self, of man expressed
    in self-determined compliance, or willful revolt,
    secure in this avowed truth, that no man is our master,
    nor can any ever be, at any time in time to come.

Allen Ginsberg and Kaufman were not antagonistic towards each other, but always reflected the love that would be a staple of the Flower Power Movement that would follow the Beat beatitude. Kaufman's poem "Ginsberg (for Allen)" gives an indication of the Zen irony with which Kaufman viewed the man, the poet, and his fame.

Ginsberg won't stop tossing lions to the martyrs . . .
The Church is becoming alarmed by the number of people
defecting to God . . .
The holy stepfather cautioned the faithful to emulate none of
the saints who hide behind the Fifth Commandment
when persecuted.
There is also a move to cut off Ginsberg's supply of lions.
The poet continues to smoke carnal knowledge knowingly . . .
*****

Why I love him, though, is equatorially sound:
I love him because his eyes leak.

Humor and tenderness were staples of the Beat poetry that inundated the coffeehouses and galleries of North Beach in the 1950s. To laugh and explore emotional and often sexual feelings had been elements missing from a good deal of traditional American poetry.

It seems to me that Allen Ginsberg's attitude towards Bob Kaufman changed after Kaufman's death. Ginsberg had seen many of his contemporaries have a difficult time with drugs, and perhaps that may have fed his antipathy. That Kaufman hardly spoke at all, to a big conversationalist like Ginsberg, may have also been hard to take. Ginsberg seemed to change a lot of his point of view towards Kaufman after he consciously studied African Americana prior to teaching at Brooklyn College.

The late photographer Jerry Stoll, who was Eileen's employer when she and Kaufman met, was forceful in his contention that Kaufman was indeed the head Beat in charge as far as political activism, poetics, and beatitudes went. Although Kaufman was not at the Six Gallery reading, considered today to be the launch of the Beat pantheon of poets, according to many that was an oversight that could have easily been amended. It is not out of the question, given the insurgent Beats and their strong desire to impact society that they may have felt let down by Kaufman's fall from grace. One only has to compare the two most powerful poems of the time, Ginsberg's "Howl" and Kaufman's "Second April," both written and famous in the late 1950s, to see the doubling of power these poems make in tandem. Kaufman may have indeed been the best mind of the generation screaming madness in the street. There are interesting edits in Ginsberg's manuscript for "Howl" as faithfully documented in the book that features the evolution of the poem. Those edits take out the frequent references to jazz and takes the poem away from any confusion with an African-American dimension. And (with the exception of the works of Jack Kerouac) conferred the debt to the music that inspired the Beat Generation to a footnote in history. That Kaufman was deep into the jazz life was reinforced by poet and confidant Jack Micheline who describes an evening in which he and Kaufman went to see Billie Holiday and were very well received by her in her dressing room where she very respectfully accepted a sheaf of Kaufman's poems.

The beef that I had with Ginsberg about the representation of Kaufman in the Beat poetry pantheon had been an ongoing one. Kaufman was missing from too many anthologies of the Beat Generation. Knowing Ginsberg painstakingly monitored the Beat legacy, I thought Kaufman's frequent omission was no accident. But after Kaufman's death Ginsberg, Raymond Foye (who had been singlehandedly responsible for Kaufman's last book, *The Ancient Rain: Poems 1956—1978*), and John Fisk, a participant and also the recordist, made a tape recoding where they all shared reminiscence about Kaufman. Ginsberg noted a fact that was not well known about Kaufman's great popularity in France where he was known as the Black Rimbaud and respected by scholar Frances Watson Taylor "as being the great surrealist American poet" who, "had a true surrealist muse." Ginsberg did not leave out his personal feelings about the poor state Kaufman's life had become, but he revealed important moments when they shared experiences, like for instance when Ginsberg, Kaufman, and William Burroughs dropped lysergic acid in an East Second Street Manhattan apartment and tripped together.

The Beats' later relationships to African Americans have long been an obvious problem. While some Black Beats like Ted Joans were somewhat steeled to the response, others were more like Amiri Baraka who as LeRoi Jones was late to the Beat Generation yet clearly became a beloved spokesperson and co-conspirator, especially after Ginsberg began to live in New York City as his main residence in the early 1960s. But LeRoi Jones's poetry, prior to his defection from the Beat Generation and New York School into the Black Consciousness movement, is full of ambivalence and harsh feeling for those referred to as his friends of that period. Given the wide latitude given to poetic expression these sentiments never seemed to be held against LeRoi Jones, the poet. When he was arrested in the Newark riots in 1967, Allen Ginsberg and other Beats were quick to come to his defense. Before and after that incident Ginsberg would often ask me about the state and feelings of LeRoi Jones who by that time was calling himself Amiri Baraka and had consciously distanced himself from the Beats and his Greenwich Village formative years. I don't believe Ginsberg ever really understood LeRoi's reasons for turning his back on the Beat Generation.

Amiri Baraka is very candid about his reasons. In his *The Autobiography of LeRoi Jones* (1995), Baraka gives great detail to his way of life and concentrations during his days in New York at the height of the emergence of the Beat Generation. His connection with the West Coast was nil. He was aware of the poets and writers of that region through his periodical *Yugen*, where he published, at the urgings of Allen Ginsberg, Philip Whalen, Gary Snyder, and others from the San

Francisco area. Why he never considered Kaufman is a mystery. He was aware of Kaufman's "Abomunist Manifesto," a popular poem long before it was published in a broadside in 1959, and certainly Ferlinghetti, but he is clear that he took direction from Allen Ginsberg in which poets to publish after the second volume of *Yugen*. Baraka as LeRoi Jones was awed by the power of "Howl" as were so many in its wake. But then again he was out of touch with the original emergence of the Beat Generation on the West Coast where Kaufman was recognized as, at least, a major figure, and who many thought of as the major poet. There is no mention of Jones/Baraka's knowledge of Kaufman's "Second April." In fact Baraka notes that as LeRoi Jones he had taken a stance, a change of direction, after the first two issues of *Yugen*, where he, as editor, had published several Black poets including himself and his close associate from Howard University, A. B. Spellman. Baraka does not deal with this issue head on, rather he says this:

> By the third issue there was not one black writer at all (though I was still an editor)! At the same time the normal trepidation I felt when confronted with anything in the u.s. which I knew histori- cally must be in some way linked to white supremacy made me wary as I entered into these new relationships. I did think that white people would be opposed to a black dude even being a writer, even saying it. I thought maybe it was like coming into some place where they wouldn't want you. That maybe there were passwords or dress codes or certain signals you had to learn.

Perhaps this will give a reader some idea of the barriers that existed in the literary world and how difficult it was and really courageous for the African-American poets, Bob Kaufman, Ted Joans, and the then LeRoi Jones (Amiri Baraka), to emerge, albeit via the Beat scene. Kaufman was the pioneer, although he is given no credit, but they all were, all coming on the scene in the late 1950s. And it is to the credit of the Beat Generation that these African-American poets were able to be a part of the movement to change traditional American cultural sensibilities.

Ted Joans did not know Kaufman was Black. Baraka, as LeRoi Jones, may have thought the same. Kaufman did not announce his race through his poetry. His appearance in New York City in the early sixties estab- lished that fact. Ted Joans would tell the story of Kaufman appearing at his loft, having been directed there by Ginsberg who had arranged for Kaufman to "crash" there. This was an important, an essential element of the Beat Generation: coast-to-coast free housing for those "on the road." Joans thought Bob Kaufman was a Jewish recipient of the beneficence of the new king of the Beats, Jewish Allen Ginsberg. It would take Kaufman many publications in Black anthologies during the heyday of the Black Arts Movement. Recognition of Kaufman as a Black poet may have began with his publication in a new edition of Langston Hughes's and Arna Bontempts's legendary anthology *The Poetry of the Negro* and continue through the sixties with *Umbra Anthology 1987–1969*, *Umbra/Blackworks: 1970–1971* and *Umbra Latin Soul 1974*. Those and other publications began to nail down Kaufman's errant African-American identity. It would take until the late seventies/early eighties for Kaufman to emphatically declare himself Black, as in his collection *The Ancient Rain: Poems 1956-1978*.

Baraka's stance as a Beat Generation-era poet was conflated by impacts of the Black Mountain School led by Charles Olson and Robert Creeley and the New York School as led by Frank O'Hara and John Ashbery. In fact, he formed a separate distinction for the New York City Beat poets who mainly lived in the East Village, Lower East Side, most definitely an unfashionable and poor part of downtown at the time. Baraka's rise in status was not hindered by his having feet in all three "schools." But for many downtown poets, intellectuals, visual artists, and jazz musicians, he was the prominent Black figure in the New York City emergent literary movements during the early sixties.

Kaufman, whose amphetamine and incarceration problems in New York City effectively undercut his emergence, was recuperating in those early sixties years once he was returned to San Francisco. Although in the late fifties Kaufman had published three significant broadsides through City Lights, it would not be until 1965 that his seminal collection *Solitudes Crowded with Loneliness* would be published by New Directions, the most distinguished publisher of the new poetry even at that time through their editions of Ezra Pound, W. H. Auden, Robert Graves, and other world-class poets. Although Baraka began to write seriously in 1957 only after Kaufman and Ginsberg were well on their way to establishing themselves as important poets in San Francisco, his prolific works in poetry, prose, and playwriting were well underway when *Solitudes* came out.

But Kaufman, after returning to San Francisco in the early sixties never left the scene again, and like Ferlinghetti, he became a perennial Beat poet on the original turf. By the time Baraka (as LeRoi Jones) made the scene in New York, Ginsberg was living in Paris and was on the way to establishing the Beat Generation of poets worldwide. Meanwhile Kaufman made it his primary business to foster the publication of *Beatitudes*.

Ted Joans remains a mysterious figure in the Beat pantheon. If Ginsberg had a problem with Kaufman, he had more of a problem with Ted Joans, who, as Baraka and many other poets are quick to confirm, was the first poet of the Beat Generation they knew about.

Joans frequented the coffeehouses on Macdougal Street in Greenwich Village, and was a fixture among blues musicians, folk singers, comedians, and the like who were featured in a row of small clubs and coffeehouses that comprised a busy low-keyed showbiz-type scene. While Joans may have emphasized the more exploitative aspects of the Beat Generation, Rent-a-Beatnik for the weekend was one ruse, some would argue for that as being Dadaistic. His subsequent role in the Black consciousness movement was very significant, especially in a world context. Joans would become the poet-in-residence of the Organization of African Unity and had established a residence in Timbuktu where he became very knowledgeable about African culture and served as a link between African and African-American poets and artists of all stripes. His oeuvre reveals deep poetic sensibilities that were not often apparent in his public persona.

Ted Joans's reunion with Bob Kaufman in San Francisco in the mideighties was legendary. It electrified the poetry scene there. The Andre Lewis photo of the two Black Beat poets embracing, cheek to cheek, graced the cover of *Poetry Flash*. This reunion was widely reported in the daily and weekly local papers. Joans spoke at the San Francisco Art Institute on "Black Beats" where he celebrated Kaufman and spoke of other unknown Black Beats who had been important to the movement, but who were unknown to most of the public. Kaufman, unlike Ted Joans, never made speeches after his activist days in the fifties and unlike Baraka/Jones did not write of his life in an autobiographical fashion. This writer believes Kaufman remained true to his vow as silent penitent unto his death. Ted Joans remained a link to Africa and Europe (especially Paris) until his death. His adherence to the principles of surrealism and Dadaism had merged with his Beat days, and in many ways overlaid them. But he was most loyal to his original inspiration as a jazz hipster who dug "Bird," the original king of the Beats. If Kaufman is missing from many Beat anthologies, Ted Joans is an invisible man.

It is very clear that Kaufman's early influences were of leftist politics, jazz, and visual art, and a sensibility that those influences forged in his poetry as well as applied to the continuity of the Beat Generation. The historical positioning of jazz as a seminal influence of the Beat Generation has all but been lost. The Beat Show at the Whitney Museum in New York City in the 1990s inappropriately had jazz as some kind of background muzak, quite contrary to the power of its influence. A sense of that power can be found in many of the prose and poetry works of Jack Kerouac, who was unflagging in his jazz sensibility that was so essential to his works.

Towards the end of Kaufman's life he was treated to a public television special on his poetry produced by Ozzie Davis and Ruby Dee and broadcast nationwide. It is said he sat up in Vesuvio's Bar and watched the program that emphasized that Kaufman was missing in action, so to speak. The two veteran and quite professional actors gave fine readings and representations of his poetry that Kaufman by then, due to physical limitations, was unable to deliver. The readings he gave toward the end of his life were often tortured tokens of his dry, evocative and quite clear voice that can be heard in a rare recording of his reading from "Second April" in 1958. It was published as a broadside by City Lights the following year,

Does The Secret Mind Whisper?, a poetic novel that was published as a broadside by City Lights in 1960, is a monument to surrealism, and a powerfully consistent work that never lets down in its seemingly improvised associations, and poetic content, in one long take without punctuation.

His late influences, this writer would say, included an acknowledgment of his significance to African Americana. Zen Buddhism is there clear and strong. And the devotion to beatitude, as the Beat thing, is always there along with the continuity of his early activism and the melodies and beat of jazz from where Kaufman always swung—that originated in his birthplace, New Orleans, home-house of jazz.

Kaufman, without any literary activism on his part, became an important part of the Black consciousness movement. His seniority as a major Black poet, coming before LeRoi Jones (Baraka) and certainly Ted Joans, place him in a line of continuity as a major figure in African-American poetry. That twentieth-century lineage is linked to Langston Hughes, Pulitzer Prize in poetry (1950) winner Gwendolyn Brooks, and Robert Hayden, who in the eighties became poet to the Library of Congress. Therefore Kaufman's seminal Beat I.D. conferred on him a triple identification when placed with his surrealist honors that were hardly known in the United States, but solemnly acknowledged by Europeans and especially French expert scholars. A triple poetic threat, yet living in a Zen humility that, this writer believes, few understood. And, of course, how could it have been for Kaufman to try and explain his position? He simply was. He lived a magical life in spite of challenges that would have defeated many a man or woman.

He had an ongoing relationship to jazz. He would often walk, snapping his fingers rhythmically to some internal jazz melody. Lynne Wildey was definitive in that he listened to jazz radio continuously.

From *Solitudes Crowded with Loneliness,* his first book of poetry published by New Directions in 1965, of the many jazz references therein "Walking Parker Home" is a complete tribute, a poetic bio of Charlie Parker, an avatar of the form.

Sweet beats of jazz impaled on slivers of wind
Kansas Black Morning/ First Horn Eyes/
Historical sound pictures on New Bird Wings
People shouts/ boy alto dreams/ Tomorrow's
Gold belled pipe of stops and future Blues Times
Lurking Hawkins/ Shadows of Lester/ realization
Bronze fingers—brain extensions seeking trapped sounds
Ghetto thoughts/ bandstand courage/ solo flight
Nerve-wracked suspicions of newer songs and doubts
New York altar city/ black tears/ secret disciples

In the same volume his poem "Mingus," after the great bass player (Charlie Mingus) of the generation of musicians that followed Parker captures a moment inspired by a performance.

String-chewing bass players,
Plucking rolled balls of sound
From the jazz-scented night.

Feeding hungry beat seekers
Finger-shaped heartbeats . . .

Improvisational performances formed the basis of his early work. He could spontaneously spout poems and then remember them, because of a unique gift of memory, a rare ability. The electric shock treatment he was administered while incarcerated in New York City and the psychotropic pharmaceuticals he was given in the aftermath of the severe attacks on his brain, had some sustained effect on his abilities. Yet throughout his vow of silence he would, on great occasion, recite at admixture, as Raymond Foye attested to, of T. S. Eliot, especially from *Murder in the Cathedral,* Hart Crane, García Lorca, and his own poetry, an admixture to great effect. It was a celebration on the rare occasions he would do this. Unlike his readings, where he struggled to see the page and emote the words through bad dentures, his spontaneous oral recitations were of another order. Majestic and commanding, a true mystery, as if some spirit deep within him was awakened.

Once (around 1975 or '76) Steve Treadway, an African-American North Beach resident, photographer Andre Lewis, poet and editor Conyus Calhoun, and this writer were seated in Enrico's, that grand outdoor cafe that for years stood on Broadway a few rows down from the Condor and adjacent to City Lights Books, next to the street that ended when the impossible steepness of the continuing thoroughfare became a series of steep steps upward to the mysterious regions overlooking North Beach. There on Broadway, Kaufman came by as we were having drinks. We bought him a drink and he received a cognac and beer chaser. He was admiring two leather bracelets on this writer's wrist that had been made by the artist Lezley Saar. I gave him one, the best of the two, and with that he launched into a great recitation of excerpts of his own poetry that silenced all within earshot. It was a marvelous moment. We toasted him and he recited some more as the twilight crept over the promontory that is North Beach and the cooling fog rolled across the sky heading out to the Pacific.

By that time Kaufman had left the drug culture far behind, and became the mystery he would be known as for the rest of his life. Kaufman's early poem, "Celestial Hobo," that had been published in *Solitudes,* seems to be some indication of this public "persona."

For every remembered dream
There are twenty nighttime lifetimes.
*****
Everyday, confused in desperate poses,
Loses its hue, to Dada prodigies of black.
There never was a night that ended
Or began.

Kaufman's vow of silence was a very serious thing and he stayed with it until he could hardly speak at all. How does one maintain a vow of silence? By stating that you are being silent because of a vow? Or by simply following the vow? Yet even with his silence he had deep friendships with many in the community who were little known or unknown.

Kaufman continued to write throughout his vow of silence. One interesting lapse in his vow was when he remarried Eileen. He wrote the poem "All Those Ships That Have Never Sailed" and read it in honor of his marriage. While that lapse is often credited as the official end of Kaufman's vow of silence he seldom had anything much to say in public, outside of reading from his poetry, after that.

All those ships that never sailed
. . .
Today I bring them back
Huge and intransitory
And let them sail
Forever.

Kaufman's attitude towards his writing did not seem conscious to anything he sought to accomplish. It was largely through the actions of others, from Eileen Kaufman, to Lynne Wildey to Raymond Foye, that his work is preserved. Perhaps there is something of Zen in that.

From the mid-seventies until his death, Kaufman often went around North Beach often looking like a beggar, a homeless person, and obviously a person who had significant physical difficulties. Kaufman was missing a great many teeth, had bad eyesight and poor hearing, and his thinness approached that of a malnourished man often shaking with palsy. But Ferlinghetti, on the other hand, was, from my perspective, always cheerful, respectful, and generous to Kaufman, who seemed to always need cigarettes, a drink, and some food. He lived in the SRO (Single Room Occupancy) hotels in the area, his favorite being the one just across the street from City Lights Bookstore, in the building that houses the infamous topless club the Condor, featuring the redoubtable, legendary stupendously breasted Carol Doda. There was one hotel down Broadway, towards the corner (where Anton Levay had his famous magic store) called the Golden Dragon that Kaufman had renamed as the title of his second volume of poems, *Golden Sardine,* published by City Lights in 1967.

The poem in this volume, "Crootey Songo," is a poetic equivalent of a speaking in tongues as this excerpt attests:

DEEREDITION, BOOMEDITION, SQUOM, SQUOM, SQUOM.
DEE BEETSTRAWIST, WAPAGO, LOCOEST, LOCORO, LO.
VOOMETEYEREEPETIOP, BOP, BOP, BOP, WHIPOLAT.

I always thought that Allen Ginsberg's antipathy had more going for it than just the difficult physicality of Kaufman. Ginsberg mentioned to me on more than one occasion Kaufman's unfortunate run-in with drugs: amphetamine. Eileen, Kaufman's wife during his formative years as a Beat poet, and again later as a post-famous Beat poet, is candid about his bout with the drug when he stopped in New York City on his way to Harvard to read as a candidate for the distinguished Guinness Poetry Award, that went, perhaps by default to T. S. Eliot. He never made the reading and never received the award, which, had he won, would have been a huge boon to Beat poetics. He may have been perceived as letting the Beat Generation down.

But he did get bogged down in New York City in a nexus of events that were truly tragic. While on his way back to San Francisco to join his wife and their young son, Parker, he was arrested in Washington Square Park for walking on the grass. A longtime regular in the San Francisco jail system for Beat activism, in New York City his defiance and disdain may have been responsible for his beating and incarceration in a mental facility. Usually walking on the grass resulted in only a fine or a day in court at most. The late John Fisk, a longtime recordist for the Poetry Project, and formerly of Pacifica's WBAI in New York City, encountered Kaufman afterwards and shared experiences about the mental facility where all inmates had their heads shaved. Fisk is specific about Kaufman's harsh treatment, and the powerful involuntary electric shocks and drugs he was given to keep him in line. By the time he returned to San Francisco he was a different man. He slowly recuperated, taking to sometimes excessive drink to numb the physical problems brought on by the powerful drugs he had been administered in New York. Fisk is very candid and specific about the palsy-type effects that were an aftereffect of those drugs. Kaufman was to never be completely free of those shocks to his system that are considered today by many to be inhumane.

"Second April," one of the three broadsides published by City Lights Books in '58, '59, and '60 that received the attention of the East Coast poetry establishment, begins with a quote from the Holy Bible: Romans 12: "Be ye not conformed to this world, but be ye transformed by the renewing of your mind." And continues:

> O man in inner basement core of me, maroon obliteration
> smelling futures of green anticipated comings, past denied,
> now time to thwart time, time to frieze illusionary motion on
> far imagined walls, stopped bleeding moondial clocks, boom-
> ing out dead hours—gone . . . gone . . . gone . . . gone . . . on to
> second April, ash smeared crowns, perfect, conically balanced,
> pyramid-peaked heads, shuddering, beamed on lead-held
> cylinders—on granite-flowered windows, on frigid triumphs,
> unmolded of shapes, assumed aspects, transparent lizards,
> shattered glaciers, infant mountains, formed once, all time
> given to disappearance, speculation, investigation of holes,
> rocks, caught freaks, in skin sandals, ten million light years
> dripped screaming, hot dust rotted eyes, ages in clawing eyes,
> insanities packed in century-long nights, pointed timeward to
> now. Hollow out trees, release captive satans, explode roses,
> sentence grass to death, stab rivers, dehydrate oceans, suck up
> deserts, nail sky to scattered earth, in air, we come to second
> April.

Kaufman continues through twenty-seven more sections of similar length as above with the numbering dominated by the early sections whose numbers are all aspects of zero. The beginning six sections builds a poetic base from which this most unusual poem emerges. Equal to any poem of the era, or the decade of the fifties in San Francisco and points East, "Second April" is one of Kaufman's greatest works.

> Session double zero is bare floors, cannery row darkness, San
> Juan bare whores in young-boy brilliance, discovering balls in
> sources of pee . . . fried stink was lunch under the bed as the
> thick-wristed sailor projected Anglo-ness on Maria's wrinkled
> heaven, I read Sade . . . against the under of the mattress, a
> thing, that's a thing, they watch, tonight death is a blonde, we
> are bending ice cubes, cubes, that's a thing, cubes, Mondrian
> dug, they killed him in California, injected natural wood set-
> tings and cal tech . . . Modigliani spurting . . . Naked Marys,

fucking me out of my mind in triple quarter tones, on my wall
sideways . . . a thing they watch, they know we break out, my
bending night is ending, one second is value enough, I am
forever busted.

This relentless poem continues in dense brilliance and often, seem-
ingly, autobiographical poetics to where it ends with:

We watch them going on watching us going on going,
wrapped in pink barley leaves, almost, the time is not near,
but nearer we are to time, and time nearer to ticks. Burning
in torch surrender to auto-fantasy, we illuminate the hidden
December, seen, flamelit in the on core of the second April,
come for the skeleton of time.

Kissed at wintertide, alone in a leeming world,
green bitches, harlequin men, shadowed babes,
Dumped on the galvez greens, burned with grass.

In "The Ancient Rain," the title poem of Kaufman's last collection *The
Ancient Rain: Poems 1956—1978*, published in 1981 while he was living, the
author gives indication that his early brilliance was still strong. He sought
to work with images and metaphors that dealt with the origins of the
American republic and of the amazing contribution of African Americans,
most notably Crispus Attucks, who was the catalyst of the revolution yet
who is largely unsung today. One significant note in Kaufman's poem is a
simple declaration of racial identity so lacking in his early work: "Crispus
Attucks is my son, my father, my brother, I am Black." Crispus Attucks
was the first to die in the making of the American Revolution.

The Ancient Rain is falling. The Washington
    Monument rumbles.
The Lincoln Memorial is surrounded by stars.
Mount Rushmore stares into every face.
The Continental Congress meets in the home of
    the Ancient Rain.
Nathan Hale stands immaculate at the entrance
    to the Capitol.

Crispus Attucks is taken to school by Thomas
    Jefferson.
Boston is quiet.
The Ancient Rain is falling.

His metaphors regarding the ancient rain seem in some ways prophetic inasmuch as he portrayed a phenomenon of nature having coming symbolically to bear on the history as it would also be in the future of America.

"The Ancient Rain is a mystery known only to itself. . . . it falls silently and secretly." Vindictive as well as curative. It "fell on the Confederacy and it was no more." And, "It is the voice of the American Revolution. It shall play forever." Kaufman prophesies "World War Three, the largest war ever" and "a star prophecy of 37 million deaths" that the United Nations seek to avoid.

The Ancient Rain wets my face and I am freed from hatreds of
me that disguise themselves with racist bouquets. The Ancient
Rain has moved me to another world, where the people stand
still and the streets moved me to destination, I look down on
the Earth and see myself wandering in the Ancient Rain,
ecstatic, aware that the death I feel around me is in the hands
of the Ancient Rain and those who plan death for me and
dreams are known to the Ancient Rain . . . silent, humming
raindrops of the Ancient Rain.

Kaufman in the last part of the poem switches to a consistent first person: "I see the death some cannot see, because I am a poet spread-eagled on this bone of the world." As war nears Kaufman hears a voice from the whirlwind:

Federico García Lorca wrote:
Black Man, Black Man, Black Man
For the mole and the water jet
Stay out of the cleft.
Seek out the great sun
Of the center.
The great sun gliding
    over dryads.

The sun that undoes
all the numbers,
Yet never
crossed over a
dream.

Kaufman concludes "The Ancient Rain" with himself as a little boy dis-
covering the great Spanish poet: "Hearing the Lorca music in the endless
solitude of crackling blueness. I could feel myself a little boy again in crack-
ling blueness, wanting to do what Lorca says in crackling blueness to kiss
out my frenzy on bicycle wheels and smash little squares in the flush of a
soiled exultation. Federico García Lorca sky, immaculate scoured sky, equal-
ing only itself contained all; the distances that Lorca is . . ."

"Crackling blueness," a progression on a Lorca concept, is the other
side of the ancient rain that both reappropriates and formulates concepts
for Kaufman that augurs favorable outcomes within the whirlwind for
those of mindfulness and identity.

One of Kaufman's most important relationships was with Philip
Whalen, who as a spiritual leader of San Francisco's Buddhist temple, qui-
etly supported Kaufman's very serious religiosity. Kaufman cleaved to
Buddhism more and more as his days grew numbered, and it became clear
to Lynne Wildey, and a few others who knew him well, that Buddhism
had long been at the core of his Beat existence.

—2007–2008

EDITORS' NOTE: Our request for this essay inspired David Henderson to reconstitute
and elaborate on a talk he gave about Bob Kaufman at Naropa in the summer of 1996,
for which the tape appears to be missing.

The editors requested David Henderson elaborate on areas such as Bob Kaufman,
the person, his relationship to literary movements such as Surrealism, the Beats, and the
African-American, as well as his relationship to jazz, his vow of silence after the assas-
sination of President Kennedy, and his relationship to Buddhism, all elements touched
on in Henderson's audio documentary "Bob Kaufman, Poet" and in his introduction to
Cranial Guitar, the selected poetry of Bob Kaufman.

AN INTERVIEW WITH EDWARD SANDERS

Junior Burke

JUNIOR BURKE: IT SEEMS LIKE AMERICA IS VERY MUCH A THEME FOR YOU; you're doing a history of America in verse. How did that come about?

EDWARD SANDERS: Well, in Naropa, 1975 . . . I thought of a lecture and called it "Investigative Poetry" because when I had written my book on the Manson Family in 1970–71, I found myself writing some of the text with line breaks although I had a typist who took my line break text and typed it into regular paragraphs. Many of the techniques I used in writing my book on the Manson Family could apply to something I called Investigative Poetry. How to work with people, how to prepare question lists, how to be very methodical, how to take notes under really stressful circumstances, how to stay calm under any circumstances. So, I wrote this manifesto ["Investigative Poetry"] and Ferlinghetti printed it. A few years went by and I did lectures and people would ask me, "Who's been writing investigative poems?" So I decided, time to start writing in the Investigative Poetry genre. I wrote a verse biography on Anton Chekhov. I wrote a book called *1968: A History in Verse*. I wrote a long book called *The Poetry and Life of Allen Ginsberg*, in poetry form. I was reading William Blake's *America: A Prophecy* and decided to write about American history in verse. And John Martin, who ran Black Sparrow Press, very graciously agreed to publish it. Three volumes have been printed. I started out with the twentieth century and now I'm almost at the end of the twentieth century and then I'll work back through the nineteenth, eighteenth, seventeenth, and sixteenth. I'm working on all six volumes at the same time right now. The next will cover the Nixon years and Carter years and some of the Reagan years and will be published in 2006. The final volume of the twentieth century will include Clinton and the first George Bush. The others will march back through time. I thought I'd write about the century I'd lived through first cause I knew most about it. I've been working on it since 1998.

BURKE: It's so thoroughly researched; what's the method?

SANDERS: I read relentlessly. Sometimes I pick up assistants who will help, but basically I do the research myself. My golden rule for this kind of thing is to immediately break the material you encounter in books and in printed sources—immediately start breaking them up into lines and try to get a sense of the text that you're going to use as an open field, charged poetry surface. And so I create big long chronologies. Only five percent can I use in the book. The stuff I say "no" to is at least twenty times more than what I say "yes" to. Each thing has a page number and source. Let's say I read something I know I want to use, I try to transform it. If I don't, I put it in quotation marks to avoid any sense of borrowing somebody else's writing. But my advice is to immediately transform it. Change the word order. I have a computer file for every one of my investigative books; all the sources for every sentence are sequentially followed by the book with the page number, the author, publication, this and that, so that I can immediately fast click it. Inaccuracy is difficult if you take that level of care.

BURKE: You came to New York through reading *Howl* in shop class in high school in [Jackson City] Missouri. What was that like, reading that text at that time in that location, at that point in your life?

SANDERS: Very mind-opening or revolutionary life-changing experience. I purchased *Howl* at the University of Missouri bookstore. There was a fraternity weekend, where you go down there from your high school and stay at a fraternity. You might get to meet sorority girls, drink a little beer. But I did go to the University of Missouri bookstore in the context of that fraternity weekend and bought *Howl*. And why did I buy it? Because I knew William Carlos Williams. I was more interested in William Carlos Williams's introduction to *Howl* than I was in Allen Ginsberg. I bought other things. I bought Samuel Beckett's *Waiting for Godot;* I bought some stuff. And I had been writing a lot of poetry. I was more interested in Edgar Allen Poe and John Greenleaf Whittier. And I was beginning to become slightly aware of something called Ezra Pound. I wasn't quite sure what the deal was, other than he was supposed to be a very good poet, but was also a traitor. Anyway, basically I memorized *Howl*; I had it all in my mind. I used to, on the weekends, drive around the town square with my drinking buddies. We'd be drinking Griesedieck Brothers Beer or Falstaff. I'd be howling away reciting *Howl*. After a while, my friends would start a regular conversation while this crazy guy was reciting this strange poem in the back seat. That sort of made me realize I could possibly have a life as a poet. I also became roughly aware of Dylan Thomas around that time. So Dylan Thomas, Ezra Pound, and then Allen Ginsberg. . . . And I never thought I'd ever meet him. I came to New York to study rocket science at New York University and it happened that NYU was next to Greenwich Village, and voilà! A year or so after coming to New York I saw Allen at poetry readings and Kerouac at poetry readings and Corso at poetry readings and Frank O'Hara and all these people, and slowly I decided to become a full-time poet.

BURKE: Your first days in New York. I assume that your impressions are similar to those you recounted in *Tales of Beatnik Glory*.

SANDERS: They didn't have regional poetry networks then. They didn't have poetry coffeehouses in every junior college in America. You couldn't stay in Pennsylvania and make it as a viable poet. You either had to go to San Francisco/Berkeley or you came to New York City. It so happened that I was accepted to New York University, so I borrowed my father's suitcase and hitchhiked with $35 to New York City in the summer of 1958 and I immediately read about the Gotham Bookmart. I had my *Howl*; I had my Samuel Beckett. I had already bought *Being and Nothingness* by John Paul Sartre and I had the Upanishads and I'd read the Beats were interested in Buddhism so I'd already got a couple of Buddhist texts from the Cokesbury Bookstore in Kansas City. So I came in with my books, but I went to the Gotham Bookmart and basically spent money, too much of my money. And that's how I came to New York. I hitchhiked in, took a bus from Newark to the Port Authority, then walked over to Forty-seventh Street to the Gotham Bookmart. I had been in New York when I was a high school junior. My sister lived here in 1956 and stayed out in Queens. I had my first taste of New York City jazz, went to the Randall's Island Jazz Festival and to a lot of Broadway shows. I had been exposed to jazz a lot in Kansas City. Because the jazz clubs would let kids, young kids, in for some reason, I don't know why. But we could get in all the Twelfth and Vine jazz clubs in Kansas City.

BURKE: You mentioned the writing of the Manson book *The Family*. You managed to portray, or suggest, a very sinister subtext of what the climate was like in Los Angeles at that time. Does that resonate for you at all?

SANDERS: Yeah, sure. I don't think it's so much there anymore. There [were] cadres of organized evil there. There were cults and people [who] believed in sacrifice of living things. There was a sense of organized evil. Evil for the sake of evil. The thing about evil, it often has to scurry underneath the cover of night. America is not into organized evil, unless you call the sequence of wars that it engages in, organized evil. But the general societal structure of America is not into organized evil in that sense. Most people want calm times of doing their laundry, watching television, just hanging out and having fun. So, there was that climate there. It's a complicated thing. I've written more about it in the subsequent editions of *The Family*. I put out an edition two years ago, three years ago with a bunch of new photographs and a hundred new pages. I've been collecting more material; I have a lot more material. I'm going to do a final edition to talk about, what was that Orson Welles movie, *A Touch of Evil*? It was kind of a touch of evil and Manson was affected by it.

BURKE: At some point you went to Woodstock and made a commitment to that community and began a publication. When did that take place?

SANDERS: Oh, I had trouble after my Manson book came out. I had a few rough years. There's nothing like success to screw up your life. So, anyway, around 1974 we moved; my daughter was getting ready to go into junior high school, was still in elementary school. We looked around and Woodstock seemed o.k. Art colony, rents were affordable, so we moved up there. I didn't move up there to be a part of the community. I just moved up there to have a kind of haven. Woodstock was known for just letting people live there. When I moved there, Philip Guston was there painting away, and Anton Refregier, painting away. And there were a lot of artists. Milton Glaser, the designer, was there, Milton Avery, the painter. . . . And a lot of jazz players. Jack Dejohnette was there and Cecil Taylor would come to teach. It seemed o.k. It was a pretty, bluestone, Catskills town. Clean water, safe; you didn't have to lock your car at night. We moved into a farmhouse that had been there since the early nineteenth century, and I was looking for the locks. This old farmhouse we were living in had never had any in one hundred seventy years. Because I was used to police locks, a couple deadbolts, maybe a siren or something, in New York City. Went up there for a little safety. In those days, women could walk in the streets at night and never get touched. It was safe; it was a good place to move. And we slowly developed a sense of community and became involved more and more. As I said, I'm in the Whitman wing of the Democratic Party, so I've been very active in Democratic Party politics for about twenty years. I basically wrote my town's zoning laws. I wrote an aerial spraying law. I helped write the environmental quality law. Then, writing a lot of speeches for candidates while trying to keep the region more or less environmentally intact. We wrote our laws. We don't let big hotels come in. It's a tourist town, so Marriot, they would all love to build hotels there. We don't allow it. We figured out legal ways of restricting developments. I don't think a Wal-Mart or a Sears could come here.

BURKE: Abbie Hoffman and Jerry Rubin. Looking back, how do you see their place in history?

SANDERS: I usually don't talk about the Yippies. You know they say politics make strange bedfellows. Antiwar movements make strange bedfellows. I didn't like to be in antiwar demonstrations with people carrying the Viet Cong flag, because I'm a pacifist. I didn't think the Viet Cong should blow up people or whatever. The Yippies were useful in the sense that they brought some of the principles of guerrilla theater that emanated from the Living Theatre and from certain radical-like malice theater groups. Street theater, the concept of guerilla theater. They picked up on that. I had my quarrels with both of them. But I wrote a book with them and I was one of the founders of the Youth International Party and knew them very intimately. Jerry Rubin dressed up in Viet Cong black trousers, a toy submachine gun and wore Indian warpaint on his face, showing up to testify at the House Un-American Activities Committee. That was a historic event. That picture of him will probably last more than anything he ever did. Abbie was the Jim Thorpe of the radicals. He was incredibly talented; he was very brilliant. He just didn't believe in himself as an artist. And so he didn't take his writing seriously. He was very charismatic, had a lot of energy. In the years before he became a real manic depressive, he had unbelievable energy. Unfortunately though, he couldn't ever slow down enough to pay attention to art, [to] creative writing. He could've been like a number of radical writers, W. E. B. Du Bois, for instance, or any writer who took on long-term radical issues and wrote about them. He had the mind to do it, but squandered his enormous talents. None of us are perfect, and I hope he's resting wherever he is.

BURKE: I would like to ask you about the Fugs . . .

SANDERS: It's like an art project. It's something we began in 1964, but a career's a long thing. A career is fifty, sixty years; seventy years depending on how long the artist lives. So I wanted to keep a band together. By luck we put together a group in 1985 that stayed together. They all have careers like Steve Taylor, a professor here at Naropa, but also a beautiful singer and excellent guitar player and arranger. My co-founder, Tuli Kupferberg, [will] be eighty-two in the fall. I think the one you saw was probably *The Fugs Final CD (Part 1)*. So we're probably going to do *Part 2*, we're going to record Tuli's new songs.

BURKE: Because some of the songs were celebrating freedom of speech and stuff like that, there was an impression early on that it [The Fugs] was more of a novelty or something. "Homemade Shit," songs like that. But when people got into it, they saw it was coming from a poetic base.

SANDERS: All those New York intellectuals like Elizabeth Hardwick, that was her favorite song. And Philip Roth got the idea for *Portnoy's Complaint*, watching Tuli Kupferberg sing "Jackoff Blues." It's a tradition of Brecht. Where I grew up in Missouri there was a whole heritage of risqué songs. I learned them often in the context of religious retreats. I came from a very religious background. You learn these songs at Christian Camp. You might learn "My First Trip Up the Mackinaw River" or a bunch of erotic tunes, so it was a tradition I already knew. We were testosterone-crazed young men; we blundered a little bit. Some are not what you'd call politically correct, like "Supergirl," and I guess "Coca-Cola Douche" might not have been the most proper song to write.

BURKE: But that's what I'm saying. People who didn't get into the nuances.

SANDERS: Well, we did Swinburne and Blake stuff. And Shakespeare.

BURKE: Greek references . . .

SANDERS: Yeah, so it's no easy answer. People criticized Brecht for bringing these kind of risqué elements to his tunes. Singing is much more conservative than writing; imagine at the Metropolitan Opera, say Philip Glass did an opera using the dialogue of one of the *Sopranos* episodes; I mean he'd get put in jail. [Sings] "Motherfucker, take that!!" They'd get blown off stage.

BURKE: It was ironic that, for a time, you were on Reprise Records, which was Frank Sinatra's label.

SANDERS: Well, I had to thank Frank for letting us on the label because they played our first album on Reprise for him, *Tenderness Junction.* Mo Ostin had to play it for him, the head of Reprise during '67, when we signed with Reprise. And Frank said, according to Mo, "I guess you know what you're doing." So, Voilà! We were on. I always felt grateful to Old Blue Eyes for that. He basically was a working class liberal from New Jersey no matter what he was. He was like a poet, mean and nice and rough and soft.

BURKE: This is the Kerouac School. One of the pieces I've seen archived is his final television appearance which was on, I believe, the William Buckley program which you were on as well. Would you care to elaborate on that experience?

SANDERS: I'd see him [Kerouac] walk by my bookstore on East Tenth Street, headed for Allen's pad just down the street and then he would call me now and then and somewhere in my archives are a couple of little poems he dictated. He wasn't totally friendly. He became a curmudgeon a little too early in life, I'm not sure why. Maybe through the influence of his mother, who was very conservative; you might even call her right-wing and certainly anti-Semitic. Anyway, he was a very torn guy by the time I came to know him in 1965 when I first had conversations with him on the phone. And I became pretty close with Allen, so Allen would tell me a lot of things about Jack, some of which I wouldn't care to repeat. . . . I think Burroughs was in the Delmonico writing his piece for *Esquire* after the Chicago riots, the Chicago demonstrations, and

Jack may have stopped off there before going to the Buckley show. We had to go up in advance and check in and speak to Buckley and figure out what we were gonna do. Jack was in that checked jacket he was buried in about a year later, and we both were on the same elevator and I didn't recognize him, because the drinking had transformed him. He looked kind of like a state trooper; he was getting a little heavy, his hair was slicked back. Anyway, we had a discussion. It wasn't that friendly and he was drunk and had been driven down from Lowell by one or more of his close friends there. I've met one of them since then and I forget his name; he viewed it as a sacred journey. He got to go down with Kerouac to this fancy hotel and meet the great William Burroughs and then come to the right-wing hero's television show. Allen's in the audience, so Allen and I discuss what to do. Kerouac had, I'm not going to repeat what he said to me in the elevator, but he was not friendly and he basically accused me of trying to copy Allen, which in a way was true. But I certainly, by then, had my own books out. I had the Fuck You Press and had published *Fuck You: A Magazine of the Arts*. I had the Fugs. I had been on the cover of Life magazine. I had been on a lot of television shows, had fans that sometimes camped outside my house. I was almost as famous as Jack Kerouac. He was kind of in a decline and was writing for girly mags at that stage in his career and living an insular life. I didn't feel the comparison was just, so I talked it over with Allen. He [Kerouac] helped me get out of the Midwest and just his *Mexico City Blues* alone and *Subterraneans* and *Dharma Bums* were a big influence on me. I said, "I'm not gonna fight with him no matter what he says to me." So the show began. We were sitting up on fairly large individual cubes, but as I remember, Kerouac fell off his, during a break. He was smoking little cigarillos, Muriel Coronellas, thirty-five cents a pack. His chair fell off the thing and he went to the floor and Buckley said, "That's it!" They wanted to throw Kerouac off and bring Allen on, and I said, "No, no, no, no! He'll be all right, he'll be fine." So we finished the show. We were very friendly afterwards. With Kerouac and Allen and others, we went to a nearby Times Square bar and drank and I never saw him again. Another guy who should have lived onward. The Catholic-Buddhist synthesis should have been interesting to explore, but he didn't live to do it. I think he might not have been such a right-wing nut. He voted for Nixon; he voted for Eisenhower. He voted for Nixon in 1960. That was the beatnik split. Ginsberg voted for John Kennedy; Kerouac voted for Nixon. And then, you couldn't imagine Kerouac in a necklace. That was the stage, the shift. All of a sudden there were no more beatniks and you were a hippie. So this idea of wearing pantaloons and Merlin-curved toed shoes and runic thumb rings and weird granny glasses with rose quartz lenses and head-dresses and caftans. And Kerouac, it was too much for him. He had a weird sense of patriotism. He was raised to viscerally hate communists, but like many anticommunists, lumped too many things under the rubric of communism. Too many cultural things that were quite separate from what he called, thought of, as authoritarian or totalitarian communism. So it was a tragedy.

BURKE: In terms of now and the future, do you feel hopeful?

SANDERS: I have a lot of Irish blood in my blood veins and was raised to be hopeful. I come from, on my father's side, a long line of farmers. And a farmer is always moaning and groaning about "Oh, is this really gonna work?" as he plows and puts in seeds. I view myself as a nonviolent socialist revolutionary. By that I mean a civilization where everybody has six weeks paid vacation. Everybody has cradle-to-grave healthcare; everyone's given access to travel and fun. An inalienable right to fun and thrills. That all philosophies as to lifestyle, say transgender and regular old hetero, are equally respected by the culture. Where the food supply is organic and the energy is as clean as possible. People, border disputes are immediately taken care of. So I'm hopeful. I think every forty or fifty years there's a big revolutionary upsurge. The child labor laws and Social Security of the thirties. The sixties, some of the good things that happened in Paris and in the United States. It's time again, about time, for another surge.

—July 8, 2005

No matter where I go this is the opening: nothing ever happens here, nobody does anything, everyone's doing something else. "Everyone says." You have to watch out for people in organizations that start their conversations with everyone or no one. First of all, it's not true, "everyone says" is usually their roommate or their cousin they just talked to on the phone, these people are not taking Gallup polls. When they use this talk they are setting up certain resistance, certain anxieties about acting, so this is a rationalization, that everyone says this won't work. No one will do it—they're saying nobody cares. And I say, oh, you mean you?—No, I care. Well, how can nobody care if you care, automatically it's disproven. To win these struggles that I'm talking about you do not need everyone and you already have more than no one. So, how many do you need? You need enough, that's all you need. I know that it's not a majority, that the concept of moral majority is ridiculous. It's a moral minority that really makes a difference. When people talk to me about the sixties and about the antiwar movement, [in places] like Chicago, I say how many people do you think were there? And they say, oh, 300,000, or gee, there were thousands, or they were all there, we're not like your generation. Believe me, generations do not make change. We had the same number of engineering majors, of business administration majors in the sixties as we had in the eighties. In 1968 do you know who the most popular Americans were on college campuses? Richard Nixon and John Wayne. There were 10,000 people in Chicago, when Kent State happened there were 800 or 900 universities that went on strike and that's terrific, that's incredible, but there are 5,000 universities in the United States. So it's never a majority, it's enough, that's what you need. Now, how many is enough? That depends on the weather, depends on what's playing on TV that night, it depends on your ability to communicate, depends on the issue, how good you are, the timing; there're a whole bunch of scientific factors, I am convinced there's a science as well as an art to organizing. But you really want to get people out of the idea of thinking that they need everybody and that nobody cares.

—Abbie Hoffman, from "Warrior in the World,"
a talk given June 20, 1986

YOU CAN'T WIN: AN INTERVIEW WITH WILLIAM BURROUGHS

John Oughton and Anne Waldman

ANNE WALDMAN: AS WELL AS A GREAT WRITER, WILLIAM, I CONSIDER YOU an investigator of paranoia, a scientist, and I'm always curious about your world picture at any given time. Do you really view the planet as a sinking ship? And do you think that certain human beings will be able to get off it?

WILLIAM BURROUGHS: Well, we hope so. I was talking to Dr. Timothy Leary* about this last night, that's what he was talking about. Everyone would get off into space in their own world and he said, "I promise you in ten years there will be worlds, worlds for bisexual vegetarians and there will be a world for Anita Bryants." Furthermore, we're all going to live indefinitely, and we will all take longevity pills in a few years.

WALDMAN: I don't believe it. What do you think?

BURROUGHS: I'll believe it when I see it.

WALDMAN: Do you have any inklings, any prophesies you might make through dreams or just your sense of things at this point? Where is his information coming from?

BURROUGHS: Oh, I don't know, he is all full of inside information.

JOHN OUGHTON: Leary is following some American scientist who wants to build orbiting stations in space which are like little planets and

---

* Timothy Leary would occasionally breeze through Boulder and participate in Kerouac School events during the summer of 1978. He appears in the Naropa documentary *Fried Shoes, Cooked Diamonds* (Mystic Star Video).

wants to get people up there somehow. How you get the energy and money to do that, I don't know.

BURROUGHS: The problem isn't getting people up there, it seems to me it is getting a piece of real estate up there. Well, I asked him about this. He said perhaps there were some problems with that . . . so he sort of passed it over.

WALDMAN: Well, who owns outer space?

BURROUGHS: Nobody.

WALDMAN: I know they've divvied up the moon.

OUGHTON: According to some United Nations accord outer space is supposed to be open, no one can sort of say that this planet belongs to us.

BURROUGHS: Well, that would be very old-fashioned colonialism . . . it terms of old-fashioned colonialism, it would be the first person to get up there which wouldn't mean a goddamn thing because there might be beings already there.

OUGHTON: It seems to me that I read in one of your prefaces or intro-ductions—maybe I'm attributing what someone else said—but it was a line about creating a new mythology for this space age in the characters that are through[out] a lot of your earlier novels. Do you feel that you have completed that mythology now?

BURROUGHS: I feel I haven't started it. So far the space age is some-thing that has only got us as far as the moon, and this in an aqualung.

WALDMAN: Is this in terms of William's own writing?

OUGHTON: Yes, some of the characters—Heavy Metal Mary is the one that sticks in my mind. In the one you're working on, *Cities of the Red Night*—does this continue and evolve some of the characters and some of the lines from your earlier work?

BURROUGHS: Some of the characters, yes.

OUGHTON: But it is a much more extended piece than . . .

BURROUGHS: Yes, it is twice to three times the length of any book I have written to date.

WALDMAN: And it travels a lot in time. It started out as a pirate novel?

BURROUGHS: No, well, it's two points of view simultaneously. I can't talk too much about it because it is very much a roman à clef. The Russian scientists have been able to travel not only in space but in time as well, but traveling in space probably would involve traveling in time, as we know it would. The finite speed of light—it's all implicit. Space travel is time travel.

OUGHTON: The earlier novels I started reading with you, *Naked Lunch* and then followed through with *The Soft Machine* and *The Ticket that Exploded*. In looking at these novels as separate things, I wondered how you decided what constituted each one as a part? It seemed to me that I could almost read them as a continuous work because of the recurring characters, the recurring lines and the structural things.

BURROUGHS: Well, actually it is more or less arbitrary—as Maxwell Perkins, the famous editor who edited Thomas Wolfe, Wolfe would go on and on; and then Perkins would go "klunk." That's the end of this novel. It is arbitrary and actually a question of selection, for example, the *Naked Lunch* was assembled out of unfinished material from about 600 to 800 pages of notes material for *The Soft Machine, The Ticket that Exploded,* and through into *Exterminator!* and *Port of Saints* and more novels. So the answer is that you have got to decide how to finish your novel.

WALDMAN: So how do you decide arbitrarily? Do you throw the dice?

BURROUGHS: No—don't throw the dice. You say this goes here and I have done enough with this particular novel and it comes to the point where you just start to produce a finished product. But actually, of course, it is all a single continuum.

OUGHTON: In dealing with the actual mechanics of publication, do you find a real problem with the editors of publishing houses in that your work is experimental, creating your own format in some ways? Were they able to deal with that and still help you in some way?

BURROUGHS: I didn't require any help.

WALDMAN: Always had your own way?

BURROUGHS: I had my own way, yes. I never felt the need for a Maxwell Perkins.

WALDMAN: Except *Exterminator!* was billed as a novel.

BURROUGHS: Well, that was not my fault. I said, why call it anything? Because you call it a novel and then critics say it isn't a novel, which in a sense it isn't. It's a collection of short pieces, really. It should have been presented as that.

WALDMAN: But you had no say finally, it was to sell copies, or?

BURROUGHS: It was just the theory that books of short stories or short pieces don't sell as well as novels. It doesn't help any to call something a novel that isn't.

WALDMAN: Was that picked up on by reviewers? I didn't see it.

BURROUGHS: Sure, although I could certainly call *Cities of the Red Night* a novel. It is a long sequential narrative. It has a definite plot.

WALDMAN: Are there any cut-up sections in it?

BURROUGHS: Certainly, the kind of cut-up is something to be used in certain instances. Very good for delirium, confused states of mind. Somebody, say, drove [to Boulder] from Denver or Greeley or somewhere and afterwards has a confused, kaleidoscopic evening and he wants to put that down, is going to be a cut-up sort of piece.

WALDMAN: What was the subject of Leary's talk?

BURROUGHS: He was talking about the future and about the space things, space worlds, and the longevity pill that he was going to have also quite soon. And also he was giving us—I don't know if he mentioned this, this is one of the more interesting ideas that he has, that private capital will be used to finance these space ventures, and that would be the best defense that I've ever heard of private capital.

WALDMAN: What is the private capital that people want to get frozen?

OUGHTON: What is in it for the capitalists, that is the question. Is it mining on the moon?

BURROUGHS: There are lots of things in it for them. They could have their own world all full of bank vaults and things, literally rolling in money with no fear of anyone stealing it.

WALDMAN: Doesn't Leary think that there is going to be some sort of war with Russia and the States?

BURROUGHS: Absolutely not, and I don't either as a matter of fact. I think it is unlikely we will have a nuclear war at this point. The big proliferation is that everyone has got a weapon now.

WALDMAN: Could be an accident.

BURROUGHS: That's possible, a Dr. Strangelove sort of accident, but the point is that anyone can make an atom bomb. You know that boy who wasn't even a physics major made one—he was majoring in economics. He had a few courses in physics. So it is pretty difficult to control it now. I was talking to Daniel Ellsberg* this afternoon. I said, "Well, if we had a

---

* Daniel Ellsberg, American military analyst employed by the RAND Corporation who precipitated a national uproar in 1971 when he released the Pentagon Papers, the U.S. military's account of activities during the Vietnam War, to the *New York Times*. Ellsberg was participating during this period, along with Allen Ginsberg, Anne Waldman, and others, in protests at the Rocky Flats Plant, where plutonium triggers were being manufactured for nuclear warheads.

very efficient international atomic police, could they do anything about it?" The answer is probably not because there is too much of this material around and it is easy to get hold of even if they try to control the sources. You can't control all the sources. It would mean, of course, guarding every bit of radioactive material in hospitals and everywhere. It would have to be under constant guard. But shit, man, it's right out here in the hills . . . and it doesn't take all that much.

OUGHTON: There's already all that plutonium unaccounted for from American plants that may have gone to Israel.

BURROUGHS: It went to Israel, that particular batch. But Ellsberg said that the CIA might have kept some of it for their own use which is quite possible. See, if they really wanted to precipitate a fascist state, all they'd have to do is set off a bomb in New York and attribute it to the dissident militants.

WALDMAN: Well, they are doing that, I think the FALN (Fuerzas Armadas de Liberación Nacional), the Puerto Rican movement, has been used.

BURROUGHS: I'm talking about an atom bomb that kills say 200,000 or 300,000 people or something like that, that would produce this terrific hysteria.

OUGHTON: You wouldn't put it past them?

BURROUGHS: I wouldn't put it past anybody who is in that position. I wouldn't put it past your big corporations. Or if they wanted to start a war with China, they'd attribute it to China. Their computers undoubtedly have told them they can't win a war. That is why I doubt there is going to be one. You don't have to rely on someone's intelligence, just put the factors into a computer. I don't mean that in the sense everything would be devastated, I mean that America would lose.

We are more vulnerable to atomic attack than either China or Russia because we haven't decentralized all that sort of thing. That is one factor. Suppose we started a war with China and Russia stayed out. Well at the end of the war, it would be a long drawn-out war, whatever the outcome of the war would be, Russia is going to be on top at the end of the war. Supposing we started a war with Russia, well, we would be pretty much wiped out and so would Russia, possibly. If we took them both on together we would be pulverized, I mean, you see, they would pour across the Bering Strait—and Russia has the straight atomic power. China has tremendous manpower. Just on the face of it we can't win.

WALDMAN: So why do they keep playing these games? It seems like they want to have a shoot-out.

BURROUGHS: I don't think so.

WALDMAN: Wouldn't it save our economy a bit for a while?

BURROUGHS: What would be left of our economy?

WALDMAN: Well, for a while though, everybody would have jobs and something to fixate on.

BURROUGHS: This wouldn't be like that kind of war, like World War II. Nothing happened to us.

OUGHTON: We could have a hell of an atomic war in four hours.

BURROUGHS: We could have just five atomic bombs on the USA, and the chaos would be unbelievable.

WALDMAN: But don't you think that the planet will have to have some sort of world socialism or something like that to survive ultimately?

BURROUGHS: No, I wouldn't say that.

WALDMAN: But there aren't enough resources for everyone.

BURROUGHS: Undoubtedly the population problem is a big problem.

OUGHTON: It is a pretty fear-stricken world we live in right now, not only the chance of nuclear war but also the concern about population. Do you think that theories like Leary's and movies like *Close Encounters* and *Star Wars* are sort of playing on a theory of deus ex machina, something will come along that will be all right and we won't have to settle all this shit ourselves?

BURROUGHS: No, Leary said the opposite. He said that we are going to have to solve it ourselves, we can't rely on the deus ex machina. He sees pollution and overpopulation as a healthy sign that is the sign of successful planning.

OUGHTON: But we have to go away.

WALDMAN: Who would want to live on some space station with just two hundred other people who all felt and thought the same way you did?

BURROUGHS: I would, God, yes.

WALDMAN: Would we have our own rooms? I'll go if you go.

BURROUGHS: Nice to have your own room. These things can be up to one thousand. They have everything on—they showed pictures of it, beautiful flowers and pools, and all kinds of things.

OUGHTON: There is the technology to do that, to create artificial climate and artificial atmosphere in outer space.

WALDMAN: I would feel very vulnerable, I think.

BURROUGHS: Why?

WALDMAN: Some alien thing could come along—it is like being on a support system—pull out the plug.

BURROUGHS: Couldn't they do that right here, just as well?

OUGHTON: It's a bigger system . . .

WALDMAN: I guess so—it is a bigger system though.

BURROUGHS: One small atom bomb on power stations and they pulled out the plug. Everything you need is gone. Food is gone, any way of cooking food is gone, other than breaking up furniture and stuff like that to start a fire. So I think we are much more vulnerable here than in outer space.

WALDMAN: But it is bigger, more room.

BURROUGHS: So it is bigger, so what? Where are you going to go and how are you going to get there? There is nothing more vulnerable than a big city, to such minor things as a blackout. Suppose that had gone on for a week to ten days and there was no immediate way of fixing it. All the food's going to spoil, the freezers, nobody can cook.

WALDMAN: It would be really stinky.

BURROUGHS: A big problem with dogs. One of the first things at any time of attack they tell you to do is to kill your dog. There are hundreds of thousands of these fuckers in New York City, suppose they were all dumped in the street—big dogs would be roaming around.

WALDMAN: Eating and preying on human flesh.

OUGHTON: Don't you think all those New York poodles have so much submission built into them that they would . . .

WALDMAN: Pass out. A blackout in China or Russia would probably be very different, do you think?

BURROUGHS: Well sure, they have done so much more towards decentralizing their population. They have never been as dependent on power and consumer goods and supermarkets as we have—we are wide open. If five bombs were dropped in the United States—one in New York, one in Washington, then taking out the big industrial complexes like Detroit and Los Angeles, the mess would be just unbelievable. In other words, they would need more troops to preserve order than they could put in the field.

WALDMAN: Why do you think it was that people went wild in the blackout and women in their fur coats—it is actually like that story of yours in *Exterminator!*—the women in their mink coats, Fifth Avenue, raiding the supermarkets literally came true.

BURROUGHS: I know the only thing, shopping without money! Rushing into the stores.

OUGHTON: You have said, or rather written somewhere, that in doing cut-ups and using the cut-up method you can sometimes cut timelines and you can create a prediction that comes true later. Have you noticed other examples of this from your work?

BURROUGHS: Oh, I have collected quite a few of them. What is happening is the old saying that what is written may be literally true and when you cut it you see it. Mostly the cut-ups that I have got have been just accidents sort of, nothing that has affected me personally, but I was cutting up some of John Paul Getty's articles in *Playboy*—that it was a bad thing to sue your own father. Well, his son did sue him and it came out two years later.

OUGHTON: After that whole thing with the missing ear, he was kidnapped and his ear was cut off.

BURROUGHS: No, that wasn't his son, that was his grandson. His son—not the Paul Getty that is the father of the boy—but another son he had. That family has had a lot of trouble. That son was killed under quite mysterious circumstances. He was supposed to have fallen on a knife at a barbecue party. It was pretty obvious that his wife had or someone had stuck a knife in him or something of the sort.

WALDMAN: These families with large money seem to have strange karma.

OUGHTON: It is almost like a virus, some of your metaphors with virus. Like look at Howard Hughes, it seems to have literally made him crazy the last twenty years of his life as far as anyone could see.

BURROUGHS: Yes, he was trying to be as straight as possible by putting himself in a position where nobody could affect him. But what he did of course was delivering himself into the hands of Mormon security. What protection did he have then?

OUGHTON: One of them has published a book called *I Caught Flies for Howard Hughes,* which is what he was hired to do—Hughes had fly-o-phobia.

BURROUGHS: It's easier to keep flies out than catch them.

WALDMAN: Actually, back to this virus as a metaphor. It seems to be everywhere, for example, do you think these plutonium leaks—there is a direct connection to a cancer virus—I don't know if you remember that article.

BURROUGHS: There's absolutely no question of the increase in cancer accompanied by increased radiation. There is a big valley in England that has a very high, abnormally high cancer and leukemia rate. So they went there and made tests, found much more radiation there than there is anywhere else in England because of some climatic condition. Not just the proximity to an installation, the climatic conditions of the valley. There's no question of that.

WALDMAN: What about building up an antivirus, or do you think we will have to mutate to conquer cancer in some ways? It just appears to me that more and more people that I know, people that I know personally, are getting it at early ages.

BURROUGHS: It is getting to be an epidemic. Wilhelm Reich has two things to say about that. One is the orgone accumulator which I think is certainly worth trying, and the other is what he calls the orgone radiation that is produced by putting very small amounts of radioactive material into one of his accumulators. While it produces an initial reaction, or the person becomes ill, that it might convey a certain amount of immunity to radioactivity.

OUGHTON: You obviously have done a fair amount of research. Has anyone in the scientific community taken it seriously enough to really test these effects, try to measure them with the orgone box?

BURROUGHS: You don't think they are looking very carefully for a cure for cancer, do you?

OUGHTON: Well, no. It's good business for them.

BURROUGHS: Well, that's it. They don't want to know about something, particularly something simple. You see, this is just human nature, that's the nature of bureaucracy—the more expensive your project the better. You got something . . . Reich's orgone box is quite simple. You could make one for $200.

WALDMAN: You can make one yourself.

BURROUGHS: No one wants to know about that. But if you've got something that requires some very expensive piece of equipment . . . The more money you get, the better, because that means then your department is more important, you need more employees, you need more money and . . .

OUGHTON: It's a symbiotic relationship between cancer and greed.

BURROUGHS: Yes, because the old American idea is the way to solve something is to get a huge amount of money and solve it. But that's not the way to solve things at all, you get a billion dollars appropriated to solve something and you'll be sure they won't solve it.

WALDMAN: God, I've never really thought of it like that. It's so awful.

BURROUGHS: It's simple. Same way with the drug problem—the more money they pour into it the worse it gets.

WALDMAN: Is it getting worse, the drug problem?

BURROUGHS: Well, not actually. People are pricing themselves out of the market and going onto the methadone program which is, of course, the same thing. I was talking to Dr. Archer, who's one of the first pioneers in the methadone clinics. I was talking about all the misinformation that methadone is not habit-forming and all that kind of thing. He said, "Well, we didn't—actually the people who started the clinic didn't put out these stories, but we allowed them to be circulated without interference because we wanted to get the program started." That is why they couldn't do it with morphine which is, of course, not as strong as methadone. Just for the name, they couldn't have used opium, they couldn't have used morphine. Now people are working round to the point where they could say, oh well . . . as long as they get their heroin, they'll keep out of people's apartments.

OUGHTON: That's what they've tried in Britain, isn't it? I mean, the heroin maintenance program.

BURROUGHS: They were using it for years and it worked very well there until the Americans got over there with their missionary workers and more or less put a stop to it, so now they have the same mess that we have, corruption. Everything results from trying to enforce an unenforceable law.

OUGHTON: What do you think is behind the government idea to try and stop all sorts of illegal drugs? I'm thinking of interfering with poppy growing in Turkey. What produces that fear, in bureaucratic minds, of drugs?

BURROUGHS: I don't think it is a matter of fear, it's their job.

WALDMAN: It's money, I guess.

BURROUGHS: Money, money, money—it's a big business. They find they will price themselves out of the market so that people are getting 150 dollars a day as a full-time thief and whore and dealer.

WALDMAN: You mean they might think they are afraid, you know they can be indoctrinated maybe to . . .

BURROUGHS: Well, I mostly . . . Dr. Schultz—he's a botanist who's been down to South America—this guy down there who was from the United Nations tried to stop the cocaine down there and Doc Schultz said he believed it himself. It was his job.

WALDMAN: What about the word as a virus?

BURROUGHS: Well, yes, the only way we have of knowing the virus is it produces symptoms, or if they are recognized as symptoms. So the word—there is quite a lot of evidence that the word is or was originally some sort of illness, sitting in the organ of consciousness and breakdown of the bicameral mind. His thesis is that the first voices were hallucinated voices, that is people hearing voices. He doesn't speculate as to the origin of this but it could have been an actual illness.

WALDMAN: These are the first words, you're saying, are hallucinated voices.

BURROUGHS: Speaking about language, see, animals talk, they don't write. In spoken words is implicit the concept of written words. Animals don't have that concept.

WALDMAN: You're talking about the written words as far as . . .

BURROUGHS: The written word, yes, the written word must in a sense come before the spoken word.

WALDMAN: That's what Robert Duncan was saying this summer.

BURROUGHS: See, animals have only signals, they can convey all sorts of things. What they can't do is to—an animal can learn in its lifetime from other animals a lot of things, but they can't collect all the young rats together and tell them about poisons, about traps, etc. That, they can't do. In other words, they don't have a means of communication beyond their range, or for other animals. In the future, you don't need written language, you don't have to have writing, but even an illiterate—there aren't any illiterate people in my way of thinking. They may not be able to write but they have the concept of writing which is storing information. They can collect the young people and tell them this, that, and the other, which they have heard from somebody else and it is passed on. Animals can't do that.

OUGHTON: So you think there is no functional difference between their kind of oral history and their written record?

BURROUGHS: Not really, none at all.

OUGHTON: You worked on exploring hieroglyphics for a while as an alternative form of signal. What kind of influence did that have on your own concept of working with words as a writer?

BURROUGHS: Well, it's not an alternative. I mean that Chinese, Arabic, and Japanese are in a sense hieroglyphic or calligraphic writing. One of the obvious things that we lose sight of is the fact that the word is an image because there isn't that correspondence between the words. The word "dawn" or "day" would be "sun" in different hieroglyphs but there is no correspondence between a word and the object it refers to in the alphabetical language. Of course, the actual grammar of the Egyptian hieroglyphs is extremely cumbersome and extremely complicated and much of it is arbitrary. The idea that this is all a picture . . . they're phonetic elements, all kinds of elements. A lot of picture writing in the only really complete hieroglyphic writing we've had, much of it's arbitrary.

OUGHTON: I called it an alternative system, I was thinking more of a person who's used to writing in, say, English, such as you, goes to the hieroglyphs as a different way of passing on thoughts and communicating to see what that might do in terms of changing his own conception of English.

BURROUGHS: Well, I think, generally speaking, a writer realizes already he has got to be visual and concrete—it simply shows you have to be visual—you have to see it, in order to play it so there is no way in pictorial language, except by being purely arbitrary, that you can even convey abstract notion. Abstract words which most writers don't use anyway or shouldn't use.

OUGHTON: Infinity for example.

BURROUGHS: Well, "justice," etc.—they don't mean anything. Everybody has their "communism," "classes," everybody has different ideas than what you've got. Therefore, there is no agreement. You talk about different things. You can argue all day or night and never realize that. Say you say, "Well, I say that's a desk and you say that's a table." We can't argue about that very long because it doesn't make any difference what we call it and I can say, "Well, we can call it x." Doesn't make any difference whether we call it a desk or a table or x or a number. But when you have something you can't see and you have one idea about it and I have another, then you can argue a bit.

WALDMAN: I try to avoid those arguments myself. I got into one the other night . . .

BURROUGHS: I simply will not engage in an argument like that.

WALDMAN: He was going on about communism and socialism. I had no idea what he was talking about after a while.

BURROUGHS: He hadn't any idea, I'm sure, because communism . . . this applies to Russia, it applies to China, it applies to anything they don't happen to like and fascism is applied to an expanding militaristic movement like Nazi Germany or Italy and then they turn around and say that a place like South Africa, all they are trying to do is hang on to what they've got and it's not an expressionist movement at all . . . this is not the same political phenomena . . . and call them both fascism. But it's not so at all.

WALDMAN: So are these the virus words?

BURROUGHS: Well, yes, they behave like viruses.

OUGHTON: They are self-maintaining per se.

BURROUGHS: Korzybinski has a lot to say about the issue of identity. He said, "Well, whatever this is, it is the chair, it isn't the label chair." To say that it is, is just an inherent contradiction in Western language. You can't say that in Egyptian hieroglyphs. You say it is as a chair, not he is my servant, which implies that he is my servant for all eternity imposing his permanent condition; he is as my servant.

WALDMAN: So when did this come about?

BURROUGHS: It came about with syllabic language.

WALDMAN: Syllabic language, from the very beginning.

BURROUGHS: What he calls the "as of" identity. You can take it out and once you realize this, it doesn't make any difference whether you use it or not. You don't have to use it all, you can rule it right out of your conversation, it just sounds kind of funny.

WALDMAN: He is as my friend.

BURROUGHS: You don't even have to say that. As yes . . .

WALDMAN: He is as yes?

BURROUGHS: "He servant" or "I here." I don't have to say "I am here." This chair is much, no contradiction there, this chair that is the object that I'm talking about when I use that word.

OUGHTON: I feel somewhat the same way when someone asks me if I'm a poet I feel that I'm only a poet when I'm actually producing and working on it. The rest of the time I'm just a being.

BURROUGHS: I know, that's what I mean. He's as my servant at a certain time.

OUGHTON: I'm sort of skipping around here. One of the other questions I wanted to ask you is about younger writers, younger novelists that interest you. One of the things that is remarkable about your work is the level to which you integrate things from science and technology, for example, like theories of virus within a pictorial narrative. Thomas Pynchon in *Gravity's Rainbow* tried a similar thing with a different set of technology. Did that interest you as a novel?

BURROUGHS: Yes, I found it kind of hard reading but it was interesting. It is one of the books that I would have liked to sort of read on vacation or something, or on a boat, like Proust or war fiction.

OUGHTON: Who are you reading now?

BURROUGHS: I don't read much so-called "serious" fiction.

WALDMAN: It is grade-B pulp stuff.

OUGHTON: Science fiction.

BURROUGHS: Science fiction, horror stories.

WALDMAN: Books about packs of dogs taking over New York City, the orphanators.

BURROUGHS: One a day.

WALDMAN: The long dark night of the soul.

BURROUGHS: It is another possessed ten-year-old boy and the governess arriving.

OUGHTON: There has been a lot of pop interest in the whole thing of exorcism and demonology over the last decade. I wonder where all that came from. Why that now?

WALDMAN: Because we are possessed. People are hearing voices all the time. Like in that girl's dream last night, things like that. If she were a less stable person . . .

BURROUGHS: Everyone hears voices all the time. Part of it is propaganda coming from the Catholic church. It's the only way to keep a hold on their . . .

WALDMAN: Reborn Christians.

BURROUGHS: Yes, sort of dust off the devil. You can't imagine—you see, I read these things all the time—how many of these there are. There was *The Exorcist* then there was *Damien* I and *Damien* II. Let's see . . .

OUGHTON: *The Amityville Horror* will be a movie, I'm sure. *Carrie.*

BURROUGHS: God, I don't know, I've read at least fifteen to twenty of these. People are absolutely shameless about copying someone. A book will come out and make money, another book will come out just the same.

The rats, for example, then there was the cats. These were very intelligent rats, about two feet long.

So then at the end of *Rats* you realize that somebody hadn't closed the door or they put the poison out, so they are going to have one or two rats left. So they have *Rats II*. Same thing happened with the cats—the cats went mad and at the end they intimidated a dog, something about a cat frightened the dog. So you realize it is going to start again. There is *The Cats, The Bats, the Swarm*, something called *Night Wings*—vampire bats, millions descend upon the people and suck all their blood. *The Birds, The Frogs, Squirm, The Killer Worm*.

OUGHTON: Last year I took your workshop on screenwriting and you mentioned *Interview with a Vampire* by Anne Rice. I went back and read that and I thought that really classy pulp style was very assured. It gave the vampire a new dimension for me.

BURROUGHS: That was a good book. It was an interesting book, showing some of the impasses of physical immortality.

OUGHTON: Would you be immortal if you had the choice?

BURROUGHS: Well, the question is not relevant—there is an argument that any kind of physical immortality is going to end up as a very bad idea indeed.

WALDMAN: It is.

BURROUGHS: Yes, physical. That is a sort of mentality something like [William Randolph] Hearst's and anyone who says they want to live forever is talking nonsense because forever is a time word. It simply means that they want to live a long time.

—August 3, 1978

The scope and influence of the New American Poetry and its attendant offshoots and cross-fertilizations with other writers of the expansive poetry world is an Indra's Net of inter-relatedness and is thus difficult to codify. Suffice it to say, however, that some of the writers most associated with the Beat movement were already very cognizant of and extremely well-read in Buddhist philosophy and psychology. Gary Snyder had majored in anthropology as an undergraduate at Reed College and then did graduate work at the University of California at Berkeley where he studied classical Chinese and pursued his Zen Buddhist practice. He received a scholarship from the first Zen Institute which led to nearly fifteen years in Japan. He and his (then) wife, poet Joanne Kyger, traveled to India with Allen Ginsberg and Peter Orlovsky where they met the sixteenth Dalai Lama. Jack Kerouac befriended Gary Snyder who provoked in him an interest in Buddhism. Kerouac's novel *The Dharma Bums*, which adopts a veiled Snyder as its central character, triggered the "rucksack revolution," which set young people off "on the road" with a resolute spirituality more at home with Buddhist and Taoist thought than with any Western philosophy. "Meditation is the art of deliberately staying open so that myriad things can experience themselves," Gary Snyder has written.

The conversations, readings, performances, collaborations, panel discussions, poems, and the like occurring with many of the poets who passed through the Naropa gates, particularly those cited as "Beats" (this is a historical and handy term, but does not convey the full complexity of the individual writers or their work), constitute what I perceive to be an as-yet unacknowledged body of uniquely articulated and salutary "dharma poetics"—that derives from Buddhist psychology and philosophy around such issues as spontaneous mind, dream yoga, the is-ness of language, the sense of "right view," of co-emergent wisdom (similar to Keats's "negative capability"), "intentionality," "first thought, best thought," "things are symbols of themselves" and the notion of "all ten directions of space" as a mode for investigative poetics. It is always interesting to observe where the meditator's mind and the poetry mind might resonate and to be able to describe the processes of mind as an artist (which Buddhism does to such discriminating degrees).

Chögyam Trungpa, Rinpoche, Naropa University's founder, clearly stated from the beginning of the visionary Naropa project that he hoped poets could make the Buddhists more articulate through original speech and mind and that the poets might benefit by sitting meditation which would provide a greater grounding to their lives which would benefit others. And that there be no conflict between poetry and spirituality. Allen and I declared in our "mission statement" on the founding of The Kerouac School in 1974: Though "not all the poetry teachers are Buddhist, nor is it required of the teachers and students in this secular school to follow any specific meditative path, it is the happy accident of this century's poetic history—especially since Gertrude Stein—that the quality of mind and mindfulness probed by Buddhist practice is similar to the probes and practices of poetry. There being no party line but mindfulness of thought and language itself, no conflict need arise between religion and poetry, and the marriage of two disciplines at Naropa is expected to flourish during the next hundred years."

Allen also wrote in 1978: "Whatever the fate of the Jack Kerouac School of Disembodied Poetics, some climactic event has taken place in American poetry which will leave its imprint of frankness and wisdom on future American lyric thought."

—Anne Waldman, from "Tendrel: A Meeting of Minds,"
a talk given July, 1999

"FRIGHTENED CHRYSANTHEMUMS": POETS' COLLOQUIUM

William Burroughs, Rick Fields, Allen Ginsberg, W. S. Merwin, Chögyam Trungpa, Rinpoche, Anne Waldman, Philip Whalen, David Rome, Joshua Zim

CHÖGYAM TRUNGPA, RINPOCHE: WANT TO SAY SOMETHING?

WILLIAM BURROUGHS: Well, as I understand it, you're a little bit, shall we say reluctant to admit all these sort of psychic practices like astral projections, feeling colors with your hands, and telepathy, and so on. My feeling about these things, frankly, is that they're simply fun, like skiing or gliding, learning Mexican cooking or something like that. Do you seriously object to these practices?

TRUNGPA: Well, I wouldn't say "reluctant," actually, the question seems to be that these phenomena we experience are made up in our psychic level, which we can't actually share with somebody. They're not as real as a dollar bill. So that seems to be the problem, always. And, also, there's a tendency to get into a new world, a new dimension that nobody can share, that people in the street can't share, can't experience. And further, how much are we making these things up, or are they actually happening? That's the kind of question. No doubt a lot of experience occurred. They do function on an individual level, but do they in terms of public phenomena? Somebody might see a TWA jet flying overhead, which is everybody's common knowledge. These other things are not exactly common knowledge. It may be common knowledge to a certain particular circle. That seems to be the problematic point. Are we going to encourage people to pursue something that is purely in their minds or to pursue something they can actually share?

And half of the world, or even more than that actually, 99 percent of the world, haven't realized who they are to begin with, so it's quite a burden.

BURROUGHS: Yes, but the simple consideration I was making was that these things are fun and they are limited. The man in the street can't do hang-gliding, he can't do ballooning, he can't do mountain climbing, but is that any reason why those who can shouldn't? And I think the same thing applies to astral travel and other things that are fun. They're not supposed to be any final answer.

TRUNGPA: Absolutely not. Everybody is on their own anyway in this world. If they feel rejection from their parents, or if they feel acceptance and enlightenment from their teacher, why not?

BURROUGHS: I guess all I am saying is that enlightenment should be fun. It isn't always, to be sure.

ALLEN GINSBERG: Now you're proposing astral travel as enlightenment?

BURROUGHS: No. I proposed it simply as fun, that's all, like any sort of travel.

PHILIP WHALEN: Why should enlightenment be fun or anything else? Why shouldn't it just be enlightenment? Like it usually is.

BURROUGHS: Incentive learning. People are more interested in doing something that's fun than not fun. Allen, what do you have to say on this question?

GINSBERG: Well, I've never experienced astral travel except in dreams. I ain't never seen no flying saucers, and all the acid-heads that come up to me with all sorts of Tarot with wings and hydro-headed birds coming from Mars with a message of apocalypse, are generally speed-freaks so I get turned off to late-nineteenth-century-style magic.

BURROUGHS: Yes, there's a great turn-off in the whole literature of occultism. Such atrocious writing, and there's this sleazy, second-rate thing that's being put down. I mean the whole literature of theosophy and so on.

TRUNGPA: I think that has been a problem, always. I think the whole reason why that thing started was a need to introduce another dimension in thinking, and that was the closest they could come up with. You know, it's such an extraordinary thing. I have experienced astral travel myself, by flying TWA.

BURROUGHS: May I ask if you've ever tried to read Aleister Crowley?

TRUNGPA: Yes. In fact, one of the closest students of Aleister Crowley happens to be a good friend of mine. And we talked a certain amount about it, not a great deal. He's rather discreet about the whole thing, but that area is very interesting.

BURROUGHS: Well, he did say something very profound. He was simply requoting the Old Man of the Mountain. He said, "Do what thou wilt. That is the whole of the law." Well, now, one person in twenty million knows what they want to do, so this is no invitation to unrestrained behavior.

TRUNGPA: Aleister Crowley himself felt the experience of torturing death. Finally, the magic of the world descended on him, which is interesting drama in some sense. There is something operating. Buddhists would say it is the act of the Vajra principle or whatever.

BURROUGHS: Well, this is simply a quote, a restatement of Hassan i Sabbah's dying words, "Nothing is true. Everything is permitted." That means if nothing is true everything is permitted and if all is illusion then you can do anything you want.

TRUNGPA: That's true, but we can't jump out the window from the Empire State Building.

WHALEN: The thing is, do you want to do anything? What do you want to do?

BURROUGHS: You are bringing up the whole question of motivation.

WHALEN: No, I'm bringing up a question of what do you want to do right now? What is it that you want to do? Supposing that we're all these illusory bodies sitting around here, which we are, and so are you, what is it you want to do?

BURROUGHS: It cannot be put into words.

GINSBERG: When I first knew Bill in 1945 or 6 he was studying Korzybski's *Science and Sanity*. Do you know that book or of it? General Semantics. The words are not the things they represent, which is like a Western presentation of the fact that the word "table," for example, is not the same as a table. So that a goose in a bottle is a verbal construction and you can get it out the same way you put it in.

TRUNGPA: That always puzzles me. How to take the goose out.

GINSBERG: You put it in the bottle. You take it out of the bottle.

TRUNGPA: I'm not so sure.

GINSBERG: The point was that Bill said then that his thought process was primarily visual and pictorial rather than verbal, and mine was primarily verbal. I was always astounded by that actually. When interrogated he says that he doesn't even have the pictures sometimes. And that you can turn it off or turn it on.

BURROUGHS: Yes, it's no problem to make your mind as blank as a plate. It's simply a question of sufficient knowledge, obviously. If you understand your brain mechanism fully you can say, "turn off the words." Very simple. It's a tape recorder, anyway. Yes, Korzybski used to come in and slap a chair saying, "Whatever this is, it's not a chair." That is, it's not the verbal label "chair." Another of his great statements was, "You think as much with your big toe as you do with your brain, and probably much more efficiently." These, of course, are Buddhist commonplaces.

GINSBERG: Or are they?

BURROUGHS: Of course they are.

TRUNGPA: Well, I think rather Zennish.

BURROUGHS: Just suppose we had a machine to wipe out everyone's past conditioning. This is quite possible in terms of present-day technology. So people don't have to do any sort of meditation. They just go to the machines. Their whole past condition, their whole bad karma, is wiped out of their brains. It must have a place in your nervous system through which it manifests itself for it to be manifest in you.

TRUNGPA: I think the question is why the nervous system developed in the beginning for it to happen that way.

WHALEN: Your nervous system comes out of that lunacy to start with.

BURROUGHS: Yes. And of course we have a nervous system that is already divided by the two sides of the brain. Gregory Bateson has talked quite a bit about the two sides. I think that's a very, very important point. You talk about compulsive verbalization, but where is it coming from? It's coming from the other side of the brain, perhaps.

TRUNGPA: Well, I think the point is who's the maker of that up there? How does the whole thing happen to be that way? And what kind of mind is going on behind it? Well, it's a question of taking at face value who actually had the brains to assemble such a machine in the beginning.

BURROUGHS: Have you read Wittgenstein? He says that no proposition can contain itself as data. In other words, the only thing that's not prerecorded is prerecordings themselves.

GINSBERG: Well, do you think given sufficient money you could get a machine that would resolve problems of echo, of language, of the word, and problems of conditioning?

BURROUGHS: It's not exactly a question of a machine. It's a question of the interaction between the machine and the individual. We've got machines. We might as well use them. Which isn't to say that you've invalidated the meditative position. But simply that there can be an interaction between that position and, shall we say, data provided by machines which would make it much more available to large numbers of people.

GINSBERG: But in a way acid is that too. As soon as people get their conditioning wiped out, they freak out. So as soon as you've got your conditioning wiped out, as soon as you turn off the machine, you'd walk right out in the street and stop and have a coke.

BURROUGHS: Not necessarily. See, you've got a series of tape recorders in your brain, and you know that you can wipe out a recording.

RINPOCHE: I think the problem is that you still have the tape recorder in your brain.

BURROUGHS: Suppose you put a magnet on it and it was wiped out?

RINPOCHE: But you still have the tape, empty tape, which is willing to pick new channels. That is always the problem. We can wipe them out, but we still have the machine that's running around willing to respond to all kinds of things.

BURROUGHS: I was not proposing some very easy way of doing it, I was simply saying that we can use machines, perhaps, to make it more efficient and more available.

DAVID ROME: Well, with due respect, some of the earlier metaphors and notions of meditation that you presented about blank mind or getting rid of the sum of past conditioning were a rather static, or decided notion of what meditation is. Whereas I think the tradition of Buddhism is really interested in the process of how it goes on right now, how we handle what is there.

BURROUGHS: Presumably if you were able to wipe out past conditioning you'd be able to go on from there, wherever you went on to.

JOSHUA ZIM: Presumably without wiping it out you'd also be able to go on. Wiping it out is a curious intention.

BURROUGHS: Most people are not able to wipe out and get beyond their past conditioning. As Bernard Shaw says, "Those who are ignorant of history will suffer its repetition," and that goes as well for any individual.

ZIM: But then you're stuck with this question of where this intent to wipe it out comes from. And that still remains.

BURROUGHS: No, there is no question there at all. It is simply biologically inappropriate to be reacting to past and future dangers, that's all. It is advantageous to be rid of your past conditioning. You don't have to say any more than that. You take some guy who's been in battle fatigue. He's still reacting to that situation and there can't be anything more biologically disadvantageous than that. And the same thing with people who are reacting at the present time to infantile traumas that happened forty years ago. And they're completely crippled by this. This is very disadvantageous.

TRUNGPA: But knowing how to walk and talk and breathe is part of past conditioning. How do you sort those things out?

BURROUGHS: You don't have to. Walking and talking and breathing are quite advantageous. Reacting to something that happened to you forty years ago is very disadvantageous. The techniques exist whereby that can be wiped right out of the brain. And once it's wiped out it's wiped out.

ZIM: Then you've swallowed the whole idea of wipeout. That's become another element of conditioning. Let's say you were lucky enough to wipe out your traumatic experience of ten years ago without wiping out how to walk and talk and breathe, and still so what? What do you do then?

BURROUGHS: What you want to do. "Do what thou wilt. That is the whole of the Law." You find out what you want to do and you do it.

ROME: Are you sure that you're still going to want to do something?

BURROUGHS: Maybe you'll just have a lot of people who couldn't move at all. So we say, "Well, what the hell. We tried." There's no way of knowing. That is why Rinpoche has spoken about a leap into the dark. You try it, say, "Well, we're going to wipe out the whole past conditioning for these people."

ROME: Now, wait a minute, you're going to wipe it out for them or wipe it out for yourself?

BURROUGHS: Well, I'll be quite content to wipe it out for myself. I would be glad to be the first experimental subject and see what happens. You see, you cannot say, "I will decide ahead of time what will happen if I make a leap in the dark." And you have spoken very much about the leap in the dark, have you not?

TRUNGPA: The dark in the sense of having no idea what's going to happen.

BURROUGHS: It may be good, it may be bad, it may be simply indifferent. Well, I've been talking too much. Let someone else talk for a while.

TRUNGPA: Why do you write poetry?

GINSBERG: I took a vow when I was fourteen years old that if I were admitted to Columbia University I would work hard on the salvation of mankind.

TRUNGPA: Did you think you were going to be famous?

GINSBERG: That was not the original intention.

TRUNGPA: But the second one?

GINSBERG: You know, I don't think I'm going to be famous. I'm already famous, so the future isn't necessarily fame.

TRUNGPA: So how did you think poetry would help people?

GINSBERG: If you can make an accurate description of the differences in behavior and changes in your own life and in your own mind, people looking at it see a sample of how somebody else behaves and how somebody else reacts and get some sense of their own changes, the variety of them, the strangeness of them. It's you who learn for other people to understand. You make a graph of the agreements and contradictions.

TRUNGPA: Do you think that's going to help society?

GINSBERG: Yes, because you lay down "what oft' was thought but ne'er so well expressed," or never expressed at all.

BURROUGHS: But Allen, let me say something about your poetry. I mean, the fact that forty years ago if someone had gotten up and sung a song "Everybody's a Little Homosexual" they would have been torn to pieces, particularly in front of college kids who were especially afraid of that. You have created this terrific cultural revolution whereby you can get up and say that, and people will applaud you. I would say that Allen's poetry has been a great force in transforming American society.

TRUNGPA: Are you talking, Bill, purely in terms of homosexuality or something else?

BURROUGHS: Not just homosexuality, but the whole matter of freedom of the word—so that you can say words like "fuck."

GINSBERG: Responsible frankness, or at least an accounting of what's going on, like a core sample.

TRUNGPA: So that will just be to help people free themselves from holding back, and culture from holding back?

GINSBERG: No. To help them free themselves for spiritual search, free themselves for dharma also, or even to awaken curiosity and insight.

TRUNGPA: Well, you have a lot of faith and hope.

GINSBERG: Well, yes I have. "Devotion is the head of meditation, as is said."

TRUNGPA: Oh, my goodness!

GINSBERG: No, it begins with some sense of devotion. I recognize your beauty the same as I recognize my own or anyone else's, and I write about that in my poetry. However you want to define the word "beauty."

TRUNGPA: Are you sure? Are you perfectly certain?

GINSBERG: No, but I do my best.

TRUNGPA: That's better.

GINSBERG: Well, that's all I say. I may try to make a record of what goes on as far as I can see it, but there doesn't have to be a record of truths. There only has to be a record of what I thought was true or what I thought about, so it serves as a model for other people who might not be thinking, or might not think you're supposed to think about that, or might not think that there's any reality to such investigations.

BURROUGHS: If anyone asks me why I write novels, I am but a simple craftsman.

ANNE WALDMAN: A writer writes.

BURROUGHS: A writer writes, that's the way he makes his living just like a doctor. Any craftsman wants to make money. It's his trade and he has to make money in order to continue to do it.

TRUNGPA: Do you regard yourself as a craftsman?

GINSBERG: Sometimes. Other times I regards myself as a bodhisattva or with bodhisattva intentions.

TRUNGPA: When was the first time you heard the word "bodhisattva?"

GINSBERG: Oh, 1951 or something. Reading Suzuki.

TRUNGPA: What did you think a bodhisattva was like then?

GINSBERG: It reminded me of the fact that I got there on the ferryboat across the Hudson from Hoboken to New York and kneeled down on my knees and prayed that if I got admitted to Columbia University I would save the working class in America.

TRUNGPA: Just the working class? Why not the others?

GINSBERG: Well, that was just the beginning. I didn't realize at the time that anybody was suffering, that the trees were suffering, that I was suffering.

WALDMAN: It's like being a reed, a conduit, and letting the wind or whatever play on you. The sufi view.

W. S. MERWIN: The first reason I do any of those things is because I want to.

WHALEN: I usually get carried away. I hear some line in my head or see something that attracts my attention or carts me off with it temporarily and I get it all on paper somehow, maybe not all at once, maybe several days later. But it's an obsessive kind of business. I can't really say that I create these things, that I sit down with the intention of saying, "Now, today is Friday and it's poem-writing time," and I get out this paper and pencil and say, "Now I'm going to think of a sublime thought," and presently the sublime thought appears and I say, "The moon is rising over the purple hills." This is a sublime statement of my sublime thought and you got poetry. With me it doesn't work that way. Sometimes I get turned on by a single word or by a phrase or by something somebody says on the bus or maybe I'll be reading something that suggests something else to me, and I take off and start writing my own thing at that point. It isn't so much a business of my being a professional poet or something or of my seeing myself that way, but just being interested in words and language and having a great deal of fun with it.

TRUNGPA: Do you memorize your poems of the past?

WHALEN: No. I can't remember. I have to write them down. And then after I write them down I can't remember them.

WALDMAN: You're freed once you write them down.

WHALEN: In a way. Sometimes on rare occasions I can remember fragments but if someone tells me, "Please recite one of your poems for us," I can't do it. I have to go find a book and look in the book and read. Allen used to be able to remember lots of his poetry and Gregory could remember his and Kerouac could remember long passages of his own writing and recite them for you. And I always envied Allen's capacity to remember classical poetry, to remember large sections of Shakespeare and Milton, Blake and so on, which I can't do. My memory is too shaky or something.

TRUNGPA: How do you feel your practice connects with the poetry?

WHALEN: Oh, it stops it. At first, in the earlier part of doing formal zazen—the first year and half, two years—I wrote very little and I resented—very deeply resented—the fact that I wasn't writing anything, and it made a great difficulty for me. It was only about six months or so ago that I started to feel free enough to write or not write.

TRUNGPA: Do you find any conflict between writing poetry and sitting?

WHALEN: You know, in some subliminal way that I can't really describe. It's gradually working itself out to where I can write if I have something to write and if not, not. It all works itself out without my having to worry about it, mess with it.

TRUNGPA: Do you write about sitting practice in poetry?

WHALEN: Oh, no. I couldn't. It's too large. It's too complicated. After I'd been through a *sesshin* I thought, my goodness, that to explain what had happened to me in those seven days would take thirty-five or forty volumes of closely printed pages, and then you'd still just have books, you still wouldn't have anything like what it was that I pushed myself through. So it doesn't work, or at least I haven't found a way of telling that or telling what it's like to be in the training period at Tassajara where your life is totally changed, where in addition to doing lots of zazen you do all three meals a day in the zendo with the bowls, plus working, plus changing out of working clothes into robes and back again and things like that, and it's very funny. I still have found no way of saying it except to tell people that they ought to try it.

GINSBERG: I'm not as deeply into practice as you are but what will I do? Some things stand out, like anything you can remember stands out. So what little you can remember is material in a sense.

TRUNGPA: You wrote a lot of poems when you were at the seminary?

GINSBERG: Yes, I wrote a lot of good poems, I thought.

TRUNGPA: Maybe that was your only thought, a time to write poetry.

GINSBERG: No, it wasn't my primary thought. Thoughts came. Occasionally they were tempting enough to write down. They were solid enough, pretty enough to write down.

TRUNGPA: Yes, I think a lot of Tibetan poets like Milarepa are spiritually moved out of the sitting practice. All kinds of things come up which they jot down, just write, just sing happily or sadly or whatever it may be and poems get written down. It's worth trying.

GINSBERG: Yes, it would seem natural. The only conflict I would find was whether or not to break up the sitting to write. I did it once, but anything strong enough to write down remained after sitting.

TRUNGPA: Well, you could do it while you were sitting on the toilet or something.

BURROUGHS: I don't see any reason why you can't sit at the typewriter.

RICK FIELDS: Rinpoche, during retreat you instruct your students not to write, why is this?

TRUNGPA: Well, when you sit meditation a lot of things churn up your mind—resentment of the past and your mother, your father, your teacher, your brothers, sisters and dharma or blood brothers or whatever.

BURROUGHS: Doesn't all that come up when you're writing?

TRUNGPA: Not necessarily. There could be a moment of very clear thought when you can actually write something without thinking.

BURROUGHS: I'd like very much to go on one of these month retreats to cut off all input.

TRUNGPA: Let's do that.

BURROUGHS: But I would like to have a typewriter.

TRUNGPA: Well, a typewriter becomes an out for us. It becomes your occupation, that's the only source of entertainment.

GINSBERG: Yes, but he's also saying the typewriter, the use of typewriters, is his zafu, that's his yoga. Is that possible?

TRUNGPA: It's possible, of course, but it's very deceptive.

WHALEN: Or you could take the ribbon out.

GINSBERG: Well, it's a practical proposition. I wonder would there be a room for Bill at Karmê Chöling?

TRUNGPA: There's no room for him to type in a retreat hut. There's only room when he comes down. He can do that, which is an entirely different situation. I think that if you're able to preserve your creative mind even when you're in a transitional period, then you are already there. You can write. But there was a woman who did her whole book in retreat, which was jammed with all kinds of resentment, all kinds of sexual fantasies, and all kinds of political ideas.

BURROUGHS: Well, sexual fantasies are bound to arise in retreat.

TRUNGPA: Sure, that's not regarded as bad, but if you have writing materials available on the spot of your sitting practice, then it's just more garbage. There's so much happening you don't have a chance while you're sitting to review anything that's happened to you before.

ROME: Why does it make sense to you to limit your input but not your output?

BURROUGHS: I didn't say that at all. I simply said that if I was on retreat I would rather like to have a typewriter in case anything useful came up.

ROME: But I think that's the point, that we give up judging anything useful in the process of doing retreat, being in meditation.

BURROUGHS: That seems quite reasonable.

TRUNGPA: Sitting practice is regarded as an unproductive period. You don't produce any commercialized industry of any kind at all. Just sit and do it, slow the world. The world doesn't have any further ideas or input in it at all. This is very hard in some sense, but I think in the long run it provides more input.

BURROUGHS: In other words you're simply cutting out your input. No mail, no radio, no nothing.

TRUNGPA: No telephone.

BURROUGHS: I could do that in New York City, rip out my telephones and say, "I'm in retreat, boys. Nobody contacts me."

WALDMAN: I've got some problems with some of the students here at the Poetics Academy coming to classes and saying that they can't write because they're so involved with their meditation, which is fine.

BURROUGHS: Why do you say that when someone is in retreat, they can't also write?

WALDMAN: It's just a temporary cut-off.

BURROUGHS: But suppose in retreat they get an idea for a great novel?

WALDMAN: It'll come back later if it's that great.

BURROUGHS: But it may not though.

TRUNGPA: The point is that we may have good ideas but we are uncertain as to which part is the real inspiration and which part is just entertainment. You would like to prove to yourself that you have something happening. If you have real inspiration it's going to last.

BURROUGHS: It may not last, it may not last. You may have something just beautiful and you'll never remember it later. Like Coleridge forgot the end of "Kublai Khan" because someone came in.

TRUNGPA: It doesn't mean that we give up ever judging anything useful or useless. But for that situation we are willing to try doing that. It is difficult to sort out what is real production, and what is just part of your fantasy. Usually your mind becomes so clear, so precise that you need some more feedback. The result is that you put in a lot of neurosis and entertainment. This usually happens with people.

WALDMAN: I think there are exceptions.

BURROUGHS: It depends on how neurotic you are to start with.

TRUNGPA: Well, it's possible that if I decided to send you to retreat, sir, maybe I would like to give you a typewriter.

WHALEN: The thing is that if you have one good idea the chances are that you'll have another one later. You lost the first one, well you get another one anyway, so why sweat?

TRUNGPA: Yes, good Buddhist thinking.

BURROUGHS: It's not always true. You may get a good idea and lose it completely. This great novel is gone because you didn't have a typewriter.

TRUNGPA: The painters would have a brush. And the seamstresses would have their needles and thread. And all kinds of things begin to happen. And maybe the master chef who's in retreat would like to have his food and cook delicious meals.

BURROUGHS: This would apply, of course, to any other profession. You've got someone up there on retreat. He's a carpenter. He shouldn't do any carpentry. You've got someone up there, a physicist. Suppose he's got a new field theory, something comes into him. He should not write this down?

TRUNGPA: No.

BURROUGHS: I'm glad you're giving me definite answers.

TRUNGPA: Maybe we shouldn't give you a typewriter when you go on retreat.

BURROUGHS: I think it'd probably be very good for me not to have a typewriter, really. It's like a film director who doesn't have a camera, right?

TRUNGPA: Very much so.

BURROUGHS: I think it's a very good exercise. I agree 100 percent, because the guy's going to be up there saying, "Oh my god, I've got the film, I've got the novel," then he realizes this is not so important.

TRUNGPA: Sure. That always happens, and usually people who practice sitting are very brilliant people. They would like to do this thing. They come up with these fantastic ideas. The whole thing may be dissolved, or the remaining ideas may be continued after they get out of this, when they have some taste of the world and a flavor of the sitting practice.

BURROUGHS: I think your point is very well taken here, very valid.

TRUNGPA: If you want to take a retreat you're always welcome.

BURROUGHS: I'm willing. I've written enough. I don't have to write anymore. Any profession can become compulsive. I think to break it completely is very good exercise.

TRUNGPA: Yeah. I would say more of a training, not even exercise. There is a difference.

TRUNGPA: Well, why do you write poetry?

WALDMAN: I don't know. I feel driven. And I feel calm with it and comfortable, healthy, sane. Some kind of discipline which hasn't interfered in other ways.

TRUNGPA: Do you feel any kind of feelings towards your audience when you write?

WALDMAN: Sometimes when I read or when something comes spontaneously, I feel that the audience is somehow part of it, and feeding it. We're all doing it together and that feels healthy. On the other hand I feel, as William was saying, professional in some way. I mean that's what I do, I write.

TRUNGPA: Well, poets generally have some vision of society. They are putting some kind of energy into the society. So what is your work actually doing for the good of society? So somebody buys your booklet of poetry. What do you expect of them?

WALDMAN: I don't think about it too much.

TRUNGPA: You don't? Really you don't?

WALDMAN: I've been lucky as far as a career in poetry is concerned. I think it has to do with being female at this time and other considerations. Publishers like to put photos on covers and so on.

TRUNGPA: Some of your poems are very powerful. They always enter my dreams.

WALDMAN: Thank you.

TRUNGPA: Always, I keep on hearing your voice.

BURROUGHS: You write poetry. Do you think of your audience when you write?

TRUNGPA: Sometimes I do when I write. Sometimes I have a separate sort of split, I should say; I'm writing for this particular person, a love poem or whatever it may be. But at the same time as the audience would hear this, they might pick up some kind of spark. And I think it's the same when I give a talk. I'm talking with an individual person in the audience while this particular talk is being taped and going to be played on the radio, so I have an awareness of that at the same time. So what I expect out of my work is that people will pay attention and they will think twice. In fact, this is exactly what is happening right now, because we're being taped. We have to make our tape not just a pile of shit but somewhat workable so we can use it again and people will have some idea as to who we are, what we are, and what we are trying to do.

WALDMAN: I also feel part of some lineage. So that when I read certain poems I'm inspired to continue in some way, or translate again through my own instrument.

MERWIN: For me the two things are almost the same because it's entirely a matter of recognition. I mean, the reason I love to do it is because the excitement, the feeling that one recognizes something in terms of language, is for me a great, great excitement. When it happens you don't question it. Part of that faith is that the recognition is something that can be shared, it's something that language is there to pass on to other people.

TRUNGPA: Well, I think that's quite safe to say and all of us are dealing with some kind of awareness of a public. Somebody's going to respond to this. It's not just purely writing in your backyard and putting it in the garbage, but there is some sense of awareness which you try to communicate.

WALDMAN: Basically, you're communicating with yourself at first.

TRUNGPA: Sure, that's why you want to write, or you have nothing to write.

GINSBERG: There is a funny line in Shakespeare, "One touch of nature. . ."

WALDMAN AND BURROUGHS: ". . . makes the whole world kin."

GINSBERG: So one touch of one's own nature written down, and other people see their own nature. The primary preoccupation is the bemusement with discovering what you were actually thinking.

TRUNGPA: Well, we could draw another line on this, if I may say so. Please criticize me. Everybody's aware of the audience somewhat, but at the same time it depends on how much you want to put out and how much you make yourself heard. There is that kind of arrogance and pride and craftsmanship that working with words is involved with. Is that possible? I mean all of us.

WALDMAN: I think that seems more true recently.

TRUNGPA: Particularly when you're well known.

WALDMAN: It's only in the last ten to fifteen years that one has been able to give poetry readings and have some sort of audience there.

MERWIN: But there's a danger in it, too. I think being aware of readers and being aware of the public are two different things. The image of the poet which comes out of his writing is very often practically eclipsed by trying to make a sort of public relations image out of it.

TRUNGPA: If you criticize the government or if you talk about homosexuality or whatever, it would be a real statement on your part, something you take pride in.

GINSBERG: Who takes pride in mirroring what went past?

TRUNGPA: Well, that still somehow has residue of the coming out.

GINSBERG: Well, I'm confused. Do you feel that this coming out is just pure ego with no value, or do you think it's a useful work that we do.

TRUNGPA: Please don't panic.

GINSBERG: I'm not panicking, now will you stop that. I was examining very closely what you were saying. I'm an expert in this area. I know my own moves.

TRUNGPA: Well, I'm trying to study the sociological or psychological set-up of poets, and how they are aware of the audience. A lot of people begin to deny this completely but it is not quite true. You would like to make a proclamation. People write me a poem sometimes. They say, "Please destroy this after you have seen it." But they really didn't want it to be destroyed.

WALDMAN: I asked my class for the next time to bring poems that they would be willing to give away. There would be only one copy of them and they would give them to each other.

TRUNGPA: So there are two split mentalities taking place.

WALDMAN: Or even more than that. Some people are concerned with language and using other people's words, like the cut-up method, and putting them in surprising orders so that one isn't even conscious of doing it.

TRUNGPA: But that's the same thing somehow. You are still writing poetry.

GINSBERG: However, I don't understand why you're making a difference between the self and the audience, because it is all self.

TRUNGPA: Well, that has always been the question of the past.

GINSBERG: Yes, well, I don't think it should be anymore.

TRUNGPA: No, we can't just make it a very simple situation that way. You are the audience, and the audience is you, obviously. That's a kind of cliché. Nevertheless, when you begin to write poetry you would like to proclaim your poems, say something. You have your booklets printed. You have the things that you would like to write down and say—say to yourself.

WALDMAN: That's not the motive.

GINSBERG: It's not so much proclaim as allow, give permission for the self to understand itself.

TRUNGPA: Whatever you use it doesn't really matter, it's the same thing. Like the poem on how you were mugged in New York City. That was a proclamation, as well as an experiential description, which is saying the same thing.

GINSBERG: What is the meaning of the word proclamation? I'm afraid you're going to say there's a shade of aggression in the proclamation which is not useful.

TRUNGPA: Not necessarily as such, but it's possible there is a proclamation in the sense that you are going to say your particular line.

GINSBERG: Right.

TRUNGPA: And your particular approach is apt, and that's your style. You are already a poet or maybe somebody's not a poet really, somebody is an amateur, but would like to be a poet or known as a poet. There is the faint hope that you might have your particular platform/pedestal. Anybody who writes poetry seems to feel that addressing from the platform or pedestal is taking place always. Nobody writes poetry just simply for its own sake.

WALDMAN: I don't think that's true.

GINSBERG: I don't agree with you.

TRUNGPA: I'm sure a lot of people don't, but please criticize me.

GINSBERG: There's another way which I find. See, I'm public—

TRUNGPA: You see, that's what I said, how else can you write poems?

GINSBERG: The other way is just oddly surprising yourself with remembering something with no actual reference to public.

WHALEN: You remember it in words, that's the important thing. You've started to remember before you've judged whether you're doing it for an audience or for yourself. The recognition happens before you think why you're doing it. So that the element of proclamation comes afterwards, if it comes at all.

GINSBERG: The way you read it, maybe.

TRUNGPA: Well, not quite, but you have hopes of hearing your voice in the back of your mind.

WALDMAN: But that's modern. In tribal societies there was always a place for the poet shaman, shamaness, whatever, who spoke, who had a role, just like being the head of the tribe, the warrior, the one who went out and made war, the agriculture man or woman, and there was no problem then.

GINSBERG: Well, oddly enough, it's very similar. I spent time with the Australian Aboriginal stone men. They had to remember the migration of the tribe over twenty-year periods, and all the water holes, and all the lizards, and where they find food. The poet now has to remember that psychologically for a larger culture, like water holes of the mind.

ZIM: Why sidestep the possibility that the writing is in fact at least partially aggressive?

GINSBERG: Get on with the business. Don't get hung up on your ego. That kind of self-consciousness inhibits you from seeing what's outside of you. Most exhibitions of that kind of thought form are just worry and self-consciousness. So you deal with it, like you do meditation or anything.

WALDMAN: In my experience, hearing poetry read and reading poetry, especially hearing poetry read—it could be in a living room with twenty people—there is usually something very modest. It's not somebody up there giving you a line or giving you some propaganda, or trying to sell you something. It's a very naked kind of sharing and can be illuminating if you're listening to it. And I think there are a lot of poets doing that. There are hundreds of poets who are not in this room, working in very modest ways, not trying to lay their trip on anybody.

BURROUGHS: A prose writer is doing a very different thing. Essentially he is creating characters, he is performing the great sacrilege in the Mohammedan religion of creating mind. People ask me, "Would you continue to write if you were on a desert island and no one would ever see it?" Answer: "Yes, for company." I would be creating characters for my own company, my own amusement. It's not the same operation as poetry. Also, a prose writer is trying to create a universe which he wants to live in, a whole universe.

WHALEN: In both of the novels I wrote it was creating universes to show why I didn't want to live there. Why I wanted out.

BURROUGHS: If you're creating a universe in which you don't want to live, you're creating one in which you do want to live. It is exactly the same operation.

TRUNGPA: You are still aiming at the audience and what they would like to hear.

BURROUGHS: I'm aiming really to a very definite audience. Say if I'm creating a character, I am aiming to the person who would be that character. I want the character that I have made to read this.

TRUNGPA: When I wrote my first autobiography I was aware of the audience as well as telling my own story at the same time.

WHALEN: But the business of creating a character by jimmying what you know, taking pieces of experience and gluing them together to make a character, is very exciting and very interesting. You figure that by the time you get through doing this nobody's going to recognize all the pieces. They'll just see the single image or person in the book. And it's a lot of fun.

GINSBERG: I think that's a very important point. You remember it and then you remember you're a poet so you write it down.

MERWIN: I think there's another thing in it too. The audience is more a part of the language than it is part of your impulse. Consequently it's part of your indebtedness because once you start using words you're using something that's given to you by other people.

TRUNGPA: That's it. If you begin to dissect that particular impulse into two parts you're aware of the audience and you're aware of yourself. Whenever you use language you always address somebody.

BURROUGHS: You don't think of the audience when you're writing. You think of perhaps an individual audience. For example, when Conrad wrote *Lord Jim* he had no idea that his hero would be taken up by Fitzgerald and become *The Great Gatsby*. They're the same person, the same person that can only exist in the prose of the writer. Therefore no movies can be made of *Lord Jim* or of *The Great Gatsby* because they only have this vicarious existence in the prose of the writer.

TRUNGPA: Maybe we should get together some kind of reading. If you could say things about what you have written already and what kind of personal experience you have felt each time. This would be very helpful to people who are going to listen to us. A lot of people who are going to listen to us feel that they need direction, they need inspiration, they're fascinated by who we are, what we are, what is poetics in any case, what it does to this society.

GINSBERG: I have a song I would like to sing.

TRUNGPA: Well, maybe you can explain why you sing, then read.

GINSBERG: Yes. I came back from India in 1963 and was chanting Hari Krishna. Robert Duncan, a poet who is a friend, said, "You use more of your body and more of yourself when you're singing Hari Krishna than in your poetry these days." So I began getting more and more pleasure out of singing, and also more and more of my body into it, and more of my breath into it. Then when you and I met seven years later you suggested improvisation and I found it was easiest to improvise while singing. In America that's the basic way of improvising in blues or in calypso. You can use rhymes, make up spontaneous mind utterances very swiftly if you're singing and also more feeling comes out.

TRUNGPA: Would you like to compose a spontaneous poem?

GINSBERG: (*singing*)

Started doing my prostrations sometime February '75
Began flying as if I were alive
In a long transmission consciousness felt quite good and true
But then I got into a sweat while thinkin' about you
Fell down with bronchitis, the first illness that came
Pneumonia in the hospital was what they said was the name
Came back to New York, got down again on my knees
But then the cold came back and I began to sneeze
I went to see the doctor, I said, "Doctor, something's wrong—
Everytime I do my prayers my cold comes along.
Hey Doctor! Look me over, tell me what's wrong with me."
He said "Well, I think you've got some trouble with your prostate, it
    might cancer be.
Why don't you get to a urologist, he'll stick his finger up your ass
He'll tell you if it's benign or whether it is something that will pass."

The urologist said "You have to go into a hospital, son."
I said "Okay, I'll find out if my race is over and done."
Went into the hospital, unconscious on the table.
They did their cystoscopic biopsy as they were able.
When I woke up, they said "Oh nothing's wrong with you.
Might as well go home tomorrow, your body is true blue.
Take this antibiotic with you when you go to your house."
Three days I lay in bed thinkin', "Well, I didn't louse
Up my situation too bad, so I'll take the pills they gave."
Couple days of taking those antibiotics I thought I'd see my grave.
103 was the temperature, I called the doctor please.
"Oh!" the nurse said, "The Doctor, he's out there on vacation taking
   his ease,"
"Why don't you go into the hospital," the substitute doctor said.
Thought I'd better do it before I fell down dead.
Went into the hospital, they stuck a needle in my arm.
Poured more antibiotic into me, they thought it'd do no harm.
Pretty soon my face fell down, the virus hit my nerves.
I couldn't drink my water without the drops would swerve
And fall down from my lips. I couldn't move my eyebrows,
Couldn't sneeze for several weeks, I didn't even know how
To wrinkle my nose or smile on the right side of my face.
Till I found it was the same herpes simplex that John Baker had a case.
In other words I'd been better off if I'd not gone to that doctor man
As it was I had four weeks of a great big blank quite bland.
Couldn't do no prostrations, couldn't even visualize my face,
But the one thing I could remember was only you, dear Mr. Grace.

TRUNGPA: Very Jewish. So, Merwin, you want to read us something?

GINSBERG: Have you written any poems since you've been here in Boulder?

MERWIN: Yes.

GINSBERG: Do you write every day?

MERWIN: I try to write every day. Usually mornings. There's a very short one I wrote after sitting today. I remember it. It's part of a series.

Blanket flower has opened.
I have imagined a heart that lit up the whole sky.

BURROUGHS: Have you ever written prose as I mean it?

TRUNGPA: I think I have, but I don't have it with me . . . Say something.

WHALEN: Frightened chrysanthemums.

BURROUGHS: What frightened them?

WHALEN: I have no idea. What do I want to say?

TRUNGPA: That's not the point. Just say it.

GINSBERG: What's going on in your head?

WHALEN: I'd seen the crick with the bridge over it that I was walking across today. That's all, just the water running under the bridge, and there's a lot of it.

GINSBERG: What's on the side of the water?

WHALEN: Grass. Then I went and sat in the part and looked at the light in the trees. I was on my way to see Chögyam Trungpa and I was too early and so I was sitting and I was looking at the light in the trees and the sun was going down and it came straight across into all the leaves and you could see each one of them and the water was going by. There were two little boys who came along and played in the drinking fountain, trying to scoop the water out of the basin of the fountain. Then they got into putting their thumbs on top of the water spout and spraying water all over everything. They had a good time. On the way back there were some girls wearing some kind of club sweaters. The sweaters had a big l that went down into a v shape, but the word that was written on them had l's in it so that's why I know it was an L and not a v. They were standing outside of Tico's dining room and the wind blew. What more? I don't have that kind of head.

GINSBERG: Actually, it sounded like one of your poems. You have the whole city going in your mind, plus the river going through it.

BURROUGHS: May I ask you now a spiritual question? Is it true that when you see something absolutely it disappears? I remember reading in one of your books about this bodhisattva or enlightened one who comes back to his room and finds all the demons there. They say, "We will not go away until you see us."

TRUNGPA: That's true, I think, very much so.

WALDMAN: Is that true of writing?

BURROUGHS: No, this has nothing to do with writing, exactly. You simply have to see a demon and he disappears.

TRUNGPA: Well, it depends on how you see. Unless you see them completely they don't disappear.

BURROUGHS: What do you think about death? Do you think that it's possible to experience death consciously so that you die consciously or is there always the blackout?

TRUNGPA: I think that it's possible to die consciously, definitely.

BURROUGHS: I agree with you. And how many people can accomplish this?

TRUNGPA: Very few.

BURROUGHS: Yes, as I've always said, if someone's not afraid of dying, they will never die.

TRUNGPA: Well, they will die, but. . .

BURROUGHS: It's the fear, it's the fear that makes the blackout. Let me just ask one more question. Isn't the basic fear that everyone has and carries through their life the fear of their own death which they know is going to happen? Like in *Anna Karenina* where the woman had this continual dream of her own death.

TRUNGPA: I think that it's certain death of the world that you experience when you die. It's not only you who's dying but your world's going to collapse and not exist anymore.

EDITORS' NOTE: In 1975, during the second summer of what was then called the "Poetics Academy" of the Jack Kerouac School of Disembodies Poetics at the Naropa Institute (now Naropa University), Chögyam Trungpa, the Institute's founder, was curious to meet and converse with the poets. This private conversation took place in Trungpa's home.

BY ANY MEANS NECESSARY

Diane di Prima

WHEN I WAS BACK HOME, THINKING ABOUT WHAT I WANTED TO talk about here, I made some quick notes and came up with the title: "By Any Means Necessary." Part of what I was thinking was that it's great that Naropa has this press and this fine printing program and all that, but it's really important to think about just using whatever you've got, whatever comes to hand, to get your work out. You know? And to get work out to me is one of the most important things—to get it into circulation once you've written it.

There's a whole lot of things that go wrong if you don't get your work into circulation sooner or later. One, you get depressed. That's big. You might not yet even notice it, but I remember at one point when I'd been too busy for about ten years to get a book out. I was running a magic school, I was teaching at New College, I had four kids still at home, and I became increasingly aware of this oppression of like four or five shelf-feet of spring binders of work that had not been published. I still haven't published most of those spring binders, but that's another story. And I can tell you that when at least some of the work is moving, it's much more possible to keep it going. Keep new work coming.

There's also: once you finish writing something it doesn't belong to you. It has its own life and needs to go where it wants to go. And the only way it can do that is if you first launch it some way. And, you know, there are all the reasons we do or don't feel whatever about publishing at any given time. I have some women students out West who are really . . . they're fine about writing but they're horrified at the idea of publishing. To them it's all mixed up with career, fame, and fortune, all those kinds of things, and they don't want that, you know. They don't want a writing career. So then what do you do and how do you work with that?

Perhaps we'll have time to talk about some of this later.

To start with I want to make a disclaimer: This talk isn't going to be about the infinite possibilities that the Net offers, mainly because I don't know anything about all that, and I'm not doing it. I have no principles against it—I just have a very old computer, and no plans to get a new one soon. I imagine getting the work out that way is fine, if you're comfortable with it. Though I myself like hard copy—I like to hold a book in my hands.

I do want to warn you all about one thing, which is the whole copyright dance on the Net. Unless you feel as an artist that all your work is in public domain anyway, that it belongs to everyone—which we're all going to have to feel sooner or later—you may want to look into this copyright thing a little. Because it's questionable how well that works with the Net right now. If it works at all. And it's quite uncomfortable to have your work glommed onto by someone you don't like, and certainly wouldn't want to give it to for free.

The reason I mention this is: years and years ago I published my first fifteen "Revolutionary Letters" through Liberation News Service, a syndicated news service that was supplying material to all the small revolutionary papers that had sprung up all around the country. And I published the "Letters" with no copyright notice. I wasn't really thinking about it. It was the sixties—we weren't thinking about that. Everyone who had a radical newspaper or magazine and wanted to print the poems, and if there was a political cause for which somebody had to raise money they published the "Letters" as a small book and sold it with my O.K. I wouldn't have minded if all the small presses in the world had published them for free, but Farrar Straus, a large, New York house, took those poems of mine without even letting me know about the book, or sending me a copy. They used them on the divider pages between chapters of a book in which they trivialized the very stuff I was writing about. And I did mind that.

So, you know, you might want to think about that when you're dancing with the Net. How does that work? Does it work? Will it ever work? And when are we going to just pay every artist a stipend so they can live, and then they don't have to worry about copyright—every artist would just get a decent salary like a plumber or an electrician, and that's it. And then all the work is immediately everyone's. That makes more sense to me.

But in the meantime, it's one thing to dance with a small press, or guys you know, who want to print your poem for free; it's another thing to have the big conglomerates ripping you off. So you might want to think about that.

O.K. So I want to talk today just about hard copy and getting the word out that way and what that's about.

As far as sending things out goes, my preference happens to be the U.S. Mail. The postal service. I don't care how many days it takes. In fact, I kind of like that it takes days. I like to collage a postcard before I send it out. I love to get and receive handwritten letters. Think about broadsides and "little" magazines—what you have then—you have something in hand. In your hand. Each time you do it, you've made an object. Even if it's a note to a friend, it's something that stays around, and sometimes other people see it or use it a long time later. That's part of what I like about it.

Of course, the negative of hard copy is that you're making artifacts, and thereby you're freezing the moment, and if you want to get into the philosophy of flow and all that it's probably better to do everything with e-mail. But there it is: I like to make beautiful, collaged postcards, note-cards. You're making an object the way you throw a pot or weave a tapestry or cast a piece of jewelry. It's something you're doing by hand—with your hands—and infusing with your energy to pass on to other people.

You can make gorgeous stuff with any medium if you play on the peculiarities of that medium instead of fighting them. For example, trying to do offset printing so that it looks like letterpress is a big waste of time. Trying to do xerox so that it looks like offset printing is a big waste of time. But if you look at the medium you have and what it will do, and just play with that, you can make something great happen with anything.

Back when LeRoi Jones [Amiri Baraka] and I were doing the magazine *The Floating Bear,* it was mimeographed. We printed it on a Gestetner, which was the state-of-the-art mimeograph machine at that time. We would get artists to draw straight onto the mimeograph stencils with a stylus, and that would be the cover of the issue. People like Al Leslie, George Herms, or Ray Johnson would come to the house and draw with a stylus—or, if we didn't have a stylus, with a dried-out ballpoint pen—directly onto the green plastic stencil. Then we'd put that stencil on the drum and print the cover through it.

Mimeograph was all done with these horrible goopy plastic stencils. It was very different from trying to get an artist to just draw on paper and then copy that onto a stencil. By that time, technology did exist to photocopy something onto a stencil—it gave the page a kind of bogus offset printing look. But by having them draw directly on the stencil, you were actually getting the feel of the stencil and the feel of the line and, you know, you were playing with the exact materials you had, and making it obvious that that's all that you were doing—not more, not less.

When I was growing up, when I was about nine or ten, I got a toy. I've never seen this toy since and I looked for it when I had kids. It was an aluminum tray, about 8 1/2 by 14, with some hard kind of gelatin. Mine came in a box with a whole lot of slick, coated paper, and some soft colored pencils. You would write on the paper and lay it face down on the gelatin, where it left an impression, and then you could pull copies. It was a child's version of a ditto machine—which was, I think, even earlier than mimeograph.

Within days, my brothers and friends and I were doing a block newspaper, and all the kids on the block were writing about the stickball games and drawing caricatures of their teachers and this thing would come out. And that's what I mean, "by any means necessary"—you know, if I could find out the composition of the gelatin they used . . . I looked for it once or twice years ago in the sixties when people were looking for cheap ways of printing stuff, but I never found it. Anyway, all of that kind of thing made me aware—and then, of course, there was high school and the newspaper you might start—and college magazines and all that. Nothing was too hard.

So, that's the sort of thing I'm talking about. One thing that stops this is folks get into: Why do this if it's not going to change everything? Change the world? But after a while I noticed that what I myself was constantly trying to do is reach other people who are of like mind, or writing in similar ways, or writing about similar stuff, and that in itself was the reason to do it. The reason it was going on at all. Sort of like cross-country or global affinity groups of some sort, to use a very old phrase.

When I was ready to publish my first book, I just did it. Some guys I barely knew had offered to publish me, but they changed their minds. And then they felt bad about changing their minds. These guys had a press, but they'd never done a book. They just had a press in a store on Cornelia Street. and they offered to do my book and then they changed their minds, so they said, "Well, we're sorry we changed our minds. If you buy the paper, we'll run it off on our press."

That left me with the whole process of getting my manuscript print-ready. I knew nothing about any of this and I didn't have any machinery for it. Not even the most basic. But at that time IBM was lending people their new Executive Typewriters for two weeks to see if they would want to buy them—it was a promotional scheme. I knew they would never lend me one in my walk-up on the Lower East Side unless I made up a good story, so I called them and said, "I'm going back to college next year and my parents want to get me one of these machines of yours, but I don't think I can run it." "Oh, yes, you can." "Well, O.K., I'm on Houston Street, you want to bring it up?" And they brought it up, carried it up all those stairs, and I typed my book, and to my credit, when I was all done and all the corrections were in except for the one word which I missed, I called them up and said, "I can't work this thing, will you come and take it away, please?" And they came and took it back. So that's how I got my camera-ready copy.

Then the guys made negatives for me and showed me how to opaque negatives, which involves sitting at a light box and filling in every little dot of light that shows through the negative, and I opaqued my own negatives. You know, you just invent as you go along. Freddie Herko did the titles with a brush and some black ink, and I threw in a friend's drawings. And then at the last moment, LeRoi Jones wanted to start Totem Press and he had no books out yet. So it was advantageous for him to have a published title, and it was advantageous for me to have an imprint other than my own on my book—in those days there was a lot more opprobrium attached to "vanity publishing." So Totem Press became the "publisher" of my first book.

You know, sometimes if you have an imprint, if you've been doing books, and there's somebody's work you really admire, but you don't have time or money to publish them on your own, and they don't have much— they can sometimes afford to get it together to pay for the paper or the binder, and you can help them co-publish their work. When I do this for a friend, I usually have them make up their own press name too and we do it jointly. My press now is Eidolon Editions. So I put Running Grass or whatever they call themselves—Running Grass/Eidolon on the title page. What this does is it gives them access to my distribution, which is small but real. Whereas if they were just Running Grass Press and this was their only book and it was obviously just them printing themselves, they would have more trouble finding a distributor.

So, there's always all these ways of helping each other, like me using LeRoi's imprint on my first book. It helped him and it helped me. Of course the story has come down that LeRoi published my first book, which is [laughs] . . . But that's O.K.

LeRoi and I also did this mimeographed newsletter called *The Floating Bear*, which I mentioned a few minutes back. *The Bear* ran from '61 to '69. When we started we didn't have a mimeograph machine, but the bookstore I worked for, the Phoenix Book Shop—they sold modern first editions—owned a Gestetner mimeograph and they liked to get modern first editions to sell later, so we gave them fifty free copies of every issue that we printed on their machine. I'm sure that more than paid for the machine over the years. We would just go down there when the store was closed and run off the next issue.

Of course we had to make stencils. Somehow LeRoi and I were co-editors, but I did all the typing. I don't know how that happened. I finally did buy a Gestetner and put it in my own house. And then various people would come by to help. Jimmy Waring, the choreographer, liked to proofread, so he would come to my house when I was done typing and do all the proofing. Then when it was time to actually do production (about every two weeks), there would be people collating, folding, stapling, people doing the whole thing. Cecil [Taylor] usually ran the Gestetner machine. Freddie Herko the dancer would be putting the mailing labels on, except he tended to throw away any label addressed to somebody he didn't actually know, because he didn't think anybody we didn't know should get *The Floating Bear*. And I would have to go and get those guys out of the wastebasket later and send those *Bears* out.

That's how it went down later. At first it was just me and Roi in the back of this bookstore and we only had 117 *Bears* to mail out—that's what we got by pooling our two address books. And we bought the stamps and just sent them out. We never bothered with things like bulk rate, although the list eventually was over a thousand. We never let the *Bear* be sold anywhere either. It was only mailed out to people we knew, and later people could ask to be put on the list. Some would send contributions. As far as I could ever figure it out, we broke about even. Thomas Merton used to steal stamps from the monastery office, and send them to me in letters. "I can't send you folks any money, but here's some stamps from the desk drawer." And like that.

And people did various things to help us, but it seems like most of the free things I ever did always broke even. I don't know how that happened, but it did. There was that whole thing of using what you had at hand, which in this case was somebody else's machine, and paying them off in kind and just keep going that way.

The last time I saw Charles Olson he said to me that the first years of *The Floating Bear* were the only time in his life that he knew that within two weeks of his writing something new or innovative or important, it would be in the hands of every writer that he cared about. And our list was just that——it was just writers and painters and choreographers and musicians and dancers and sculptors and the like. A few critics crept on at some point, but they always had an excuse: like that they also did creative work on the side or something.

So when I could I bought a Gestetner, and that not only did *The Floating Bear*, it also provided me with a livelihood. When you buy machinery, you can usually figure out how to earn a living with it. I started running off scripts for all the off-off-Broadway—not off-Broadway but off-off-Broadway theaters. These were very small theaters running below the lowest Actors' Equity rates. I typed stencils for the plays and ran off the necessary number of copies, right in my house. At that point I had had my first kid—I was a single mom, and it was 1958 and that was how I earned our living. Someone would bring by a script, and I would throw Jeanne over my knees and jiggle her if she cried while I typed. I'd type the script, run it off, collate it, all in my office/study and someone would come to the house and pick it up. It was way faster than they could get it done anywhere else, probably cheaper, and it provided me with a very reasonable way of making a living that didn't require going out of the house and leaving Jeanne with a babysitter or anything.

Then somewhere along the line, a few years later, I decided I wanted to buy a press. What I was thinking about on the way over here today to give this talk was: what I kept going for when I bought equipment was the top of the line of the cheapest method of printing. Not the top of the line of an expensive method, but like a Gestetner was as good a mimeograph as you could get. Mimeo being the cheapest method. And when I looked for a press—what everybody was using then was an A. B. Dick offset press, which was tinny and a sealed unit: you couldn't get at the innards to fix anything, it either worked or it didn't. It tended to fall apart every minute. I'd worked on them in offices, and hated them.

Instead I bought a decent press, a used Fairchild-Davidson offset press, and it came with a week of classes. And so I took my week of classes. I was the only girl there, and the other guys were all there because they wanted to have a trade and I was . . . they had to have a stool for me to stand on so I could see the top of the press and adjust the pressure, because I was too short. How I got the money for my press was, I just called a bunch of painters that I knew. Painters were making money then. And I said, "I found the printing press I want and it's $1,200," which was quite a bundle in 1963. Within one afternoon of calls I had $1,200. And I also told them, "And it comes with classes. I'll be able to print right away." I think they liked that. And within one afternoon I had my press and that's how that went.

After I finished taking the classes on my already-bought press at the loft of the guys who sold it to me, they delivered it to the store I rented around the corner from my house, and set it up for me, and I was in business. The first thing I printed was a flyer for a performance at our theater that night, and I still remember what a thrill it was to watch those pages with their beautiful drawing come flying out.

Then I had to learn a ton of stuff about cold type—making camera copy that looked more professional—so I took a job. I needed a job anyway. (What with the New York Poets Theatre and the press and three kids, we were broke.) I got a night job at a typesetting business that specialized in cold type. There, I learned the skills I needed, like "stripping" corrections into copy. In those days, the IBM Executive Typewriter had made it possible to type copy that had proportional spacing—it looked more like lead type than typewriters used to. But each Executive Typewriter had only one font of type, and in only one size. You had to have a different typewriter for italics for instance and "strip in" the italicized words. It was very labor-intensive.

Poets Press, my first imprint, printed about thirty-two poetry books. Most of them were first books by various people. I published first books by Audre Lorde, Clive Matson, David Henderson, A. B. Spellman, Herbert Huncke. Huncke's book was a trip because I was determined, since it was prose, to justify the right-hand margin. And how you did that with an Executive typewriter was, you counted how many hairline spaces were left over at the end of each line, then you averaged them out between all the words in that line. You made little notes in the margins as to how often to hit the hairline space bar (different from the regular space bar) between the words and then you typed the whole page over. Each line was different. The counting was different. So it was interesting, you know. All those things were like meditations in their way.

Again, just like buying the Gestetner, it gave me the chance to earn money with my machinery. I did fliers for people, and eventually did some "real" printing for others: sometimes a literary magazine, and also a lot of odds and ends.

With the very first book Poets Press did, I was pushed into getting even more of the machinery into my own hands. The book was *The Beautiful Days* by A. B. Spellman. When we sent the camera copy out to get plates made, the first place refused to do the job and sent it back, because A. B. had used the word "dick" in a poem. The dude who made plates said, "Well, you know, this is obscene. I have clients that are churches and what if something that you send me gets mixed up with something of theirs? I'll be in the big trouble." So, that inspired us soon after to look into getting a plate maker and then a copy camera, and by that time we had the entire thing except for binding in our own hands. In our storefront on East Fourth Street.

Later we took the whole shop up to Kerhonkson, New York, where it supported us for a year, till we moved on.

But it's important, you know, not just to print the book, but to make sure it gets out there somehow. In those days, I don't know why, but it wasn't so hard to get the books around. By about the third or fourth book, when a Poets Press book came back from the bindery, I had 600 standing orders for it. There were special collections libraries, individuals, and bookstores around the country to send it out to. I soon had to start with a printing of 2,000, instead of 1,000, so that we'd have plenty of copies left for the author who I paid with ten percent of the books, and for the bookstores in the neighborhood and readings and all that.

The hardest part of the work, actually, was invoicing, and shipping, and keeping track of those 600 copies and where they went and who had paid and who still owed. I don't know whether it was because there were so few small presses that so many people wanted the books, or the quality of the work, or the intense curiosity of the times, but that was definitely how it went.

With my own first book, before I had a press, I just took it around the city in my stroller with my baby. And within a year the whole nine hundred plus copies of *This Kind of Bird Flies Backward* were gone. A couple of years later somebody reprinted it.

One of the biggest kicks I got out of having a press was making broadsides. You could make a broadside, you could put it up any place—go out with a pot of glue or a staple gun, and start sticking it up wherever you wanted—really getting the word out, or giving it away free, in the back of the theater.

You know, I'm not trying to say that this is so great what I did, but that you have to think of what the means are that are at your disposal and just use them. At one point when we were living probably way too expensively—I had a very interesting husband at that point who liked to spend lots of money—we did a series of limited editions. I dreamed up doing a series of limiteds that were simply very skinny little holographs. One of the poets I knew would come by and handwrite his poem or bunch of poems for me— about 12 pages on regular 8 1/2 by 11 inch unlined sheets. We'd reduce it, handwritten, print 100 copies signed by the poet, plus 25 special ones that were colored or had little doodles drawn in by the author or were special in some way and 25 more for the poet to do as she pleased with. The writer got some money, we got a bunch of money, and the Phoenix Book Shop (the same bookstore I'd worked for years earlier but now it was owned by Bob Wilson)—the bookstore dealt them for us, so they made a bunch of money too. Bob had collectors already waiting for most of the copies.

So it was like printing dollar bills, you know. And, you didn't even have to deal with typesetting, you just took those handwritten sheets and made a book. We did about a dozen of those little books, one a month. I was living in the Hotel Albert with four kids and this expensive husband, and there wasn't really room or time to typeset or do anything. This was a way of keeping the whole thing going. Poets Press did some regular books at the same time but these limited editions kept that—the press and the whole scene running—including a few people who were living at the hotel, separately from us, and assisting with the whole operation.

Then we all went back to mimeo. And from mimeo to xerox, because it was the time of the Diggers and the time of the Communication Company, and it was kind of a point of honor in San Francisco to get a sheet out on the street every day with the latest info, the latest news, the latest inspiration, what to do next to disrupt the system in some way. And these were either mimeoed or xeroxed, whatever was around at the moment, and they were done overnight.

In the summer of '68 Lew Welch wrote one telling everyone they should move out of the cities and occupy the national parks. He called that one "A Moving Target Is Hard to Hit." We were all writing them; they were on the street every morning—maybe 1,000 copies a day handed out to whoever walked by.

Similar stuff was going on in New York with the Communication Company. Similar stuff was going on in Detroit with the Artists Workshop. There was an incredible amount of street literature. Many of us collected it. I'd like to know what happened to it all. I know what happened to my copies: they got left behind by a friend who borrowed them and didn't take them with him when he left some furnished room somewhere. And yet he'd borrowed them because they were such important history. Paul Krasner did an issue of *The Realist* with some of the Digger papers. But, you know, nobody's really done much with that material or written much about it.

At the same time there was this thing called Liberation News Service. Because there were about 200 weekly underground newspapers coming out around the country. Every reasonably large town had one.

Liberation News Service was another, smaller, syndicated news service, like AP. Essentially, they took the material they received and redistributed it. If you had a news story that you felt was important or in my case the "Revolutionary Letter" poems, you mailed them in to them. They preferred that you sent them 150 copies, so they could just collate everybody's material and send it out to the papers who subscribed. The newspapers used what they wanted. I still have copies of photos of Jean Genet with the Black Panthers that Liberation News Service sent out when Genet visited Oakland around 1969. Stuff like that.

If you sent something to Liberation News Service, you didn't know where or if it was going to appear. It was impossible to keep track. I don't know who published what "Revolutionary Letters," but I kept sending them out. The only change I made was I started to add a little copyright notice that said basically, "These poems may be used freely by any noncommercial press." It was pretty loose, but I felt like it was better than nothing. I had that going for years and I sometimes didn't even read the underground papers, for news I would just read Liberation News Service.

An interesting piece of research would be to trace how the underground newspapers got squelched, you know. It was different in different towns, but a lot of Cointelpro-type stuff went down around that.

We did at that time notice that it was all starting to break down. Communication was breaking down between different parts of the country. In spite of the Web I think that's still the case. I mean, people in one area don't really know what's happening someplace else. They don't have the feel of it, the energy of what's happening.

We started talking about renting a furnished room and putting a phone in it for people to call in with the news. So you'd be able to call and say, "Hi, I'm in Morocco and such and such is happening here." Or, "Hi, I'm up here in Vancouver and they just raided the offices of the Indian movement."

I don't think that room thing ever got started. The idea was that it should be a room, it should be nobody's house, because you didn't really want to be raided. And we were, all the time, being raided. It was a big drag.

To get back to this "By Any Means Necessary" thing—it would help a lot if we all knew what was going on right now. I don't. I go down to L.A., and my daughter Dominique who does a radio show down there says, "Well, I'm doing the show in the community this week instead of in the studio because of the riots in the high schools. I want to get people to talk about what's going on." And I go, "What riots in the high schools?" I'm only 300 miles away in San Francisco, but that stuff doesn't come through on the news or anywhere else. Or I tell someone in L.A. I'm reading at the memorial for Judy Bari, and they say, "Who?" These are people who are conscious, ecologically conscious, economically conscious, socially conscious, but information doesn't go out of a given area of concern, or a given geographical area, so it's important to think about how to make that happen again. Some kind of communication.

Then there's the practical aspect of getting the stuff out that I wanted to talk about. I teach privately in San Francisco and once or twice a year there'll be somebody with a real manuscript who's ready to make a book. And I keep saying, "Well, so-and-so from the group that I taught last year has a manuscript ready. And how about, instead of doing your own vanity press book, if four or five of you pooled your $500 or your $750 or your $1,000 each, whatever, and made a small press, and then you published each other. You could help each other get readings, you would have a legitimacy that you won't have if you do one book, and you do one book, and nobody's ever heard of any of you."

It's a really old idea, you know. It's like the collective or something. But, it's hard for people to think about it. It seems to me that we have a real taboo about thinking about interdependence—it's against our American system or something. But there is the fact that it's not that hard for just four or five people. You don't have to agree about everything. You have to agree that you like each other's work enough to stand printing each other's books, and that you could maybe stand reading with some of the others.

A lot of this is hit-and-run. It doesn't have to be a life's work. A lot of this is hit-and-run. You rent a storefront for four months till you've shown your work and all the people you really care about. Their paintings. People take turns sitting in the storefront to keep it open. Then disappear. Forget about the rest of the lease. You know, it's not forever.

Or don't get a lease. We used to do a theater season that ran three or four months. We never had leases. We'd do from February to May and then the rest of the year we'd be recuperating and raising money for the next season.

None of this has to do with becoming the new movement. The new established order. It has to do with getting the work out there that wants to get out.

And then the question is, you know, what is that? And why? And that's something everybody has their own ideas or feelings about. Why you want the work out and why it's important—what your own vision is of what art is for. I'm not going to give you any information about that, because I don't think my information is of any use to you, beyond that affinity group idea. You know, Pound said that poetry is news that stays news. But what makes something news keeps changing.

Sometimes poetry is news because we're breaking down the syntax or playing with the language. Sometimes it's news because we're extending the content of what can be said in a poem. Sometimes it's news because we just reinvented the line or we've uninvented the line and we're only going to write prose poems for the rest of our lives. Sometimes there's a philosophical point of view behind a whole bunch of work. Those are all kinds of news, but what makes any of it stay news is that level of enthusiasm and energy in the intent. Energy of intent that goes into the writing of the stuff. You know, something like that has to also go into getting the work out. Something similar.

I think that's mostly all I had to say. I want to put one other thing out there that relates to all this in some way, though I can't directly say how.

Years ago somebody asked me to write a statement on poetics for some anthology. And, I was in the midst of raising three kids and running a theater and a press, and the statement that I wrote—nobody has ever accepted or published it. I wrote one sentence: "The requirements of our life is the form of our art."

You know, we make the shape of the thing depending on what's available, what time's available, what space, what money, what materials. The requirements of our life. And they said, "Surely you mean 'are.' The requirements of our lives are" . . . No—I mean "is." The requirements of our life is the form of our art."

Wally Berman had a press that only printed that big, so he did a tiny magazine called *Semina* which now you can't buy for love or money on this planet. You know, the requirements of any of our lives—what we got and what we don't got. Making all that into an advantage in the game of making stuff, and making stuff happen.

—July 9, 1997

REMEMBER THE FUTURE: ARCHIVAL POETICS AND THE WAR ON MEMORY

Steven Taylor

EMORY IS THE OBJECT OF WAR. WAR IS THE ATTEMPT TO REPLACE one archive with another. You want to rewrite the memory of the people whom you wish to dominate. ("Hearts and minds" is the current rubric.) In the period of slavery in North America, African memory was systematically taken apart through the mechanical suppression of speech, the separation of kin, and the laws against the use of drums. Other historical examples would be the book burnings of the Nazi ascendancy and the Chinese Cultural Revolution, and prior to that, the burning of persons of particular persuasions, like Hypatia, a teacher of mathematics and Platonic philosophy whose father, Theon, was the last librarian at Alexandria before the *museion* complex was destroyed. In 415, Hypatia was seized on the street, hacked to pieces, and burnt. At the time, being an archivist of pre-Christian thought was, obviously, a rough gig. These days, we don't burn scholars, we revoke their tenure, but issues of access to memory are as urgent as ever.

The war on memory takes various tacks. There is the struggle between one archive and another, and there is the attempt to reconfigure particular memories to signify differently. The media generation's memory warriors have learned that popular memory can sometimes be reprogrammed by simple insistence on even the most outlandish propositions. Back-room strategist Karl Rove resigned his White House position in 2007 to go public with the obligatory memoir, and claimed that Congress, not the White House, was responsible for the rush to war in Iraq. In cases where historical facts would be too obvious to be rewritten, there is amnesia by decree, which attempts to bypass the struggle over memory altogether. A case in point was the 2001 executive order that empowered the president and vice president to render permanently secret whatever White House papers they decide should be kept from scholar-historians and the public. (In 1978, after Nixon's shenanigans, the Congress had passed legislation limiting the secrecy of executive branch papers to twelve years. President Bush's order effectively nullified that legislation.) In 2007, when Congress members voiced opposition to the ban on access to executive archives, the White House complained that too much was made of the issue, given that only sixty-four pages of material had been made permanently secret. Making those pages public could go a long way toward our understanding the mess we got into under Bush.

Reason, language, and life take place in communities of memory. The author is the archivist in multiple senses, and certainly in many cultures, the poet, the singer of tales, is the one who knows the tribal genealogies and who invokes the ethos of your time, the quality of your society, the moral character of the people; the poet historian is the keeper of your culture, the keeper of reality. Ed Sanders addresses this in his book *Investigative Poetry*. Ed says that lawyers have an expression, when they argue a case that sets an important precedent, they say they are making law. Sanders extends this idea, and says that poets make reality. Wanda Coleman spoke along this line when she introduced herself at the 2006 Summer Writing Program convocation. She said, "I make words, I make reality."

The idea of world as word, or language as reality, has been with us for as long as there have been words, magic, religion, and science. In the beginning was the Word, and the Word was God, an ancient poet sang. This line was updated for the modern era by German idealist philosophy and the psychology and linguistics descended from it. Universe is mind, and mind is language. This idea plays in multiple dimensions. I heard an environmental activist say, "It's all conscious, the whole environment is conscious." And we have physicists saying things like "reality is ultimately composed of information." As Gregory Bateson says in his lecture on the ecology of mind that I have brought along from the audio archive, "the metaphoric is the absolute . . . it's all stories."

Ecology of mind and the metaphorics of reality were understood by poets before writing was invented. Allen Ginsberg used to talk about traveling to Australia, meeting Aboriginal Australian songmen, and learning that the tribal song man knows where the water is on the long migrational loop of your people; if your song man dies before he can pass the song along to an apprentice, your people are finished. The sense of that level of importance of the songster has come to us in the Sanders reference, and in Whitman's evocation, in *Democratic Vistas,* of the literatum, in whom Whitman placed his hope, above the politician and the priest, for the realization of democratic humanity.

The singer of tales has been valued all along except by priests and politicians. The poet archivist represents a community of memory that predates church and state and, if we play it right, will outlive them. The Tewa Indian anthropologist Alfonso Ortiz said that rather than seeing the tribe as a step in the evolution toward the state, we could see the tribe as an alternative to the state. Tribes, particular communities of memory, act against the vast, homogenizing fog of amnesia that is the state.

The Kerouac School's audio holdings represent a community of memory centered on the twentieth-century renaissance of aural literature that was part of a larger movement that Allen Ginsberg referred to as a "democratization of the arts." I'll note two aspects of this here. First, beginning in the latter half of the nineteenth century, we see a blurring of high and low cultural forms, where Baudelaire is calling a newspaper illustrator the most vital painter of his day, Manet is painting rag pickers and prostitutes, and a generation later, Satie is composing songs for barroom performers, the Futurists are championing the circus and the variety theater, and fifty years on, Jim Dine is dressed in clown makeup drinking from a bucket of paint. The point is that as art came out of the more exclusive realm of the salon, it became more performative and politically engaged.

The second thing I want to note with regard to democratization in the arts is that in the latter half of the twentieth century, a lot of apparatus for making art available on a massive scale became widely accessible and portable, like movie cameras and tape recorders.

In the 1920s and thirties, European avant-gardists, like the Surrealists, took to film. The establishment of the 16MM format after about 1923 helped make do-it-yourself cinema a medium of broad exchange. In 1946, Maya Deren booked a movie house in Greenwich Village to show what she called "Three Abandoned Films" (after Apollinaire's observation that a work of art is never completed, just abandoned). Deren toured her films around the country, setting a precedent for self-financed and distributed movies (a trend that mirrored the little magazines of the period, and continued with the DIY ethos of the fifties and sixties and forward). Edison's recording phonograph, which finally caught on in the marketplace in the 1890s, had allowed only a couple of minutes of recording per cylinder;

subsequent technologies increased uninterrupted recording capacity, but the tape recorder, widely available after 1948, enabled recordings of an hour or more of audio at a time. Now there are audio archives of concert-length readings from the 1950s on.

Allen Ginsberg told me that the democratization of the arts came from attempting to do things on a small scale, which was the philosophy of the underground film. That you could bypass the entire Hollywood business which was public and vast, but you could entertain yourself and your friends, which is the same thing as the revival of poetry readings on a small scale. So the best thing to do is do your own thing with a garage band in your own little club in a small town, decentralized culture. The Beat ethos that Ginsberg helped to shape can be described as a resistance to the war on memory, a kind of romantic quest to remember what Greil Marcus has called "the old, weird America," the pre-corporate-speak polyglot collage of regional cultures, particular histories, strange cuisines, and backstreet dreams whitewashed by Eisenhower's highway system, television, and the adaptation of the industrial war machine to the domestication of everyone everywhere.

The resistance to the mechanisms of whitewash is memory; not nostalgia, but memory in the sense of particular history as a basis for judgment. We see this now in China, for example, where students are rediscovering the ancient texts once suppressed by the communists, and are learning again the importance of historical imagination. "Learning the texts, for them, is learning to think. . . . They understand why Confucius . . . said that he 'had faith in antiquity.' History does not just provide actual lessons from the past, but, more important for the students, history gives them the chance to consider the right and wrong of human judgment even though the deeds were done long ago."

A sense of historical vision is essential to democratization. The Beat vision was based on "remembrance of things past." In the mid-1940s, a teenaged Allen Ginsberg and his friends Jack Kerouac and William Burroughs concocted their "New Vision" based in Arthur Rimbaud's idea of the poet as seer, and Guillaume Apollinaire's championing of the "New Spirit" that he saw in the paintings he called "Cubist" and which he translated into a poetry that wed directness of expression with juxtaposed images that resist easy synthesis, a poetics that would, after his death, inform the movement Apollinaire named before it occurred, Surrealism.

If the New Spirit in the arts goes back to Apollinaire, democracy in the arts goes back to Whitman, who championed an open form delivered in the American vernacular. The Objectivists, who emerged in the period between the world wars, favored direct treatment of ordinary reality in the native idiom. Later, in 1950, Charles Olson described the new poem as a transmission of energy that is measured not in the old European forms of rhyme and syllable count but on the length of the breath. Olson uses the metaphor of a dance, that the syllables dance on the poetic line. Breath, energy, dance—the trend to performance is evident here too, for all of Olson's bookishness. Meanwhile, Kenneth Rexroth had declared that "it is very important to get poetry out of the hands of the professors, and out of the hands of the squares . . . and into the life of the country."

In the 1920s, Rexroth teamed up with Langston Hughes to read poetry with live jazz. He went on to correspond with Pound and Williams, and was published in Objectivist venues, continued to read and record with jazz ensembles, and published articles championing jazz. In San Francisco in the 1940s, Rexroth and poet/dramatist Madeline Gleason befriended a group of younger poets based in Berkeley, Robert Duncan, Jack Spicer, and Robin Blaser. In April of 1947, Gleason presented Rexroth and the Berkeley group in a gallery reading along with other young poets.

In the 1950s, Robert Duncan taught at Black Mountain College in North Carolina, linking the San Francisco poets with what became known as the Black Mountain group. The school's faculty had included visual artists Josef and Anni Albers who were refugees from the Bauhaus, the groundbreaking German school of architecture, design, art, and performance that had been closed by the Nazis in 1933. In 1952, Black Mountain participants Charles Olson, John Cage, Merce Cunningham, and Robert Rauschenberg set the template for what became known, after Alan Kaprow's use of the term in 1959, as "the happening." It was the idea that you could have a set of apparently unrelated events going on at the same time. Olson read his poems while Rauschenberg showed his paintings, Cunningham danced, and Cage lectured on Zen.

Meanwhile, in San Francisco, the poetry readings continued, and in the autumn of 1955, Rexroth presented a new group of poets at an old garage that had been taken over by six artists, hence the name of the venue, the Six Gallery. The evening was publicized by an unknown New York poet, a newcomer to the San Francisco scene, who had a background in marketing, and who understood that a postcard advertising the gathering in hyperbolic terms might draw an audience. That poet was Allen

Ginsberg, and the occasion was the premiere of his poem "Howl." Jack Kerouac was in the audience (see *The Dharma Bums,* chapter two), as was poet and publisher Lawrence Ferlinghetti, who subsequently published *Howl* and was busted for obscenity. The trial and acquittal and attendant publicity helped make Ginsberg and the Beats the new hot thing at the bohemian end of American literature.

The renaissance of aural poetry, begun by the San Francisco poets, became associated with the Beats, and the readings moved to New York. In 1960, Mickey Ruskin opened the Tenth Street Coffeehouse, hosting open readings on Monday nights and readings by invited poets on Wednesdays. Ginsberg told me that reading poetry in a coffeeshop was considered so unusual that one of the daily papers ran an article with a photograph of some of the poets. The readings moved through a series of venues, arriving more permanently, finally, in 1966, at the St. Mark's Church-in-the-Bowery at Second Avenue and Tenth Street.

St. Mark's Church has a long and distinguished history as a center for performance and progressive politics. Harry Houdini, Isadora Duncan, and Frank Lloyd Wright had appeared there, and the poet W. H. Auden was a member of the congregation. When the poets moved in and founded The Poetry Project, the presiding cleric, the Reverend Michael Allen, had recently returned from riding freedom buses in the South, and was preparing to go to Vietnam with Joan Baez. At the time, the church also housed the Black Panther's breakfast program, the Motherfucker's dinner program, and a child care service. Ginsberg told me, "There was a community, a forum where people could articulate their relationship to the big national problem of the Vietnam War. Sixties mouths could meet people who had been pacifists in World War I, people who knew Catholic worker saint Dorothy Day. You got a taste of prior eras, prior movements, prior communities and their moments of glory; publications, parties, social activities, and love affairs, decades old." Sixties activism is here connected with history.

So this sense of democratization in the arts, this renaissance of aural literature, coincides with the availability of recording equipment. The Poetry Project's readings at St. Mark's were first recorded on a big reel-to-reel deck by Paul Blackburn. Then, subsequently on cassette equipment, and last time I looked, digital audio tape. So there's a forty-year collection of biweekly readings and various gala occasions, initially stashed in the church basement with the corpse of Peter Stuyvesant, and now collected at the Library of Congress. Anne Waldman, who had been at St Mark's from the first, serving for years as artistic director, brought that practice of recording to Naropa in 1974, so now we have thousands of recordings of several generations of writers performing and discussing literature.

In 1948, in an auditory hallucination of William Blake, Ginsberg had experienced the voice of the poet as a time machine. But we don't have to hallucinate to get on the time machine. There's this window of time that opened here at Naropa, and was captured in the archive. We're only three decades old as an institution, but our archive holds the voices of people who were born at the start of the last century, and it has their students, and their students' students, and twenty minutes from now, it has you. And it will have your students too, if we get it right. This is our community of memory.

There's a three-millennia-old urge to totalitarianism that says that the demos is flighty and unstable and poets are to be exiled. This position claims access to a fixed truth for an elite class of rulers whose self-proclaimed rectitude argued even in the birthplace of democracy for rigging elections. In this mind, literature is useful only as fables to teach moral lessons to dullards. Stalin's minister of culture pushed a similar program in the 1930s. The play of language, which is the free exercise of memory and imagination, was anathema to these oligarchs. Today we live with their descendants. Allen Ginsberg told me, "You have to write your own history, nobody's going to do it for you." At the time I took it to be a statement focused at my particular situation as a young writer, and our immediate milieu. Now I see he was speaking to something much larger; ours is the work of memory against the mass amnesia that made the twentieth century the bloodiest in human history. The imperative to give voice, and to preserve it, can be summed up in Allen's command on occasions when I hesitated to perform, "Speak, poet!"

—June 21, 2007

You can see eternity. We look out the window; that's eternity, right? Big. Endless sky. Infinite. So you can say that definitely is it; it's got all the qualities that we think of as eternal, sky that goes beyond the mountains to the end of the universe. Just look out the window. You got it. this is the room. A room floating in that endlessness. But on the other side there's endlessness over there, too. So we're in the middle of endlessness. And there's infinity back that way, and if you got to the other side of the building it's infinitely *that* way in that direction, too. And we're floating right in the middle of it. So definitely in terms of space this is right in the middle of eternity.

—Allen Ginsberg
from "William Blake's 'Auguries of Innocence,'"
from a talk given April 19, 1991

NOTES

The First Reading of the Environmental Movement: the Six Gallery Reading. Excerpted from a panel. Transcribed by Laura Wright, edited by Michael McClure.

Kerouac's Sound. Transcribed by Laura Wright, edited by Clark Coolidge.

SIDEBAR: Allen Ginsberg on William Blake. Originally published in *The New Censorship,* vol. 5, no. 4, July 1994, transcribed by Randy Roark.

Basic Definitions. Transcribed by Laura Wright, and edited by Gary Snyder. © Gary Snyder 2009.

Pulling it Down or The Good Manners of Vampires. Transcribed and edited by Laura Wright. Excerpted from a talk entitled "Razor."

Women and the Beats. From a panel entitled "Women and the Beats." Transcribed by Laura Wright, edited by Laura Wright, Hettie Jones, Joanne Kyger, and Anne Waldman. Hettie Jones's section was originally entitled "Babes in Toyland."

SIDEBAR: Joyce Johnson. From "Beat Women: a Transitional Generation," a talk given at Naropa June 24, 1998, and subsequently published in *The Rolling Stone Book of the Beats* as "Beat Queens: Women in Flux." Excerpted from the book.

Allen Ginsberg's Language Games. Transcribed by Laura Wright, edited by Marjorie Perloff.

Recollections and Gossip: First Meetings with Jack Kerouac. Excerpted from a panel. Transcribed by Laura Wright, edited by Laura Wright and David Amram.

SIDEBAR: *Ted Berrigan.* Excerpted from a talk transcribed and edited by Joel Lewis, originally published in *On the Level Everyday: Selected Talks on Poetry and the Art of Living* (Talisman House, 1997).

Reading, Writing, and Teaching Kerouac in 1982. Transcribed by Laura Wright, edited by Ann Charters.

Kerouac, Catholicism, Buddhism. Excerpted from a panel. Transcribed and edited by Laura Wright.

BIOGRAPHIES

DAVID AMRAM has composed over one hundred orchestral and chamber works, written two operas, and early in his career wrote many scores for theater and films, including *Splendor in the Grass* and *The Manchurian Candidate*. He plays French horn, piano, guitar, numerous flutes and whistles, percussion, and a variety of folkloric instruments from 25 countries. He has collaborated with such notables as Leonard Bernstein, Dizzy Gillespie, Lionel Hampton, Charles Mingus, Dustin Hoffman, Thelonious Monk, Willie Nelson, Jack Kerouac, Betty Carter, Odetta, Elia Kazan, Arthur Miller, and Tito Puente.

AMIRI BARAKA Born in Newark, New Jersey, USA, he is the author of over forty books of essays, poems, drama, and music history and criticism, a poet icon and revolutionary political activist who has recited poetry and lectured on cultural and political issues extensively in the USA, the Caribbean, Africa, and Europe. Baraka is known as the founder of the Black Arts Movement in Harlem in the 1960s. His books include *Transbluesency, Selected Poetry of Amiri Baraka/LeRoi Jones, The Music,* a collection of poems and monographs on jazz and blues authored by Baraka and his wife and poet Amina Baraka, *The Essence of Reparations* (essays), *Somebody Blew Up America,* and *Tales of the Out & the Gone.*

TED BERRIGAN was a central figure in the second generation of the New York School of Poets. He was the author of more than 20 books including *The Sonnets, Bean Spasms* (with Ron Padgett and Joe Brainard), *In Brief, Red Wagon,* and *A Certain Slant of Sunlight. The Collected Poems of Ted Berrigan* was published in 2005. He died in 1983.

JUNIOR BURKE is a novelist, lyricist, and dramatist. He serves as Chair of Naropa University's Writing and Poetics Department, as well as

Director of their low-residency MFA in Creative Writing. He is founder and executive editor of the online literary magazine *not enough night* (www.naropa.edu/notenoughnight) which features some of the boldest voices in American and international letters. More about his work can be found at www.juniorburke.com.

WILLIAM S. BURROUGHS met Allen Ginsberg in 1943. With his wife, Joan Vollmer, he moved to Mexico City, where he wrote his first book, *Junky*. He ended up living in Tangiers, where drugs were cheap, and where he wrote what was to become *Naked Lunch*. With Brion Gysin, Burroughs explored the "cut-up" method of composition; using this technique he wrote *The Soft Machine, The Ticket that Exploded,* and *Nova Express.* Other titles include *Interzone, The Wild Boys, The Third Mind* (with Gysin), *Cities of the Red Night,* and *The Western Lands.* From 1983 until his death in 1997, Burroughs lived in Lawrence, Kansas. He was resident faculty at Naropa in the early 1980s.

LORNA DEE CERVANTES is the author of *From the Cables of Genocide: Poems on Love and Hunger* and *Emplumada*, which won an American Book Award. She was also co-editor of *Red Dirt*, a cross-cultural poetry journal, and her work has been included in many anthologies including *Unsettling America: An Anthology of Contemporary Multicultural Poetry, No More Masks! An Anthology of Twentieth-Century Women Poets,* and *After Aztlan: Latino Poets of the Nineties.*

ANN CHARTERS, professor of English at the University of Connecticut, has been interested in Beat writers since 1956, when as an undergraduate English major she attended the repeat performance of the Six Gallery poetry reading in Berkeley where Allen Ginsberg gave his second public reading of *Howl*. She has written a literary study of Charles Olson and biographies of black entertainer Bert Williams, and (with her husband, Sam Charters) the Russian poet Vladimir Mayakovsky. She was the general editor of the two-volume encyclopedia *The Beats: Literary Bohemians In Postwar America* and has published a collection of her photographic portraits of well-known writers in the book *Beats & Company.* She has also edited Jack Kerouac's *On the Road* for Penguin Twentieth Century Classics and *The Portable Beat Reader.*

CLARK COOLIDGE Educated at Brown University and attended the Vancouver Poetry Conference in 1963. His books include *Space, Own Face, Mind: The One that Enters the Stories, Alien Tatters, One the Nameways, Volumes One and Two,* and *Far Out West,* among others.

GREGORY CORSO was born in New York City and spent most of his childhood in orphanages and foster homes. His troubled adolescence included a stint of several months in the Tombs, the New York City jail, for a case involving a stolen radio, and three months of observation in Bellevue. At seventeen, he was convicted of theft and sentenced to Clinton State Prison for three years. During his incarceration, he read avidly from the prison library and began writing poetry. After his release in 1950, he met Allen Ginsberg, through whom he also became acquainted with William Burroughs and Jack Kerouac, as well as other New York writers and artists. His major publications include *Gasoline, The Happy Birthday of Death, The American Express, Long Live Man, Elegaic Feelings American, Herald of the Autochthonic Spirit,* and *Mindfield.* He died in 2001.

DIANE DI PRIMA lives and teaches in the Bay area. She is author of forty-four books of poetry and prose, and has been translated into over twenty languages. An expanded editions of her classic, *Revolutionary Letters,* has just been published by Last Gasp Press. *Opening to the Poems,* a book of essays and exercises on writing poetry, will be published by Penguin in 2009. Diane was awarded the Fred Cody Award for Lifetime Acheivement and Community Service in 2006.

LAWRENCE FERLINGHETTI is the co-owner and founder of the legendary City Lights Bookstore and publishing house, which published early literary works of the Beat Generation. His numerous books of poetry include *A Coney Island of the Mind, Pictures of the Gone World,* and *A Far Rockaway of the Heart.* He is the former Poet Laureate of San Francisco.

RICK FIELDS was an early member of the Naropa community, editor of *Loka* magazine, investigative journalist, and author of *How the Swans Came to the Lake,* a definitive study of the arrival of Buddhism in America. He died in 1999.

ALLEN GINSBERG met William S. Burroughs, Neal Cassady, and Jack Kerouac, the core group of writers who later became associated with the Beat movement, while he was a student at Columbia University in the 1940s. His first book of poems, *Howl and Other Poems*, published by City Lights, overcame censorship trials, and its signature poem, "Howl," became one of the most widely read poems of the 20th century. In 1974 Ginsberg co-founded the Jack Kerouac School of Disembodied Poetics at Naropa University with Anne Waldman, with imput from Diane di Prima. In his later years he became a Distinguished Professor at Brooklyn College. His honors include a National Book Award, the Woodbury Poetry Prize, a Guggenheim fellowship, NEA grants, and a Lifetime Achievement Award from the Before Columbus Foundation. Some of his later books include *White Shroud: Poems, 1980-1985*, *Cosmopolitan Greetings: Poems, 1986-1992*, *Journals Mid-Fifties 1954-1958*, *Selected Poems, 1947-1995*, and *Death and Fame: Last Poems, 1993-1997*. His *Collected Poems, 1947-1997* was published in 2007. He died in 1997.

DAVID HENDERSON, one of the original members of Umbra, resides in New York City. He is the author of poetry books *De Mayor of Harlem* and *Neo-California*, among others, as well as the introduction to Bob Kaufman's *Cranial Guitar*. An updated and revised version of his Jimi Hendrix biography, *'Scuse Me While I Kiss the Sky, Jimi Hendrix: Voodoo Child* was recently published by Atria Books.

ABBIE HOFFMAN was a social and political activist, co-founder of the Youth International Party ("Yippies"), a member of the "Chicago Seven," and eventually a fugitive from the law after being implicated in a cocaine deal gone wrong and busted by undercover agents. He lived underground as "Barry Freed" for six years, working on environmental campaigns, until his surrender in 1980. He is the author of *Steal This Book*. He died in 1983.

JOHN CLELLON HOLMES ws an essayist, poet, and novelist. In 1952, after the publication of his novel *Go*, Holmes wrote an article for the *New York Times Magazine*, "This is the Beat Generation," in which he introduced this phrase to the world. Later in life, Holmes lectured at Yale and gave workshops at Brown University. His final book of poems, *Dire Coasts*, was published in 1988. He died in 1988.

JOYCE JOHNSON is the author of three novels, including *In the Night Café*. Her other books include *Minor Characters*, and *Door Wide Open: A Beat Love Affair in Letters, 1957–1958*. She is working on a definitive biography of Jack Kerouac.

HETTIE JONES's twenty-four books for children and adults include her memoir of the Beat scene, *How I Became Hettie Jones;* the poetry collection *Drive*, which won the Poetry Society of America's Norma Farber Award; *Big Star Fallin' Mama, Five Women in Black Music*, honored by the New York Public Library; and *No Woman No Cry*, a memoir she authored for Bob Marley's widow, Rita. Recently published are *From Midnight to Dawn, The Last Tracks of the Underground Railroad* (with Jacqueline Tobin), and a third poetry collection, *Doing 70*. Jones is the former chair of the PEN Prison Writing Committee, and the editor of *Aliens at the Border*, a poetry collection from her workshop at the Bedford hills Correctional Facility. She teaches at the 92nd Street Y Poetry Center and in the Graduate Writing Program of The New School.

EDIE PARKER KEROUAC was Jack Kerouac's first wife. Her memoir, *You'll Be Okay*, was published by City Lights in 2007. She died in 1993.

JOANNE KYGER was one of the few women involved with the San Francisco Renaissance constellation of writers around Robert Duncan and Jack Spicer as well as one of the acknowledged female "Beat" poets. She lives on the coast north of San Francisco, writing poetry, editing the local newspaper, traveling to Mexico, and has taught at the Jack Kerouac School of Disembodied Poetics in Boulder and the New College of San Francisco. She is the author more than twenty books of poetry and prose, including *Going On: Selected Poems, 1958-1980* and *Just Space: Poems, 1979-1989, Strange Big Moon: Japan and India Journals, 1960-1964, God Never Dies* (Blue Press), *The Distressed Look* (Coyote Books), *Again* (La Alameda Press), *As Ever: Selected Poems* (Penguin Books), and most recently *About Now: Collected Poems* (National Poetry Foundation).

MICHAEL MCCLURE gave his first poetry reading at the age of twenty-two at the legendary Six Gallery event in San Francisco. His first book, *Passage*, was published in 1956. He has published more than twenty books, including *Meat Science Essays, Rebel Lions, Simple Eyes, Three Poems, The*

Mad Cub, and *Scratching the Beat Surface*, the only book-length account of the period written by one of its active members. His controversial plays, including *The Beard* and *Josephine: The Mouse Singer*, were among the major theatre events of the sixties and seventies. In the early nineties he began collaborating on live poetry set to music by Ray Manzarek, the keyboardist from the Doors.

WILLIAM S. MERWIN's books of poetry include *A Mask for Janus*, *The Moving Target*, *Lice*, *The Carrier of Ladders*, *Opening the Hand*, *Selected Poems*, *Travels*, *The River Sound*, *The Pupil*, and *Migration*. He is also well known for his translations, among them *The Cid*, and *The Life of Lazarillo de Tormes*.

JOHN OUGHTON has worked for Coach House Press, briefly for the Charlottetown, PEI newspaper *The Guardian-Patriot* and in communications for York University and the accounting firm then named Deloitte Haskins & Sells. He twice attended the Jack Kerouac School of Disembodied Poetics Summer Writing Program. He now teaches English at Centennial College in Toronto, and runs a micro-mini press, Sixth Floor, which produces chapbooks.

MARJORIE PERLOFF is Sadie D. Patek Professor Emerita of Humanities at Stanford University and currently Scholar-in-Residence at the University of Southern California. She is author of a dozen books about modern and postmodern poetry and poetics including *The Poetics of Indeterminacy: Rimbaud to Cage*; *The Futurist Movement: Avant-Garde, Avant-Guerre, and The Language of Rupture*; and *Wittgenstein's Ladder: Poetic Strangeness and the Language of the Ordinary*. Essays on Allen Ginsberg are included in *Poetic License* and *Howl at One-Hundred*.

DAVID ROME was the personal and literary secretary to Chögyam Trungpa and close friend of Allen Ginsberg.

EDWARD SANDERS achieved fame in the countercultural world of the 1960s as poet, magazine founder, and leading force of The Fugs, a satirical folk-rock band. Later, he achieved national recognition for his 1971 book, *The Family*, a study of mass murderer Charles Manson and his followers that critic Robert Christgau called "excellent" and "terrifying." His poetry has been likened in its energy and ambition to William Blake,

Walt Whitman, Allen Ginsberg, and the investigative poetics of Charles Olson, blending slang, neologisms, classical Greek, and Egyptian hiero- glyphs. He has also written novels, short stories, and song lyrics. Recent work includes *The Poetry and Life of Allen Ginsberg: A Narrative Poem*, and *America: A History in Verse*.

GARY SNYDER attended Reed College where he roomed with Lew Welch and Philip Whalen. Snyder pursued graduate studies in classical Chinese at the University of California, Berkeley and worked for the U.S. Forest Service for several summers. His friendship with Jack Kerouac, Allen Ginsberg, Kenneth Rexroth, and Philip Whalen during this time is the sub- ject matter for Jack Kerouac's novel *The Dharma Bums*. Later Snyder received a scholarship from the first Zen Institute to travel to Japan where he lived for fifteen years. He received the Pulitzer Prize for poetry in 1975 for his book *Turtle Island*. Recent publications include *Back on the Fire: Essays; Danger on Peaks: Poems;* and *The Gary Snyder Reader: Prose, Poetry and Translations, 1952-1998.*

JANINE POMMY VEGA moved to Greenwich Village at the age of fifteen to be part of the Beat scene. She is the author of sixteen books and chapbooks since 1968, including *Mad Dogs of Trieste, The Green Piano,* both from Godine Books, and *Tracking the Serpent,* a prose travel memoir from City Lights. Her new CD *Across the Table,* performances with musicians from Woodstock, Bosnia, and Italy, has just been released. She translated the recently published *Estamos Aqui: Poems by Migrant Workers,* and is working on a new anthology of poems from prison. She has been the director of Incisions/Arts, an organization of writers working with people behind bars, and has taught inside prisons for many years.

STEVEN TAYLOR is a poet, musician, song writer, professor, and eth- nomusicologist. He has published two books of poems and a musical ethnography, *False Prophet: Field Notes from the Punk Underground.* He has com- posed music for theater, film, radio, drama, and installations, and has made more than a dozen records with various artists. He has toured and recorded with Allen Ginsberg, Anne Waldman, Kenward Elmslie, the Fugs, and the New York hardcore band False Prophets. He was member for many years of the year-round core faculty and served as chair of the Department of Writing & Poetics MFA program at Naropa, and is currently on the faculty of the Kerouac School's Summer Writing Program.

CHÖGYAM TRUNGPA, RINPOCHE was the eleventh descendent in the line of Trungpa *tülkus*, important teachers of the Kagyü lineage, one of the four main schools of Tibetan Buddhism. He was forced to flee Tibet in 1959; in 1963 he moved to England to study comparative religion, philosophy, and fine arts under a Spaulding Fellowship at Oxford University. In 1969, he published *Meditation in Action*, the first of fourteen books on the spiritual path published during his lifetime. In 1970 he moved to the United States, where he established his first North American meditation center, Tail of the Tiger (now known as Karmê-Chöling) in Barnet, Vermont. In 1974 he founded the Naropa Institute (now University) in Boulder, Colorado. He died in 1987.

ANNE WALDMAN grew up on Macdougal Street in Greenwich Village and spoke to Allen Ginsberg on the telephone in 1962 trying to lure him to a reading at Bennington College where she was a student; he was heading out of the country. They later met at the Berkeley Poetry Conference where she took a vow during the legendary Charles Olson reading to work on behalf of poetry and the "underground" poetry community. She became assistant director in 1966 then director, in 1968, of the Poetry Project at St. Mark's Church-in-the-Bowery, working there a decade while also co-founding the Jack Kerouac School in 1974. She has been a student of Buddhism since 1962, and an ambassador for the oral revival of poetry, appearing on stages from Berlin to Caracas, from Mumbai to Beijing. Her books include *Fask Speaking Woman*, *Iovis* (Books i & ii), *In the Room of Never Grieve*, *Marriage: A Sentence*, *Structure of the World Compared to a Bubble*, *Outrider*, *Red Noir*, and *Manatee/Humanity*. She is the editor of *The Beat Book*, and co-editor of *The Angel Hair Anthology* and *Civil Disobediences: Poetics and Politics in Action*. She collaborates extensively with her son, musician and composer Ambrose Bye. Her literary and cultural archive resides at the Hatcher Graduate Library in Ann Arbon, Michigan. She is the artistic director and chair of Naropa's Jack Keroac School's Summer Writing Program.

PHILIP WHALEN attended Reed College with Gary Snyder and Lew Welch and graduated with a BA in 1951. He was one of the readers at the Six Gallery in 1955. Whalen was ordained a Zen Buddhist priest in 1973 and became head monk, Dharma Sangha, in Santa Fe, New Mexico in 1984. In 1991 he returned to San Francisco to lead the Hartford Street Zen Center. His books include, *Canoeing up Cabarga Creek: Buddhist Poems 1955-1986*, two novels (*You Didn't Even Try* and *Imaginary Speeches for a Brazen Head*), *Off the Wall: Interviews with Philip Whalen, Enough Said: 1974-1979*, and *Heavy Breathing: Poems 1967-1980*. In 1999, Penguin Books published his *Overtime: Selected Poems*. His *Collected Poems* was published by Wesleyan University Press in 2007. Both the collected and selected editions were edited by Michael Rothenberg. He died in 2002.

LAURA WRIGHT is a poet, map librarian, volunteer firefighter, and graduate of the Jack Kerouac School of Disembodied Poetics. For a number of years she curated the Left Hand Reading Series in Boulder. She is the author of *Part of the Design* as well as various chapbooks. Her translation of Henri Michaux's *La vie dans les plis* is forthcoming from Action Books.

JOSHUA ZIM, a devoted student of Chögyam Trungpa, was the first information officer at Vajradhatu and the first editor-in-chief of the *Vajradhatu Sun* (a bi-monthly publication of Buddhist news, now called *Shambhala Sun*). He died in 1985.

COLOPHON

Beats at Naropa was designed at Coffee House Press,
in the historic Grain Belt Brewery's Bottling House in Northeast Minneapolis.
The text is set in Village.

FUNDER ACKNOWLEDGMENTS

Coffee House Press is an independent nonprofit literary publisher. Our books are made possible through the generous support of grants and gifts from many foundations, corporate giving programs, state and federal support, and through donations from individuals who believe in the transformational power of literature. Coffee House receives major general operating support from the McKnight Foundation, the Bush Foundation, from Target, and from the Minnesota State Arts Board, through an appropriation by the Minnesota State Legislature and from the National Endowment for the Arts. Coffee House also receives support from: three anonymous donors; the Elmer L. and Eleanor J. Andersen Foundation; Bill Berkson; the James L. and Nancy J. Bildner Foundation; the Patrick and Aimee Butler Family Foundation; the Buuck Family Foundation; the law firm of Fredrikson & Byron, PA.; Jennifer Haugh; Anselm Hollo and Jane Dalrymple-Hollo; Jeffrey Hom; Stephen and Isabel Keating; Robert and Margaret Kinney; the Kenneth Koch Literary Estate; Allan & Cinda Kornblum; Seymour Kornblum and Gerry Lauter; the Lenfestey Family Foundation; Ethan J. Litman; Mary McDermid; Rebecca Rand; the law firm of Schwegman, Lundberg, Woessner, PA.; Charles Steffey and Suzannah Martin; John Sjoberg; Jeffrey Sugerman; Stu Wilson and Mel Barker; the Archie D. & Bertha H. Walker Foundation; the Woessner Freeman Family Foundation; the Wood-Rill Foundation; and many other generous individual donors.

NATIONAL
ENDOWMENT
FOR THE ARTS

This activity is made possible in part by a grant from the Minnesota State Arts Board, through an appropriation by the Minnesota State Legislature and a grant from the National Endowment for the Arts.

MINNESOTA
STATE ARTS BOARD

TARGET.

To you and our many readers across the country,
we send our thanks for your continuing support.

Good books are brewing at coffeehousepress.org